Literary and Visual Representations of HIV/AIDS

Reading Trauma and Memory

Series Editors: Aimee Pozorski, Central Connecticut State University, and Nicholas Ealy, University of Hartford

Reading Trauma and Memory offers global perspectives on representations of trauma and memory while examining the tensions, limitations, and responsibilities that accompany the status of the witness. This series attempts to bridge the gap between trauma studies and new directions in the fields of memory studies, popular culture, and race theory and seeks submissions that closely read literature and culture for representations of traumatic wounding, the limits of memory, and the ethical duty to depict historical trauma and its effects.

Given its breadth, this series will appeal to scholars in a number of interdisciplinary fields; given the specific angle of trauma and memory, it will capture those who see ethics and responsibility as key factors in their scholarship. Such areas include Holocaust studies; war trauma and PTSD; illness and disability; the trauma of migration and immigration; memory studies; race studies; gender and sexuality studies (which has recently had a resurgence with the #MeToo movement); studies in popular culture that take up television and films about witness; and the study of social and historical movements.

We are seeking projects that question how to honor the past through close readings of literature focused on trauma and memory—which would necessarily take on international perspectives. Examples include a consideration of literature, justice, and Rwanda through a postcolonial and trauma lens; recent thinking on the phenomenon of *American Crime Story* and the resurgence of interest in the OJ Simpson trial that parallels the narrative of the Black Lives Matter movement; readings of the attempts of popular culture to address issues of historical injustice as exemplified by *12 Years a Slave* and HBO's *Westworld*.

Recent titles in the series:

Literary and Visual Representations of HIV/AIDS: Forty Years Later, edited by Aimee Pozorski, Jennifer J. Lavoie, and Christine J. Cynn
Occupying Memory: Rhetoric, Trauma, Mourning, by Trevor Hoag

Literary and Visual Representations of HIV/AIDS

Forty Years Later

Aimee Pozorski,
Jennifer J. Lavoie,
and Christine J. Cynn

LEXINGTON BOOKS
Lanham • Boulder • New York • London

Published by Lexington Books
An imprint of The Rowman & Littlefield Publishing Group, Inc.
4501 Forbes Boulevard, Suite 200, Lanham, Maryland 20706
www.rowman.com

6 Tinworth Street, London SE11 5AL

Copyright © 2020 by The Rowman & Littlefield Publishing Group, Inc.

All rights reserved. No part of this book may be reproduced in any form or by any electronic or mechanical means, including information storage and retrieval systems, without written permission from the publisher, except by a reviewer who may quote passages in a review.

British Library Cataloguing in Publication Information Available

Library of Congress Cataloging-in-Publication Data Available

ISBN 9781498584463 (cloth)
ISBN 9781498584487 (pbk)
ISBN 9781498584470 (electronic)

Contents

Acknowledgments		vii
1	Literary and Visual Representations of HIV/AIDS: An Introduction *Christine J. Cynn and Aimee Pozorski*	1
2	Countering the Plague: AIDS Theatre as a Site of Memory *Dirk Visser*	13
3	Poetry before Protease *Nels P. Highberg*	29
4	Early Representations of IT: AIDS, the American Canon, and Robert Ferro's *Second Son* *Ryan Calabretta-Sajder*	43
5	*Borrowed Time, Body Counts*, and *The Nearness of Others*: Three Approaches to AIDS Memoirs *Jennifer J. Lavoie*	61
6	Guibert before Guibert: AIDS and Literary Creation *Mariarosa Loddo*	77
7	The Dream, the Disease, and the Disaster: On Yan Lianke's *Dream of Ding Village* *Shelley W. Chan*	89
8	Abortion and Family as HIV Prevention Strategies: Kitia Touré's *Les gestes ou la vie* *Christine J. Cynn*	105
9	When "Safe" Isn't Safe: Reflecting on the Role of Science in the Production of Harmful Discourse of HIV/AIDS *Alison Patev*	125

10 Exceptional PrEParations: Pharmaceutical Interventions, Neoliberal Queerness, and Truvada 145
Andy Eicher

11 "We Should Be Embracing the Infected, the HIV-Positive, and Showering Them Not Only with Love, but with Medical Care and Psychosocial Services": An Interview with Michael Broder 163
Jennifer J. Lavoie

Index 175

About the Contributors 183

Acknowledgments

We are grateful to all of the contributors to this volume, a passion project for the three of us.

We thank the panel on AIDS representation and ethics—as well as audience participants—at the Northeast Modern Language Association conference in Baltimore, Maryland, in spring of 2017: Michael Broder, Travis Alexander, Jennifer Lavoie, Nels P. Highberg, Susan Gilmore, and Brittany Hirth.

We would also like to acknowledge the participants in the American Comparative Literature Association seminar on the topic of narrative medicine and disability studies held in Utrecht, Netherlands, in July of 2017: Alexander Aguayo, Elizabeth Brewer, Ryan Calabretta-Sajder, Shelley W. Chan, Andy Eicher, Nels P. Highberg, Mariarosa Loddo, and Dirk Visser.

This volume would not have been completed without the continued dedication of our families and their shared commitment to our work.

We thank the many departments at Lexington Books who produced this collection: first and last, our commissioning editor Holly Buchanan, as well as the executive board, designers, copy setters, proofreaders, and marketing team.

We appreciate the support of Central Connecticut State University, the Gender, Sexuality and Women's Studies Department at Virginia Commonwealth University, and the gifts of time, money, and encouragement that enabled the completion of this volume.

This collection emphasizes the importance of cultural productions—and of analyses of these works—in the struggle against HIV/AIDS. We hope that it can provoke continuing discussions about the many issues implicated in the ongoing epidemic.

Chapter One

Literary and Visual Representations of HIV/AIDS

An Introduction

Christine J. Cynn and Aimee Pozorski

In the past decade, a flurry of art exhibitions, as well as film, theatre, and television productions, have centered on the HIV/AIDS epidemic in the United States, especially as it extended from the 1980s through the 1990s.[1] The exhibitions and documentaries in particular have been accompanied by new scholarship on HIV/AIDS, memory, and nostalgia; on the central role of the visual arts in activism around HIV/AIDS (especially in ACT UP); and on how HIV/AIDS participates in and transforms ongoing aesthetic and political debates.[2] The rich and influential scholarship on HIV/AIDS and the visual arts indexes the significance of the visual arts to AIDS activism, and of HIV/AIDS to the many visual artists who in their work addressed both the epidemic and the issues and anxieties it provoked. In contrast, much less sustained attention has been devoted to literary texts, which have not been so easily assimilated into educational and activist interventions and have not been as literally visible.

This collection seeks to fill a gap in the important scholarship on HIV/AIDS: it brings together essays by both established and younger scholars on visual, as well as on literary representations of HIV/AIDS. It expands discussion of the issues generated and amplified by the epidemic to consider how HIV/AIDS has been portrayed in the United States, but also in Western and Southern Africa, Western Europe, and East Asia. During the early years of the epidemic in the United States and Western Europe, literature mostly by gay white male writers sought to combat stigma, demand state accountability, commemorate those who had died, and advocate for the finding of a cure.

As we argue here, more contemporary portrayals of HIV/AIDS in global contexts reiterate and distance themselves from these prior significations of HIV/AIDS as they continue to address issues seemingly far removed from healthcare.

Most of the essays gathered in this collection began as seminar papers at the 2017 annual conferences of the American Comparative Literature Association in Utrecht, Netherlands, and of the Northeast Modern Language Association conference in Baltimore, Maryland. Meeting a diverse group of thinkers and activists during such a tumultuous time in US and global politics solidified our sense of the importance of conversations among academics committed to a topic that for too many has begun to be taken for granted as a nonissue. A few of us have children and students who, having grown up in the United States after the discovery of highly active antiretroviral therapies, are totally unaware of the history of struggles against HIV/AIDS. Nevertheless, we are all too aware that theirs is a generation confronting increasing social and economic inequities and in the aftermath of neoliberal cutbacks in social welfare programs, intensifying precarity of those already marginalized—the populations most affected by HIV/AIDS. We are also all too aware that testing and treatment have not been universally accessible either in the United States or globally.

Much of the significant work on our topic produced in the last twenty years has been published in the form of individually authored articles and monographs, and we wondered, where did the edited collections go? How does the unique format of an edited collection generate productive discussions of pressing contemporary concerns like HIV/AIDS? This volume and its comparative focus signal our commitment to sustained conversations between different authors about visual and literary productions across regions and languages. At the same time, we recognize certain limitations in scope; as the product of MLA and ACLA annual conferences, this volume reflects the organizations' locus in the United States, and the contributors to this volume are all based in the United States or Western Europe. Nevertheless, the collection includes essays centering on work that draws attention to how HIV/AIDS has been framed in response to and beyond US and Western European literary and political debates. In this current moment, when the humanities in particular have become increasingly under attack as irrelevant, and a rarefied luxury, we insist on the necessity of collective critical work centered on close readings of texts that pose vital questions, demand responses, and imagine alternative futures that extend beyond national borders. In bringing analyses of literature into ongoing discussions around HIV/AIDS and the visual arts, we argue for the importance of thinking through some of the connections between the visual and the literary in debates on aesthetics and politics, even as we acknowledge their incommensurability.

Edited collections such as this one focusing on cultural representations of HIV/AIDS began to appear in the late 1980s. Perhaps the most influential in terms of its timeliness, *AIDS: Cultural Analysis, Cultural Activism,* was first published as a 1987 special issue of *October*, and the following year as a book edited by Douglas Crimp. The collection raises critical questions that still inform discussions about representations of HIV and the role of visual art in political and artistic interventions during times of crises. In the title essay, Crimp critiques prevailing assumptions about how cultural producers can participate in the struggle against HIV/AIDS: "Within the arts, the scientific explanation and management of AIDS is largely taken for granted, and it is therefore assumed that cultural producers can respond to the epidemic in only two ways: by raising money for scientific research and service organization or by creating works that express the human suffering and loss" (3). Moving beyond the either/or model of art as commodity to generate revenue, on the one hand, or as testimony or commemoration, on the other, Crimp challenges the status of the artist as original, individual creator and insists on the central role of collectively produced visual art as "*activist* responses to AIDS" (4).

Padraig O'Malley's edited collection, *The AIDS Epidemic: Private Rights and the Public Interest,* which appeared just a year later, began as a special issue of the *New England Journal of Public Policy* in 1988. Less interested in the arts, O'Malley's contribution takes as its focus political rights and citizenship:

> The epidemic raises fundamental questions regarding the nature of individual freedom, our responsibilities to others, the always delicate balance between private rights and public interest, and society's obligations to its "out" groups—those members it has stigmatized, discriminated against, ridiculed, and treated as less than full and equal citizens. (5)

Appearing in the same year, the collection edited by Ronald R. Butters, John M. Clum, and Michael Moon takes the idea of responsibility to a new level by considering what is at stake linguistically in discussions about responsibility—not simply in the sense of being responsible to others who are sick, but also in the sense of how and at what points responses to the AIDS epidemic are possible or necessary. In the introduction to the collection, *Displacing Homophobia: Gay Male Perspectives in Literature and Culture* (1989), Butters asks: "Is there any need for gay linguistics in general? The authors of the following essays write in a context in which such a question has likewise been asked, disparagingly and discouragingly, concerning literary criticism, history, and cultural studies" (4). The collection, significantly, features Lee Edelman's invaluable and often-cited essay, "The Plague of Discourse: Politics, Literary Theory, and AIDS," in which Edelman analyzes the ACT UP slogan, "Silence=Death" and its unstated corollary that aligns discourse with defense: "We must be wary, then, of the temptations of the literal as we are of the ideologies at work in the figural; for discourse, alas, is the only defense with which we can counteract discourse, and there is no available discourse on AIDS that is not itself diseased" (92). Edelman's essay resonates today, as literary and cultural critics have increasingly been called upon to examine the assumptions behind their rhetoric, especially as they refer to disabled and ill bodies.

Edelman contributed another foundational essay to Timothy Murphy and Suzanne Poirer's collection, *Writing AIDS: Gay Literature, Language, and Analysis* (1993). In this collection, as Murphy and Poirer explain, the art of writing and the politics of AIDS are not mutually exclusive, but rather inextricably bound: "Running through nearly all these essays is the awareness that not only is AIDS writing a literary act involving conscious decisions about what to say or what not to say and how to couch what is said, but that writing about that writing is also a political act" (5). As Edelman highlights in "The Mirror and the Tank: 'AIDS,' Subjectivity, and the Rhetoric of Activism," scholars and activists "ought not to ignore the unstable relation between necessity and luxury that problematizes the question of what is defensible in the midst of an epidemic that takes as its target precisely our modes of defense" (34). In focusing on the word "luxury" as a desire to read and think critically about cultural reactions to the threat of AIDS, Edelman responds to Leo Bersani's essay, "Is the Rectum a Grave?" which appeared in the 1988 Crimp collection. In this latter essay, Bersani writes about the role of reading in an epidemic: "Analysis, while necessary, may also be an indefensible luxury" (199), a critique later addressed by Stuart Hall in his 1992 essay, "Cultural Studies and Its Theoretical Legacies."

Rounding out the "later" collections in this tradition are Emmanuel S. Nelson's *AIDS: The Literary Response* (1992), a collection dedicated to "the creative response of gay male artists"—a focus, Nelson argues, is "inevitable, since much of the literature of AIDS has been created by gay men; but is also morally and politically necessary" (1). This collection crucially contains essays on *As Is* and *The Normal Heart*, on Larry Kramer's polemical politics more generally, and on the NAMES Project AIDS Quilt.

After 1992, although many single-authored works centered on literary and visual representations of HIV/AIDS, and on the political implications of taking up such projects, no edited book collections took up these questions. In 2007, however, Valerie Raoul et al.'s *Unfitting Stories: Narrative Approaches to Disease, Disability, and Trauma* appeared. Funded by the Peter Wall Institute of Advanced Studies at the University of British Columbia, Vancouver from 1999 to 2004, this collection does groundbreaking work in its combination of disability studies, narrative medicine, and trauma via a sophisticated understanding of storytelling (3–10). While Raoul et al.'s edited volume *Unfitting Stories* is not solely focused on representations of HIV/AIDS and includes very few essays that take up this topic in particular, it does include Lisa Diedrich's "Between Two Deaths: AIDS, Trauma, and Temporality in the Work of Paul Monette," which offers a theoretically sophisticated model for reading US literary texts on AIDS in the twenty-first century (53–60). It further points to a recent trend in scholarship on HIV/AIDS—a turn back to the early years of the epidemic and a rethinking of both the power of interdisciplinary perspectives and the role of narrative in raising cultural awareness.

While previous collections convey a sense of urgency in the face of the silence of the US government and public, our collection both looks back at representations of HIV/AIDS from the 1980s and early 1990s and incorporates readings of more contemporary visual and literary texts. The first half of this collection contains critical readings of literary responses to HIV/AIDS while the second broadens the scope to consider film and politics. In arranging the essays this way, we underscore how literature constitutes a very powerful response to AIDS that raises its own set of political, as well as aesthetic questions.

The collection opens with Dirk Visser's "Countering the Plague: AIDS Theatre as a Site of Memory," which focuses on a reading of Larry Kramer's *The Normal Heart*, originally produced in 1985 with a revival in 2011, and the works of Robert Chesley including *Jerker* (1985), *Night Sweat* (1984), and *Stray Dog Story* (1982). Visser argues that, while *The Normal Heart* is the most performed play about AIDS and thus able to claim historical accuracy, it is problematic in that it does not represent the larger body of drama from that time period. Visser uses the work of Aleida Assmann to discuss the difference between "functional memory" and "storage memory." *The Normal Heart* has become part of functional memory, which is part of the present, whereas the works of Chesley and others have been relegated to storage memory. Visser argues that these plays provide a more complex approach to the AIDS epidemic and the rhetoric, and therefore provide alternatives to the narrative of *The Normal Heart*.

Also taking up work relegated to "storage memory" in his essay, "Poetry before Protease," Nels P. Highberg focuses on poetry and scholarship written in the United States during the late 1980s and early 1990s, as a reminder of the time before protease. In his chapter, Highberg returns to poetry and scholarship of the past as a kind of recovery process, but also to trace a genealogy of AIDS representation, which seemed to change as the advent of protease inhibitors in the mid-1990s radically altered the medical realities of certain populations infected with HIV. His project responds to a troubling cultural amnesia of the time "before" through a study of poetry of the past, ultimately suggesting that literature from that traumatic time can teach us how to reflect on our contemporary traumas, those that have arisen in recent decades that we could never imagine then.

Ryan Calabretta-Sajder's "Early Representations of IT: AIDS, the American Canon, and Robert Ferro's *Second Son*," focuses on Robert Ferro's final novel, *Second Son,* published right before Ferro's own death from complications of AIDS in 1988 (also roughly two months after the death of his lifelong partner). As Calabretta-Sajder argues, while all of Ferro's noted novels center on mostly Italian American gay characters in the 1980s United States, Ferro's works remain marginalized in the queer and Italian American communities, as well as in US literary studies. Calabretta-Sajder identifies *Second Son* as the first AIDS novel in the United States and shows how queer theor(ies), AIDS literature, and Italian American studies might enrich understandings of the role of class, as well as of a "magical-realistic" ending providing hope for an entire generation of those affected by the epidemic.

A US canonical AIDS author, Paul Monette, is the focus of the opening section of Jennifer J. Lavoie's "*Borrowed Time, Body Counts,* and *The Nearness of Others*: Three Approaches to AIDS Memoirs." Lavoie posits that while there has been discussion of early gay memoirs, including those centered on AIDS, such as Monette's *Borrowed Time* (1988), less has been devoted to more contemporary memoirs, such as Sean Strub's *Body Counts* (2014) and David Caron's *The Nearness of Others* (2014). Though the first two texts are considered AIDS memoirs and both authors spend a great deal of time depicting the realities of life with HIV/AIDS, Lavoie sees a shift in method between the earliest works and those published within the last decade, especially with authors who contracted HIV after the development of effective medical treatments. Drawing on Monette, Strub, and Caron as exemplary cases, Lavoie addresses the shift in representations of AIDS as the central focus of the author to AIDS being just another aspect of life due to the change in politics and biomedical realities, a change that Lavoie argues is reflected in both the chronologies and contents of the books.

Turning from American literature to highlight the work of the great French writer Hervé Guibert, Mariarosa Loddo in "Guibert before Guibert: AIDS and Literary Creation" considers Guibert in the context of the outbreak of HIV/AIDS in 1980s France that resulted in a large number of autobiographical accounts and memoirs written by people who had contracted the virus. In her reading of two works that are not Guibert's best known works, *Incognito* (*L'incognito*, 1989) and *The Man in the Red Hat* (*L'homme au chapeau rouge*, 1992)—Loddo counters the common misperception that Guibert was unconnected to activism around HIV and argues that Guibert's writing about his personal experiences with AIDS is in fact political. Loddo goes farther to theorize that Guibert is not just writing about illness; his personal works reflect the ways in which illness writes itself.

The relationship between the personal and the public takes a different cast in Shelley W. Chan's "The Dream, the Disease, and the Disaster: On Yan Lianke's *Dream of Ding Village*," an essay that focuses on *Dream of Ding Village* (2006), a Chinese version of *The Plague* and a macabre story filled with death caused by AIDS, by the award-winning yet controversial writer Yan Lianke. As Chan argues, the daring novel launches its critique of the "blood economy" that encouraged people to sell blood to make money in the poverty-stricken areas of central China in the 1990s. Intending to make "the people rich and the nation strong," this policy ended up a "blood disaster" and "national calamity," in the words of Dr. Gao Yaojie, China's most outspoken AIDS activist.

Chan argues that by blaming shortsighted and irresponsible policy makers and practitioners, the novel makes it clear that many HIV patients in China are victims of the "blood economy" rather than of a "moral disease" resulting from their own so-called immoral lifestyle. Examining the experimental structure of the narrative, Chan's essay analyzes how the novel creates a wider and deeper blurred space between reality and unreality to highlight humans' irrational and crazy materialistic desires, which led to an absurd and ill-practiced modernization in the grotesque post-Mao China. At the same time, Chan also discusses the author's attempt of self-censorship, and how the practice of self-censorship affects the narrative in the artistic and realistic dimensions.

After Chan's article, we shift focus on literary representations from the late 1980s through the beginning of the twenty-first century, and we address the politics of film and video with Christine J. Cynn's essay, "Abortion and Family as HIV Prevention Strategies: Kitia Touré's *Les gestes ou la vie*." As Cynn argues, in Côte d'Ivoire, early education around HIV/AIDS represented the solutions to HIV as self-discipline and self-denial, rigor, and maturity. Such messages reinforced ongoing structural adjustment programs promulgating neoliberal conceptions of free individuals who needed only to be educated to be induced to behave rationally and efficiently. As a 1989 campaign poster warned, "Say no! Protect yourself!" However, directives to self-manage were not always consistent or coherent, and not surprisingly, for certain gendered bodies, injunctions to self-manage did not always suffice. The HIV-positive pregnant woman in particular provoked intense anxieties and fears around contamination, expressed in contradictory and shifting messages.

Cynn's chapter focuses on the 1993 four-part series, *Les gestes ou la vie* (*Gestures or Life*) scripted and directed by Ivoirian writer and filmmaker, Kitia Touré. Each of the four segments urges HIV testing, explains various prevention methods, and attempts to combat stigmatization of people living with HIV. One of the twenty-six-minute-long segments titled "Raisons de la peur" ("Reasons for Fear") focuses on convincing pregnant women to test for

HIV, and if they test HIV-positive, to terminate their pregnancies. Although approved by the state, these astonishing officially unofficial (or unofficially official) messages directly contravened both state and religious prohibitions of abortion. The directives further implied acceptance, even endorsement, not only of legally banned procedures but also of female sexuality not securely oriented toward reproduction.

Alison Patev similarly addresses the medical establishment in her essay, "When 'Safe' Isn't Safe: Reflecting on the Role of Science in the Production of Harmful Discourse of HIV/AIDS," which argues that scientists, particularly those who work to treat or end disease, are seen as benevolent and all knowing. However, in the case of HIV/AIDS, scientists have perpetuated a number of messages in society that may be harmful to individuals, their sexual partners, and people living with HIV or AIDS (PLWH, PLWA). For example, promoting "safe sex" implies a dichotomy of safe versus dangerous. Safe individuals are those who are presumably seronegative and cannot infect anyone, while seropositive individuals are therefore dangerous because they could pass the virus to others. This message, and others just like this, are created and perpetuated by scientists. Patev examines how scientists and health organizations, such as the CDC, have driven discourse surrounding HIV and AIDS, both in the United States and in African nations. Through critical analysis of several sources, Patev's essay demonstrates how science has perpetuated harmful messages about who can become infected, modes of HIV transmission, and the AIDS epidemic in African nations.

Patev's essay secondarily shows how these negative messages are disrupted. Art is one medium that has the power to disrupt messages produced by science. The essay goes on to analyze three works of art that subvert messages about HIV/AIDS. This includes two videos, *Doctors, Liars, and Women* (1988) by Jean Carlomusto and *DiAna's Hair Ego* (1991) by Ellen Spiro, and a collection of poetry, *Thy Condom Come* (2000) by Kgafela oa Magogodi. Finally, Patev speculates on how science, specifically HIV prevention programs, can be cognizant of the harmful discourse and can create messages that undermine existing messages and shift the discourse to be less damaging. Throughout Patev's chapter, personal, narrative reflections on HIV prevention supplement evidence about the cultural production of HIV/AIDS, as well as the disruption of negative messages.

Andy Eicher considers the cultural production of AIDS in a reading of the short video *A Short History of Truvada* (2015) by Andy Egelhoff. Eicher's essay, entitled "Exceptional PrEParations: Pharmaceutical Interventions, Neoliberal Queerness, and Truvada," reveals that, in 2012, biopharmaceutical giant Gilead Sciences received FDA approval for their decade-old HIV maintenance drug, Truvada, to be prescribed for the prevention of contracting HIV. This treatment regimen—PrEP, or "pre-exposure prophylaxis"—promises to prevent the spread of HIV between serodiscordant sexual partners when taken consistently and correctly, and has been heavily marketed to the gay male community. While this intervention promises to end a decades-long epidemic that has been understood as a plague to the queer community (i.e., the HIV crisis), Truvada has largely escaped a queer/crip critique. This chapter seeks to critically examine Truvada and its relationship to the queer body and community, while also resituating the relationship of HIV/AIDS to the queer community through an examination of the video performance by queer artist Andy Egelhoff ("SPRKL BB"), as well as the earlier AIDS film *Zero Patience* (1993).

Egelhoff's video, Eicher argues, interrogates the relationship between humans, nature, and the queer cyborg. His chapter seeks to analyze the work through the lens of queer and crip theory and critical disability studies to further critique the medicalization of queer bodies within the broader "neo-liberalization" of healthcare. Reminiscent of prototypical nature film aesthetics—extreme close-ups of "organisms," cryptic sound effects, and species-specific behaviors carefully captured by the voyeur's camera lens—this short film purportedly proffers the viewer a "short history" of the HIV prevention/management drug Truvada. By analyzing it alongside the earlier AIDS film *Zero Patience*, Eicher delineates the ways in which the imperative for pharmaceutical interventions extends back to the early days of the HIV/AIDS epidemic.

Our collection ends with a conversation between Jennifer J. Lavoie and Michael Broder, which connects the imperative for pharmaceutical interventions with the imperative for testimony. The interview returns to a conversation from nearly thirty years ago, when Cathy Caruth, Thomas Keenan, Douglas Crimp, Laura Pinsky, and Greg Bordowitz theorized about the nation's failure to address the AIDS crisis of the 1980s as a failure of witness. In the post-Trump moment, Lavoie and Broder reflect on what it means to read AIDS literature in terms of its call for responsibility, both in art and, most especially, in politics: a call that at one time was consistently ignored, but that remains relevant now more than ever.

According to a recent study, only a small percentage of the US public currently views HIV/AIDS as a pressing health concern. Nevertheless, the epidemic continues to disproportionately affect already marginalized communities. The US Centers for Disease Control and Prevention report that although only an estimated 2 percent of the US population, gay and bisexual men accounted for 70 percent of new infections in 2014. Although African Americans make up 12 percent of the US population, they accounted for 45 percent of HIV diagnoses in 2015. Globally, in 2016, an estimated 36.7 million were living with HIV/AIDS, 69 percent in sub-Saharan Africa.[3] The disparities in HIV incidence and prevalence suggest that HIV/AIDS persists as an urgent, if underrecognized, concern.

This collection takes up HIV/AIDS representation in the United States and abroad. It considers the ways in which such related concerns as adequate healthcare, political representation, ethics, and aesthetics affect scholars and citizens at home—wherever they may live and in the most domestic sense—as well as in the larger political sphere. In this way, we hope to look both inward and outward, both locally and globally.

In 1991, Dennis Ciscel, a community activist and healthcare provider, described in a chapbook entitled *Tiny Stories* (1992) what it means to care for those living with AIDS, and particularly the experience of watching morning come in with them on his mind: "Forty times, and forty times forty times / I have watched morning and felt morning come in / but never before has it begun singing so clearly / outside of my window" (11). The chapbook overall depicts the physical and mental barriers that prevent an adequate representation of the "tiny old stories" of those diagnosed with AIDS in the 1980s in Austin, Texas. Reading his poem, "Introduction," the first in the collection, almost forty years after the first reported cases of what were later defined as AIDS-related illnesses reinforces not only the repetition of seeing the "morning come in," but also the steady passage of time. "Forty times, and forty times forty times" Ciscel, and advocates like him, have demanded an ethical witness to this health crisis—largely in the form of governmental and public responses. Our collection underscores how such demands remain relevant in the United States despite the decades that have passed, and how demands for witnessing—and for action—have been differently framed in more contemporary global contexts. It is because HIV/AIDS remains close to all of us that we hope this collection, which seeks to incorporate the literary into discussions of the visual, makes some small difference in raising awareness and in showing the transformative potential of art, literature, and film.

NOTES

1. *Art AIDS America* showed in the Bronx, Tacoma, and Chicago between the fall of 2015 and 2016. The New York Public Library mounted *Why We Fight: Remembering AIDS Activism* in the fall 2013 to spring 2014, *Gran Fury: Read My Lips* exhibited at New York University in 2012, and *ACT UP New York: Activism, Art, and the AIDS Crisis, 1987–1993* at Harvard University in 2009. Smaller shows of artists living with HIV/AIDS include 2016 exhibitions in New York City, *A Deeper Dive* at the Leslie-Lohman Museum of Gay and Lesbian Art, and *Persons of Interest* at the Lesbian, Gay, Bisexual and Transgender Community Center. Film and television productions include *Test* (2013), *Dallas Buyers Club* (2013), and *The Normal Heart* (2014), as well as documentaries such as *We Were Here* (2011), *Vito* (2011), *How to Survive a Plague* (2012), *United in Anger* (2012), *Larry Kramer in Love and Anger* (2015), *Uncle Howard* (2016), and *When We Rise* (2017). A 2017 London revival of *Angels in America* opened on Broadway in 2018.

2. Important scholarship includes: *Art AIDS America*; Lisa Cartwright, "Learning from Philadelphia"; Christopher Castiglia and Christopher Reed, *If Memory Serves*; Karma Chávez, "ACT UP, Haitian Migrants and Alternative Memories of HIV/AIDS"; Ryan Conrad, "Revisiting AIDS and Its Metaphors"; Douglas Crimp, *Before Pictures*; Avram Finkelstein, *After*

Silence; Deborah Gould, *Moving Politics*; Lucas Hilderbrand, "Retroactivism"; Sarah Schulman, *The Gentrification of the Mind*; and Tommaso Speretta, *Rebels Rebel*.

3. See The Henry J. Kaiser Family Foundation, "HIV at 30: A Public Opinion Perspective"; CDC, "HIV among Gay and Bisexual Men" and "HIV among African Americans"; and UNAIDS, "Fact Sheet—Latest Statistics on the Status of the AIDS Epidemic."

WORKS CITED

Assmann, Aleida. *Cultural Memory and Western Civilization: Arts of Memory*. Cambridge University Press, 2011.
Bersani, Leo. "Is the Rectum a Grave?" *October*, vol. 43, 1987, pp. 197–222. *JSTOR*, www.jstor.org/stable/3397574.
Butters, Ronald R., John M. Clum, and Michael Moon, editors. *Displacing Homophobia: Gay Male Perspectives in Literature and Culture*. Duke University Press, 1989.
Cartwright, Lisa. "Learning from Philadelphia: Topographies of HIV/AIDS Media Assemblages." *Journal of Homosexuality*, vol. 63, no. 3, Mar. 2016, pp. 369–386. EBSCO*host*, doi:10.1080/00918369.2016.1124693.
Castiglia, Christopher and Christopher Reed. *If Memory Serves: Gay Men, AIDS, and the Promise of the Queer Past*. University of Minnesota Press, 2011.
Centers for Disease Control. "HIV among African Americans," *HIV/AIDS*, February 14, 2018, https://www.cdc.gov/hiv/group/racialethnic/africanamericans/index.html.
———. "HIV among Gay and Bisexual Men." *HIV/AIDS*, February 8, 2018, www.cdc.gov/hiv/group/msm/index.html.
Chávez, Karma R. "ACT UP, Haitian Migrants, and Alternative Memories of HIV/AIDS." *Quarterly Journal of Speech*, vol. 98, no. 1, Feb. 2012, pp. 63–68. EBSCO*host*, doi:10.1080/00335630.2011.638659.
Ciscel, Dennis. *Tiny Stories*. Plainview Press, 1992.
Conrad, Ryan. "Revisiting AIDS and Its Metaphors." *Drain*, vol 13, no. 2, 2016. drainmag.com/revisiting-aids-and-its-metaphors/.
Crimp, Douglas, editor. *AIDS: Cultural Analysis, Cultural Activism*. MIT Press, 1988.
———. *Before Pictures*. University of Chicago Press, 2016.
Edelman, Lee. "The Mirror and the Tank: AIDS, Subjectivity, and the Limits of Activism." *Writing AIDS: Gay Literature, Language, and Analysis*, edited by Timothy Murphy and Suzanne Poirer. Columbia University Press, 1993, pp. 9–38.
———. "The Plague of Discourse: Politics, Literary Theory, and AIDS," *South Atlantic Quarterly*, vol. 88, no. 1, Winter 1989, pp. 301–317.
Finkelstein, Avram. *After Silence*. University of California Press, 2017.
Gould, Deborah. *Moving Politics: Emotion and ACT UP's Fight against AIDS*. University of Chicago Press, 2009.
Hall, Stuart. "Cultural Studies and Its Theoretical Legacies." *Cultural Studies*, edited by Lawrence Grossberg, Cary Nelson, and Paula Treichler. Routledge, 1991, pp. 277–294.
The Henry J. Kaiser Family Foundation. "HIV at 30: A Public Opinion Perspective." *HIV/AIDS*, June 1, 2011, www.kff.org/hivaids/report/hivaids-at-30-a-public-opinion-perspective/
Hilderbrand, Lucas. "RETROACTIVISM." *GLQ: A Journal of Lesbian & Gay Studies*, vol. 12, no. 2, Apr. 2006, pp. 303–317. EBSCO*host*, search.ebscohost.com/login.aspx?direct=true&db=aph&AN=19606197&site=ehost-live&scope=site.
Katz, Jonathan David and Rock Hushka. *Art AIDS America*. University of Washington Press, 2015.
Murphy, Timothy F. and Suzanne Poirer, editors. *Writing AIDS: Gay Literature, Language, and Analysis*. Columbia University Press, 1993.
Nelson, Emmanuel S., editor. *AIDS: The Literary Response*. Twayne, 1992.
O'Malley, Padraig, editor. *The AIDS Epidemic: Private Rights and the Public Interest*. Beacon, 1989.
Raoul, Valerie, Angela D. Henderson, and Connie Canam, editors. *Unfitting Stories: Narrative Approaches to Disease, Disability, and Trauma*. Wilfred Laurier University Press, 2007.

Schulman, Sarah. *The Gentrification of the Mind: Witness to a Lost Imagination.* University of California Press, 2013.
Speretta, Tommaso. *Rebels Rebel: AIDS, Art, and Activism in New York, 1979–1989.* AsaMER, 2014.
UNAIDS. "Fact Sheet—Latest Statistics on the Status of the AIDS Epidemic." www.unaids.org/en/resources/fact-sheet.

Chapter Two

Countering the Plague

AIDS Theatre as a Site of Memory

Dirk Visser

INTRODUCTION: A NIGHT AT THE THEATRE

It is August 2012. I am in an Amsterdam theatre, where, on the occasion of Gay Pride Week, Larry Kramer's play *The Normal Heart* is enjoying a week of sold-out performances in the Netherlands. Audience members around me are visibly and audibly moved by the play's heartrending closing scene. As we leave the auditorium, I overhear a young man saying to his companion, "You know, this story wasn't made up. Everything really happened." From his comment I deduce that he has attentively read the playbill, which contains a synopsis stating: "*The Normal Heart* is a moving and true story" (*The Normal Heart* 17, my translation). Also in the playbill is a copy of a pamphlet that the playwright himself handed out to the audience on the occasion of the play's 2011 Broadway revival, the first sentence of which reads: "Please know that everything in *The Normal Heart* happened" (*The Normal Heart* 19). Clearly, in Amsterdam and in New York, the play was presented as a docudrama, a truthful rendering of events.

What lends *The Normal Heart* authority besides its claim to historical accuracy is the fact that it is the most performed play on AIDS dating back to the 1980s. Yet its authoritative position is problematic. This problem is not simply in that it fails to represent a large body of mostly forgotten drama of the time, but also in that it plays a prominent role in the cultural memory of the AIDS crisis in the United States and Western Europe. Its frequent revivals put it firmly in the category of cultural memory that Aleida Assmann defines as functional memory, an important element of which is that it "provides values that can support identity and norms" (123). It is here that the main problem of *The Normal Heart*'s authoritative position in the cultural memory of the AIDS crisis lies. Not only are the norms it propagates on gay sexuality far from universal—they were disputed as much at the time of its first production as they are now—but they also echo the plague rhetoric that was prevalent in the 1980s: the association of AIDS with blame and guilt.

In order to bring this problem to the fore, and to suggest a possible solution, it is necessary to juxtapose *The Normal Heart* with artifacts of memory that belong to the category Assmann labels as "storage memory." Unlike functional memory, which is closely linked to the present, storage memory "contains what is unusable, obsolete, or dated; it has no vital ties to the present and no bearing on identity formation" (127). Also, storage memory serves as "a potential reservoir for future functional memory" (Assmann 130). Assmann opines that an exchange between functional and storage memory "brings out the potential of each and may create a corrective balance that is beneficial to both" (132).

Before such an exchange can take place, it is necessary to unearth from the archive plays that belong to the domain of storage memory. Samples of storage memory that could well function as countermemory to *The Normal Heart* are the AIDS plays by Robert Chesley. Produced at the same time as Kramer's play, but now largely forgotten, they take a more complex approach to the epidemic, and particularly to the plague rhetoric surrounding it, thus providing an alternative to the norms that *The Normal Heart* propagated at the time of its first production and that it continues to propagate today through its frequent revivals.

DISEASE, PLAGUE, AND THEATRE

From the earliest moments of the health crisis, AIDS clearly was not simply regarded as a mystifying new medical phenomenon, but as a moral issue as well. The media especially framed the disease in terms of blame and punishment. This aspect of blame, Susan Sontag has argued, is a major characteristic of plagues: "It is usually epidemics that are thought of as plagues. And these mass incidences of illness are understood as inflicted, not endured. Considering illness as a punishment is the oldest idea of what causes illness, and an idea opposed by all attention to the ill that deserves the noble name of medicine" (133). The yellow press in particular played no small part in this blame game, identifying what it called the gay "lifestyle" as the alleged cause of the epidemic. In *Policing Desire*, a study of AIDS and the media, Simon Watney discusses this kind of reporting in detail. However, a respectable newspaper like the *New York Times* was not immune to linking disease with blame either. Its article of July 3, 1981, which is generally taken as the starting point for AIDS reporting, shows clear signs of plague rhetoric. After having described the symptoms of a newly discovered cancer, the article goes on to profile the patients, or "victims," as it calls them: "[M]ost cases had involved homosexual men who have had multiple and frequent sexual encounters with different partners, as many as ten sexual encounters each night up to four times a week" (Altman 4–5). In thus framing the disease, it associates this cancer with sexual excess and homosexuality, an association that persists in the public mind today.

Those battling AIDS were faced with a disease and plague at the same time. And whereas scientists mainly focused on the disease, artists made an important contribution to dispelling the plague rhetoric. Looking back to the early 1980s, performance artist Tim Miller even claims: "In fact, I think that we were the first responders. Long before science kicked in in any useful way, the people that were helping were care providers and artists, and we had this explosion of theater and dance and music. For many years, the cultural response was the only response we had" (qtd. in Hall). In other words, Miller grants culture an essential role in the fight against AIDS.

Miller is not the only person to stress the importance of the cultural response to AIDS. Various reviewers and academics have echoed his words. Nicholas de Jongh draws attention to the role AIDS drama played in opposing the rising conservatism of the 1980s and its call for a return to "family values," a phenomenon which de Jongh classified at the time as an emergency. In this emergency, according to de Jongh,

> plays about AIDS have acquired a more urgent definition, significance and aspiration. . . . There are plays in which minority voices battle to fight an orthodoxy that regards AIDS as a mere local difficulty, principally affecting a reviled minority. It is a crucial business. It is a battle for life, and to persuade the orthodox majority that The Family inevitably includes homosexuals. The theatre, with its traditional elite audience of persuaders and influences [sic] has a potentially vital role. (179)

With this statement, de Jongh moves from disease to plague. In his view, in a "battle for life," theatre should combat the rhetoric that marks homosexuals as outcasts. Interestingly, he seems to assign the audience, the "persuaders and influence[r]s," a major role in the process of changing mind-sets.

Similarly, John Clum sees a dual role for theatre. In his view, AIDS drama both educates audiences about the disease and helps to dispel plague rhetoric. He claims that "[g]ay AIDS dramas dismantle the misapprehensions about AIDS while affirming the Person With AIDS. They also, in the process, deconstruct oppressive constructions of homosexuality that have been perpetuated by popular dramatic representations" (Clum 34). And Alan Sinfield discerns yet another function, which he labels the "therapeutic mode" of AIDS drama:

> Most plays featuring AIDS . . . aspire to represent the human reality of the epidemic. They hope thereby to draw the attention of the wider community to the emergency and, above all, to help gay people with the (inter)personal dilemmas of bereavement, stigma, loss of health, and impending death. The main orientation is toward individual therapy. (317)

The one element that these visions on AIDS drama share is that they acknowledge the way in which AIDS drama looks beyond the disease itself—although that is part of the "therapeutic mode"—and addresses issues that are related to the rhetoric of plague. De Jongh focuses on the rhetoric that places gay men outside the sacrosanct unit of the heterosexual nuclear family and which allows them only a second-rate position in society. Clum refers to the plague rhetoric when he mentions the "misapprehensions about AIDS" (34).

Even though AIDS is no longer the same disease that it was in the 1980s, the drama that was produced at the height of the epidemic still has the potential to intervene in the rhetoric surrounding AIDS today. In addition to reminding audiences of the way in which gay men in the 1980s fell victim to disease and plague alike, it can counter contemporary instances of plague rhetoric, exemplified by the historiographies marking gay marriage as the culmination point of gay liberation and, implicitly, as the end of the AIDS crisis. Such narratives all too often summarize the history of gay men in America along the following lines: Gays used to be oppressed, then came Stonewall and the sexual freedom of the 1970s, a freedom which could not but lead to AIDS. Nowadays, we have gay marriage, and the hedonist days of the 1970s are over, as is AIDS, which is a direct consequence of promiscuity. By associating AIDS with sexual license, and presenting gay marriage as a point of closure, such historiographies, while declaring the disease over, revive the plague. Now, as in the past, the theatre can offer resistance to such rhetoric.

A third contribution that a revival of AIDS drama could make is showing the great variety of responses to the epidemic. However, for drama to be able to fulfill this potential, plays from storage memory need to be retrieved. With the exception of *The Normal Heart*—which, as I argue below, reinforces plague rhetoric rather than fights it—such revivals are rare if not nonexistent. Complementary to new AIDS plays being produced today—Tim Pinckney's *Still at Risk* and Matthew Lopez's *The Inheritance* among the most prominent produced in 2018—a revival of forgotten plays could make a significant contribution to the cultural memory of the AIDS crisis as it played out in the 1980s.

FUNCTIONAL MEMORY: *THE NORMAL HEART*

As pointed out in the anecdote that opened this chapter, not only is *The Normal Heart* the most prominent AIDS play from the 1980s, but it is also the most authoritative. However, it is also the most problematic because of its preoccupation with finding guilty parties to blame for the epidemic. In its search for culprits, the play all too frequently buys into the plague rhetoric of the time, which presumes that gay men brought the disease upon themselves. Parties that are particularly singled out are the New York City authorities for their inaction in the face of a health crisis, and the gay community itself, for having infected each other with HIV through their supposedly wanton lifestyle, for turning a blind eye towards the seriousness of AIDS, and for refusing to amend a lifestyle revolving exclusively around sex.

For example, in a scene where the main character, Ned Weeks, a thinly disguised alter ego of the playwright, is discussing the emerging health crisis with physician Emma Brookner, he describes the gay community as "millions of men who have singled out promiscuity to be their principal political agenda, the one they'd die before abandoning"—a remark which is followed by Emma's rhetorical question: "Are you saying you guys can't relate to each other in a non-sexual way?" (Kramer 1985, 12). Immediately after this exchange, during which the image of gay men in New York as a bunch of sex-crazed, irresponsible, and emotionally stunted men has been firmly established, the play tries to mitigate this representation with a comment that, unfortunately, only makes things worse. Weeks first explains that "[i]t's more complicated than that" since "[f]or a lot of guys it is not easy to meet each other in any other way" (Kramer 1985, 12): a remark which suggests that their focus on sexual contacts is not primarily a character weakness of gay men themselves. The words "it is not easy" imply that it is society which makes it difficult for gay men to meet in any other way. However, he then concludes by saying that "[i]t's a way of connecting—which becomes an addiction" (Kramer 1985, 12), a comment that reestablishes a link between homosexuality and illness.

Kramer's depiction of gay men as suffering from sex addiction—a phenomenon that is generally viewed both as an illness and as a moral failure—provides the foundation for the idea that it was their irresponsible behavior that led to the AIDS crisis. In following this cause and effect reasoning, *The Normal Heart* not only echoes the plague rhetoric, but also positions itself within the tradition of realistic drama. As John Clum points out,

> Since realistic drama is usually postulated on some scheme of moral, social or psychological cause and effect, diseases in drama tend to have moral, social, or psychological causes, thus mirroring society's tendency to link disease and morality. It is not surprising, then, that causality becomes central to AIDS

drama, as it is central to much of AIDS discourse, in which the cause of AIDS becomes not the retrovirus but the mode of transmission: nonprocreative, transgressive sex. (39–40)

Causality indeed is central to *The Normal Heart*. The play opens with a scene in which the protagonist, hunting for the cause of the new, mysterious disease that is affecting mostly gay men, visits a hospital to be enlightened by the medical authorities. And from that same scene onwards, it is made clear that there is a causal relationship between the gay sexual subculture of the 1970s and AIDS. What transforms the representation of this causal relationship into plague rhetoric is the moral high ground that *The Normal Heart* takes in its description of those participating in this sexual subculture as incapable of anything else but short-lived sexual relationships, and of those engaged in gay politics as "the great unwashed radicals of any counterculture" (Kramer 1985, 11).

That over the years Kramer has held on to his moralistic outlook on AIDS is borne out by *The Normal Heart*'s 2014 reincarnation as a TV drama, for which Kramer wrote the screenplay. A new opening scene written specifically for this new version reinforces the idea that a hedonistic gay community has brought AIDS onto itself. It juxtaposes the character of Ned with a community that seems only interested in partying and sex. As the title sequence rolls, the camera zooms in on a Fire Island beach party in full swing. On the edges of the party, men are obviously engaged in various al fresco sexual activities—nothing too explicit, however. This is a film made for television, not a piece of radical theatre. At various points in these scenes, Ned is depicted as the responsible outsider: he does not partake in the sexual frolicking on the beach or in the bushes, but instead finds himself the object of criticism for his speaking out against this hedonist culture.

The TV version of *The Normal Heart* leaves no doubt that gay sexual culture inexorably leads to death. After having introduced its audience to the free and easy life at Fire Island, the TV drama shows its dire consequences: a young man suddenly drops dead on the beach where a party has just taken place. As if to pinpoint the exact cause of death, the film then cuts to Ned Weeks on the ferry home, reading the *New York Times*'s first article on AIDS. By following the party scene with the death scene, the film, like the original play, suggests a causal relationship between the two, thus not only echoing the plague rhetoric of the time, but also repeating what Dion Kagan calls "a key trope in gay and AIDS history writing" (217).

Another way that *The Normal Heart* prefers to employ plague rhetoric rather than resist it lies in its advocacy of gay marriage. The play, both in its original version and in the TV adaptation, at various times voices the idea that monogamous relationships would have prevented AIDS. Blame for not having acquired gay marital rights is apportioned both to the government and to the gay community. "Maybe if they'd let us get married to begin with none of this would have happened at all," says Tommy, one of the protagonist's few supporters (Kramer 1985, 60), while Ned Weeks berates his peers for having fought for sexual liberation instead of marriage. Here again the play frames the issue in terms of blame.

The Normal Heart contrasts what it sees as the gay community's pursuit of superficial sexual pleasure with Ned's search for true love. Having established that the sexual abandon of Fire Island and the bathhouses led to AIDS, the play counteracts this with the loving relationship between Ned and Felix. Sexuality is part of this relationship as well—an ironical footnote to Ned and Emma's collective call to the gay community to stop having sex to halt the AIDS crisis—but the play clearly distinguishes between the supposed loveless sex in the gay scene and sex within marriage. However, making such a distinction is another instance of plague rhetoric, as Alison Redick remarks:

> [T]he widely accepted idea that promiscuous or public sex is inherently less safe than monogamous or private sex places blame for the potential rise in HIV transmission upon a "lifestyle" instead of specific sexual practices. This is the foundation for the treacherous prevention strategy that sustains the illusion that sex with someone familiar is somehow safeguarded against transmitting HIV. (97)

The closing scene, which shows Ned and Felix's wedding, underscores the play's philosophy. The marriage ceremony does not herald a happy and sexually safe future, but instead Felix succumbs to AIDS, his past sexual transgressions extracting their toll. Ned and Felix's marriage is doomed, not because the marriage itself is imperfect, but because of Felix's lifestyle before committing to Ned.

At a time when gay marriage has become a reality, current revivals of *The Normal Heart* perpetuate the rhetoric of blame in a way that could not have been foreseen when the play was first produced. Whereas in 1984 the play's promarriage stance could only be interpreted as "if only we had fought for/ had been granted the right to marry, then the AIDS crisis would not have occurred," in the twenty-first century, the same viewpoint suggests "now that we have achieved gay marriage, we are immune to AIDS." In this sense, *The Normal Heart* today provides a (false) sense of closure, which, as Marita Sturken remarks, is one important aspect of docudrama.

> The cinematic docudrama exerts significant influence in the construction of national memory in the United States. For much of the American public, docudramas are a primary source of historical information. They afford us a means through which uncomfortable histories of traumatic events can be smoothed over, retold, and ascribed new meanings. Like a memorial, the do-

cudrama offers closure, a process that can subsume cultural memory and personal memory into history. (85)

Sturken identifies two significant characteristics of docudrama: its importance as an educational tool, and its tendency to provide closure. In its most recent reincarnations, *The Normal Heart* offers closure in its implicit suggestion that gay marriage is the cure to AIDS, and smoothes over the fact that gay marriage is still a controversial issue within the gay community.

In the introductory paragraph, I remarked on the way in which *The Normal Heart* is marketed and perceived as an authoritative docudrama on the AIDS crisis. Whether it deserves its status as "a primary source of historical information" is questionable. Not only do current revivals, both onstage and on TV, repeat the plague rhetoric of the original version, additional scenes written for the TV version once more underscore this rhetoric; further, the play's argument on gay marriage offers closure in a way that perpetuates the rhetoric of blame while simultaneously lulling the audience into a false sense of security. Through its suggestion that promiscuity leads to disease and death and that marriage might have prevented the AIDS crisis, the play once again attributes blame to those who fell victim to the disease. The history lesson that it teaches its audience, who through the notes in the playbill are encouraged to take its portrayal of events at face value, is that gay men once engaged in irresponsible behavior that irrevocably led to disease and death. Additionally, current performances suggest that now that gay men can safely retreat within the confines of gay marriage, AIDS has become something belonging to a murky past of alleged sexual excess, with those who died from AIDS to blame for their disease. An artifact of cultural memory that makes such strong claims to authority while perpetuating the plague rhetoric from the 1980s is in dire need of countermemories that remember the AIDS crisis from a different perspective.

STORAGE MEMORY: THE AIDS PLAYS BY ROBERT CHESLEY

The Normal Heart did not always have the authoritative position that it enjoys today. Since its first performance, it has met with fierce criticism, academic and journalistic alike. Today, whereas Kramer's work is still widely discussed, the works of his contemporaries, which approach the AIDS crisis from different angles, and which could serve to mitigate the authority of *The Normal Heart*, seem to have disappeared from memory. One of the playwrights whose work was often juxtaposed to *The Normal Heart* was Robert Chesley. Discussion of his plays can be found in the overviews of gay drama published in the 1980s and 1990s (Clum, Sinfield, Román). However, attention to his work has waned. Recent monographs on AIDS drama and performance (Haas, Kagan, Campbell, and Gindt) make no reference to either Chesley or his work. Nevertheless, because they could challenge the authoritative position of *The Normal Heart* through their different approach toward the AIDS crisis, Chesley's plays deserve to be removed from storage memory in order to take their place in American culture's functional memory once more. Though Chesley's work, like Kramer's, is not uncritical about elements of gay culture of the 1970s, it strongly resists the plague rhetoric that attributes blame for the health crisis to this culture, while offering more complexity in the way it represents the AIDS epidemic.

As discussed in the previous section, Kramer is highly critical of the gay sexual culture of the 1970s. His criticism of this culture dates back to the pre-AIDS era when in his controversial novel *Faggots* (1978) he lambasts it for its focus on sexual hedonism, which in his view cannot lead to love. In *The Normal Heart* he carries this argument further and posits that it is this very attitude that led to AIDS. In contrast, an early play by Robert Chesley takes a very different approach to the gay sexual subculture. *Stray Dog Story*, though it shares some of Kramer's criticism, represents this culture in a nonpatronizing way. Also, because it does not mention AIDS—surprisingly for a gay play first produced in 1982—it also does not suggest a causal relationship between gay sex and AIDS.

Stray Dog Story tells the fairy tale (pun most probably intended) of Buddy, a dog that finds his wish to be a human granted by a fairy dogmother. However, his human life ends up much more miserable than his dog's life. After his owner is murdered by a group of queerbashers, Buddy, now physically a human being but still a dog at heart, tries to bond with various members of the New York gay community, only to find himself shunned because, unfamiliar as he is with the community's unwritten rules, he fails to follow its strict codes of conduct.

In a scene where Buddy is taken home by Brett, a gay man into S&M games, Chesley's play suggests that at least some inhabitants of the New York gay scene are well versed in sex but incapable of handling love. When the sex play that Brett initiates goes awry because its heavy-handedness scares Buddy, Buddy explains that he wants "to be yours always," a declaration of love which in its turn shocks Brett into replying: "It's just—a pretty heavy fantasy—for a first date" (Chesley, *Stray Dog Story* 26).

Similar as *Stray Dog Story* may seem to *Faggots* in its portrayal of sex and love, the major difference between the two is that whereas *Faggots* is deadly serious in its argument, in Chesley's play the scene is played for comic effect (though there may well be an element of truth beneath the humor). Nowhere in *Stray Dog Story*, nor in any of his plays, does Chesley juxtapose a supposedly negative lifestyle with a morally superior loving marriage. Because it does not mention AIDS at all, it also does not suggest a causal link between gay sexual culture and disease.

Unlike *Stray Dog Story*, two other plays by Chesley do explicitly refer to AIDS, though in an entirely different manner than *The Normal Heart*. *Night Sweat* (1983) and *Jerker* (1986) explicitly resist the plague rhetoric while presenting a more complex outlook on the AIDS crisis. *Night Sweat* is based on Robert Louis Stevenson's novella *The Suicide Club* (1882), which relates how its protagonist hears about a club where those who are tired of life come to seek death. Every night, a sinister card game decides which of the club members will die and who will perform the execution. *Night Sweat* follows the plot of Stevenson's novella closely, but moves it to the era of AIDS. The Suicide Club now becomes the "Coup de Grâce" club for gay men with AIDS, where a director as sinister as the one in *The Suicide Club* offers them the opportunity to die in "the Experience," an erotic fantasy of the victim's own choosing, which the director cynically markets as "the ultimate moment of life" (Chesley, *Night Sweat* 19).

In choosing this suicide club for its setting, *Night Sweat* plays on the fascination that plague rhetoric incites for the murkier side of gay life, particularly for those eager to catalogue the sexual practices of gay men and to use AIDS as evidence for their argument that these sinful ways lead to death. Other instances where this fascination is reproduced include fictional films such as *Cruising*, where a serial killer roams the leather bars of New York, and a documentary like *Gay Sex in the 70s*, which shows a keen interest in the clubs, discos, and bathhouses where all kinds of sexual activity took place, and which the documentary suggests inevitably resulted in AIDS. Jonathan Dollimore has commented on this fascination:

> Almost as important as the promiscuous activity itself is its location. . . . In fiction especially the gay underworld has often been a place of both death and redemption. . . . Such places echo in the mythology of the modern city underworld—residually wild, but above all shadowy and transient, full of some magic and rather more loss. Epitomizing that world is the basement club. (296)

Dollimore's observations on representations of the gay underworld apply to how Kramer's *Faggots* describes the New York gay scene of the 1970s: explicit in sexual detail on the goings-on in the clubs and bathhouses, but condemnatory of this culture at the same time. Chesley's *Night Sweat*, with its creation of the Coup de Grâce club, similarly refers to the basement club, but, unlike Kramer's novel, leaves out every sense of enjoyment, representing it solely as a location of death. It is, therefore, hardly surprising that some found the play's choice of setting and subject matter unpalatable. In the preface to *Night Sweat*, Chesley remarks that "[r]eaction to its original production, in New York, was very divided. Some people loved it, but even closest friends behaved as if I had placed something at their feet which it was best to step over and politely ignore. My best buddy told me he wished I had never written it" (10). The implicit allusion to dog excrement underscores how repulsive this particular audience member found Chesley's play.

However, what Chesley does in *Night Sweat* is to use the location of the sinister gay club to sever the supposed link between gay sexual culture and death. He does so by taking two well-known tropes (the suicidal and the homicidal homosexual) from classic gay drama only to use them as means to combat the rhetoric of blame. The classic character of the murderous homosexual villain, best known from plays such as Patrick Hamilton's *Rope* (1929, later filmed by Alfred Hitchcock), plays on the myth of the homosexual as predator. The trope of the suicidal homosexual, such as Blanche's husband in Tennessee William's *Streetcar Named Desire* and the schoolteacher in Lillian Hellman's *The Children's Hour*, depicts the homosexual as a tragic figure whose unnatural ways can only lead to death. The AIDS epidemic revived these tropes, with plague rhetoric suggesting simultaneously that gay men had killed each other through deviant sexual acts, and that they had killed themselves by these same acts.

In Stevenson's original story, the villain of the piece is the owner of the suicide club. Chesley's *Night Sweat* builds on this by casting the director of the Coup de Grâce club in the same role. He is the one responsible for organizing the demise of his "clients," for falsely advertising these murders as the ultimate sexual experience, and for justifying his heinous acts by insisting that his clients "have chosen to be victims, *insist* upon it!" (Chesley, *Night Sweat* 53). In addition to the director, *Night Sweat* features a second murderer, a homicidal homosexual who proves to be suicidal as well. It is the character of Jeppy Williams, former owner of the "Sepulchre Baths." While being interrogated by the inquisition, who are part of his "experience," he confesses that "I killed you all! . . . I sold you *all* down the river! Because you *deserve* to die, faggots!" (Chesley, *Night Sweat* 59). Both the director's and the bathhouse owner's comments reproduce plague rhetoric, suggesting that it is gay men themselves who have brought upon their own deaths because of their depraved lifestyle.

The manner in which *Night Sweat* takes issue with the plague rhetoric is significant. Whereas *The Normal Heart* is a piece of naturalistic drama, focusing on cause and effect (cf. John Clum's comment above), *Night Sweat* is very much a nonrealistic play, set in a nightmarish landscape.[1] In his elaborate study of the homicidal homosexual in theatre, Jordan Schildcrout remarks on the potential of nonrealistic plays, claiming that such plays are:

> rich sites of interpretation because they problematize conventions of realism by combining them with nonrealistic theatricality and intimations of the metaphysical, thus encouraging the audience to interpret the drama both literally and figuratively at the same time. . . . Thus, these plays position the homicidal homosexual as a character who exists simultaneously as a literal character and

a symbolic representative of metaphysical forces. In doing so, these plays challenge the symbolic order that positions the queer as evil. (132)

Whether or not *Night Sweat* encourages its audiences to ponder on the metaphysical, it certainly does not offer clear-cut answers to major problems, in the manner of naturalistic drama like *The Normal Heart*. Instead, through its complexity, which makes it impossible for an audience to interpret the drama literally, it encourages spectators to find meaning on a different level, provided they are not immediately put off by the play's gruesome imagery. That deeper level may not necessarily be metaphysical, despite what Schildcrout seems to suggest. Through its portrayal of the director and the bathhouse owner, *Night Sweat* also invites the audience to reflect on the politics of AIDS. Because of the characters' obnoxiousness, they played into the plague rhetoric that gay men are destined for death, while simultaneously reminding the audience that characters spouting this kind of rhetoric are well and truly alive in the real world. Much more than representing metaphysical forces, they also represent conservative political figures, such as Senator Jesse Helms, who through their antigay words and actions exacerbated the AIDS crisis rather than mitigated it. It is they that *Night Sweat*'s homicidal homosexuals resemble much more than those tragic figures of classic drama.

It is not only in their choice of genre, but also in their sexual politics that *The Normal Heart* and *Night Sweat* differ. Kramer, as discussed earlier, claims that the sexualized life in the gay scene cannot lead to love, but rather to AIDS, and that at a time of plague, gay men should take a "just say no" approach to sex altogether. Chesley, on the other hand, encourages his audience to resist the plague rhetoric that labels gay sex as unequivocally negative. For Chesley, gay sex is not separated from love. Instead, it is a gift to be enjoyed to the full.

Chesley's sex-positive stance is given dramatic shape through the characters of Richard and Allan. Richard is a young man who because of AIDS has lost the will to live and signs up for an "experience" at the Coup de Grâce club. However, as his death scene, entitled "the ultimate disco," is being prepared, the club is invaded by the Sisters of Perpetual Indulgence, a group of AIDS activists who are not a product of the author's imagination but who were active in San Francisco at the time. It is they who rescue Richard from his fate and reunite him with his lover, Allan. Their relationship, however, could not be more different from Ned and Felix's in *The Normal Heart*. While Ned and Felix's marriage juxtaposes monogamous bliss with sexual abandon, which in Kramer's view is separate from love, the character of Allan in *Night Sweat*, although he professes his sincere love for Richard, makes no sexual claims on him. Instead, he encourages Richard to live as full a sexual life as possible, proclaiming: "Live until the very *moment* you die! And make love! Make love in every possible, safe and sensible way! Enjoy it all, from the most delicate cruising to the heaviest S and M trips!" (Chesley, *Night Sweat* 66). For Allan, there is no separation between sex and love. He does not encourage Richard to "have sex" but to "make love," a turn of phrase that emphasizes that sex need not be monogamous to merit the label of love.

Allan's closing statement that "you *can* wake up from this nightmare" (Chesley, *Night Sweat* 67) severs the automatic link between sex and death that the Director, and those employing plague rhetoric, presumed. However, *Night Sweat* does not offer a neat closure in which Richard and Allan now set off towards the sunset. Richard's final words, with which the play ends, are "I want to live" (Chesley, *Night Sweat* 68), but the play does not make clear whether he really wakes up from his nightmare and leaves the club. Despite Allan's claim that gay men should embrace life and love, the play does not shy away from the harsh reality of AIDS at the time. Instead, its open ending provides the audience with food for thought.

Chesley's second AIDS play, *Jerker* (1986), leaves the nonrealism of *Night Sweat* and takes on the issue of sex and love through a piece of realistic drama. The play consists of a number of telephone conversations between two men engaging in phone sex. Instead of heeding Larry Kramer's call to stop having sex, they have found a safe way of enjoying it. As might be expected, the first few scenes consist of erotic fantasies—resulting in the radio station that originally broadcast the play receiving calls for prosecution—but as the play continues, it changes in character. In a scene where the characters reminisce about the sexual heydays of the 1970s, the play takes issue with plague rhetoric:

> Bert: But, you know, everyone's putting it down nowadays. *(Mimicking.)* "The party's over! The party's over! *(Own voice.)* Well, fuck it all, *no! That wasn't just a party!* It was more, a *lot* more, at least to some of us, and it was *connected* to other parts of our lives, *deep* parts, *deep* connections. . . . It was *loving*, even if you didn't know whose cock it was in the dark, or whose asshole you were sucking. And *I don't regret a single moment of it: not one.* (Chesley, *Jerker* 98–99)

In this scene, *Jerker* explicitly contradicts Larry Kramer's view that it was impossible to find love in a culture that revolved around sex. For Bert, similar to Allan in *Night Sweat*, love and sex are not separate, but intertwined. J.R., the other character and a Vietnam veteran, makes this a political point when he claims that the Vietnam War, not gay sex, was immoral.

By the end of the play, J.R. and Bert's relationship has developed far beyond superficial contact. Even though the men have never met in person, over their phone conversations, a sincere love has blossomed. However, their relationship is tragically cut short. In the final scene, Bert's phone call remains unanswered, the operator's voice telling him that the number he dialed has been disconnected, suggesting that Bert has died of AIDS. However, *Jerker* does not allow Bert's death to become a vehicle for plague rhetoric. Unlike *The Normal Heart*, where Felix's death in the closing scene confirms the idea that his past sexual transgressions have now exacted retribution, *Jerker*, through its celebration of sexuality and the characters' refusal to repent for a supposedly sinful past, explicitly resists such rhetoric. In its sex-positive attitude, it provides a powerful countermemory to Kramer's play, and therefore deserves to be recovered from storage memory.

CONCLUSION

In *The Haunted Stage* Marvin Carlson explores how theatre can function as a "memory machine." Though his study focuses solely on the ways in which new performances call forth memories of earlier performances (of the same play, of earlier plays by the same author, of earlier performances by the same actors), his claim that theatre is a memory machine holds true for AIDS drama as well. The primary function of this kind of drama is not to evoke memories of earlier performances, but to conjure up past events—either historical events, such as those depicted in *The Normal Heart*, or fictional events set at a particular point in the past, as depicted in plays by Robert Chesley. In this respect these plays function as pieces of docudrama, evoking the early years of the AIDS crisis.

The play that most prominently functions as docudrama is *The Normal Heart*. However, its prominence is not unproblematic, considering the three roles I suggested that drama from the early days of the AIDS crisis could play today: inviting the audience to look beyond AIDS as a mere disease, intervening in current instances of plague rhetoric, and showing the great variety of responses to AIDS. While certainly fulfilling the first role—the play focuses largely on AIDS as plague rather than as disease—*The Normal Heart* at various points subscribes to plague rhetoric rather than resists it. Its protagonist, the author's alter ego, depicts the gay community as sexual radicals who are blind to the fact that their behavior is the very cause of the disease. Additionally, if not propagating gay marriage outright as the solution to the AIDS crisis, the play does argue that if the gay liberationists of the seventies had campaigned for marriage instead of sexual freedom, the health crisis might have been prevented. Finally, *The Normal Heart* falls short of the third role that AIDS drama could play today: offering a variety of viewpoints. Instead, it hammers home the protagonist's viewpoint on the epidemic, without leaving room for dissent. In view of Assmann's statement that functional memory "provides values that supports identity and norms" (123),

The Normal Heart's advocating values that echo the plague rhetoric of blame is worrying.

Plays that put forward a different view, such as those by Robert Chesley, have been relegated to the domain of storage memory. Though by their radical nature less appealing to a mainstream audience, these plays nevertheless have the potential to provide a corrective to the viewpoints put forward by *The Normal Heart*. Chesley's plays firmly oppose Larry Kramer's argument that the gay sexual subculture of the 1970s caused the AIDS crisis, and provide a much more positive view on gay sexuality. Juxtaposing Chesley's plays with *The Normal Heart* could illustrate Sturken's statement that cultural memory is "the means by which divisions and conflicting agendas [of a particular culture] are revealed" (1). However, as long as plays diverging from Kramer's limited view of AIDS remain relegated to the archive, these divisions and conflicting agendas remain obscured, and Kramer's play retains its undeserved authoritative position.

In other words, as I have suggested here, the cultural memory of AIDS, as contained in the vast but mostly forgotten body of AIDS drama, is in need of expansion. However much *The Normal Heart* may market itself as *the* historically accurate play about AIDS, such a stance does not do justice to the variety of viewpoints presented onstage at the same time, and of which this essay has discussed only a few. Chesley's plays might be more controversial, and even unpalatable to some, yet readmitting them into the realm of functional memory would result in a more diverse, certainly more complicated, and perhaps even messy, but all in all more honest representation of the early AIDS years.

NOTE

1. In fact, the first performances of *Night Sweat* explicitly suggested that the events in the play were a dream. Though not in the published script, the performances featured a character who would be asleep throughout the play, and wake up after the main characters' final words, "I want to live" (Chesley, *Night Sweat* 68).

WORKS CITED

Altman, Lawrence K. "Rare Cancer Seen in 41 Homosexuals." *While the World Sleeps: Writing from the First Twenty Years of the Global AIDS Plague*, edited by Chris Bull. Thunder's Mouth Press, 2003, pp. 3–5.

Assmann, Aleida. *Cultural Memory and Western Civilization: Arts of Memory*. Cambridge University Press, 2011.

Campbell, Alyson and Dirk Gindt, eds. *Viral Dramaturgies: HIV and AIDS in Performance in the Twenty-First Century*. Palgrave, 2018.

Carlson, Marvin. *The Haunted Stage: The Theatre as Memory Machine*. University of Michigan Press, 2003.

Chesley, Robert. *Jerker, or the Helping Hand* (1985). *Hard Plays/Stiff Parts: The Homoerotic Plays of Robert Chesley*. Alamo Square Press, 1990, pp. 71–118.

———. *Night Sweat* (1984). *Hard Plays/Stiff Parts: The Homoerotic Plays of Robert Chesley*. Alamo Square Press, 1990, pp. 9–69.

———. *Stray Dog Story* (1982). *Plays by Robert Chesley*. Broadway Play Publishing, 2005, pp. 5–46.

Clum, John M. *Still Acting Gay: Male Homosexuality in Modern Drama*. St. Martin's Press, 2000.

Cruising. Dir. William Friedkin (1980). Warner Bros. DVD. 2008.

de Jongh, Nicholas. *Not in Front of the Audience: Homosexuality on Stage*. Routledge, 1992.

Dollimore, Jonathan. *Death, Desire, and Loss in Western Culture*. Routledge, 1998.

Gay Sex in the 70s. Dir. Joseph Lovett. Wolfe. DVD. 2006.

Haas, Astrid. *Stages of Agency: The Contribution of American Drama to the AIDS Discourse*. Universitätsverlag Winter, 2011.

Hall, Tom. "Meet Performance Artist Tim Miller." *Artswfl.com*. April 4, 2017. http://www.artswfl.com/theater-film/fgcu-theatre-program/tim-miller-artist-in-residency-devised-performance-piece/meet-performance-artist-tim-miller/meet-performance-artist-tim-miller

Hamilton, Patrick. *Rope*. (1929) Samuel French, 2003.

Hellman, Lillian. *The Children's Hour* (1934). *Forbidden Acts. Pioneering Gay and Lesbian Plays of the Twentieth Century*, edited by Ben Hodges. Applause, 2003, pp. 173–237.

Kagan, Dion. *Positive Images: Gay Men and HIV/AIDS in the Culture of "Post-Crisis."* I.B. Tauris, 2018.

Kramer, Larry. *Faggots* (1978). New Grove, 2000.

———. *The Normal Heart*. 25th anniversary edition. Nick Hern Books, 2011.

———. *The Normal Heart*. HBO Films. DVD. 2014.

Lopez, Matthew. *The Inheritance*. Faber and Faber, 2018.

The Normal Heart. Playbill. Amsterdam, 2012.

Pinckney, Tim. *Still at Risk*. 2018. Unpublished manuscript.

Redick, Alison. "Dangerous Practices: Ideological Uses of the 'Second Wave.'" *Policing Public Sex: Queer Politics and the Future of AIDS Activism*, edited by Ephen Glenn Colter. South End Press, 1996, pp. 91–104.

Román, David. *Acts of Intervention: Performance, Gay Culture, and AIDS*. Indiana University Press, 1998.

Schildcrout, Jordan. *Murder Most Queer: The Homicidal Homosexual in the American Theater*. University of Michigan Press, 2014.

Sinfield, Alan. *Out on Stage: Lesbian and Gay Theatre in the Twentieth Century*. Yale University Press, 1999.

Sontag, Susan. *Illness as Metaphor and AIDS and Its Metaphors*. Anchor Books, 1990.

Stevenson, Robert Louis. *The Suicide Club* (1882). Dover, 2000.

Sturken, Marita. *Tangled Memories: The Vietnam War, the AIDS Epidemic, and the Politics of Remembering*. University of California Press, 1997.

Watney, Simon. *Policing Desire: Pornography, AIDS and the Media*. 3rd ed. Cassell, 1997.

Williams, Tennessee. *A Streetcar Named Desire* (1947). Methuen, 1996.

Chapter Three

Poetry before Protease

Nels P. Highberg

In his 1994 poetry collection, *Ghost Letters*, Richard McCann begins with an extended poem of five parts entitled "Nights of 1990." He describes an unnamed friend dying in the hospital. In a single-lined stanza, McCann writes, "On the door to your room a discreet white sign warned: *Caution: Bodily Fluid*" (8). These lines come after pages where McCann presents varied images of the human body: "this articulation / of vertebral tumors, this rope of bulbous knots" (McCann 3). He relates, "When you straddled my hips and rose above me / I knew I had no choice but / To submit to touch again" (McCann 5). There is the image of "the body I saw in the street, / trousers down around its shit-smeared ass, flies / swarming over; bleeding, half-conscious body" (McCann 7). There is the scene where the poem's speaker kneels before a man "in the wet uncut grass" in a field by a train station (McCann 4). McCann presents the human body as a site of redemption, revulsion, passion, connection, and fear, conflicts and confusions that fueled the work of many other poets struggling to represent AIDS in their poetry then, now, and into the foreseeable future.

I start with this poem, not because of these images but because of the reference to the year in its title: 1990, a date right in the middle of the first years of the AIDS crisis in the United States, not only in terms of the crisis itself, but also in terms of its representation. With an eye toward representation, in particular, poetic representation, I focus here on poetry and scholarship written in the United States during the late 1980s and early 1990s, which were, quite simply, a different time, especially in regard to gay white cisgender men living in the United States and Western Europe. As I will suggest toward the end of this chapter, more recently published poets in the United States do different things—represent HIV/AIDS differently—not because

AIDS is no longer a crisis, but rather because it is a different crisis for them now than it was in the years surrounding 1990.

In this chapter, I concentrate on what was happening *then*, not just in terms of poetry, but also in terms of scholarship, as I see uncanny ways in which both modes of writing grapple similarly with the emergent crisis. Something seemed to change, however, in the intervening years, as the advent of protease inhibitors in the mid-1990s radically altered the medical realities of those infected with HIV—much like the FDA approval of pre-exposure prophylaxis (PrEP) in 2012, especially for gay white cisgender men living in the United States and Western Europe. As a graduate student in the humanities in those first years before protease, I encountered most of the texts, both poetic and scholarly, that fuel this chapter, texts that I, along with the cultural consciousness of the United States generally, seem to have forgotten when protease inhibitors came on the scene. That is a problem, a problem of forgetting, of amnesia of the time "before," that I intend to rectify. There lies immense value in studying the poetry of the past, even when we seem to have come out of the particular crisis of that time. As I will argue here, the words—poetic, scholarly, theoretical, critical—written during that traumatic time can teach us how to reflect on the words written about our contemporary traumas, those that have arisen in recent decades that we could never imagine then.

We need, in other words, to fight forgetfulness by remembering. To that end, the final pages of this essay feature a list of single-authored books and edited collections published in the years before the advent of protease inhibitors. This is work, in other words, that remains lost and forgotten from a time *before*—poetic works that we need to return to in order to find answers to our current problems with HIV/AIDS representation and, in particular, remembrance. The authors are mainly gay cisgender white men, which parallels broader structural inequities in literary and cultural institutions then and now, but works by African American men, Latino men, and white women also appear on the list.

I will first, however, turn to a brief history of medical advancements, which, as Jennifer Lavoie also argues in this collection, almost seem to parallel shifts in literary writing about AIDS in the United States. The genesis for the essays in *Forty Years Later*, whether directly or indirectly, can be found in the fear, ignorance, and denial that surrounded the first cases of what came to be known as AIDS after they were first reported in 1981. In the subsequent years, chaos limited progress. In 1983 and 1984, French and American scientists began battling over who should be allowed to claim discovery of the retrovirus believed to cause AIDS, a retrovirus that would not earn the name human immunodeficiency virus (HIV) until 1986; this battle for ownership of discovery would not end until each side agreed to share it in 1987. Four years were spent in court battles and political maneuverings over ownership rather than in the lab or with patients themselves. The president of the United States at the time, Ronald Reagan, was effectively ignoring the existence of the disease, waiting until 1985 to mention AIDS publicly for the first time and until 1987 to speak about it with any depth. Activists fought long and hard to increase research funding and social services and to demand basic respect for the mostly marginalized peoples living with HIV, but the number of people dying from AIDS-related complications simply kept growing and growing.

Protease inhibitors provided the first seismic shift in decreasing the number of those dying from HIV and increasing the number of those who were living with it. In 1987, the US Food and Drug Administration (FDA) approved the first drug meant to impede the progress of HIV's seemingly inevitable destruction of the human body, azidothymidine (AZT); many patients and doctors worried that the possible side effects of AZT (e.g., fatigue, anemia, lactic acidosis, hepatic steatosis) and HIV's ability to mutate quickly and easily enough to develop resistance to AZT would trade one set of problems for another. The first protease inhibitor met FDA approval in December 1995, with two more out in 1996 and one in 1997. Encouraging results were practically immediate. People were still dying, but survival seemed possible for the first time in fifteen years. With the gift of time, something never an option for the thousands who died before and just after protease inhibitors became available (and since), it is now possible to collect the abundance of poetry, plays, novels, short stories, memoirs, and essays created about the collective and individual effects of living in a world with AIDS and to examine how literature about AIDS addressed the abundant traumas of such a dark time.

In this chapter, I turn particularly to poetry. Perhaps this focus is a bit arbitrary. As the work by my peers also included in this collection makes obvious, there are many options for analyses of diverse literary genres. I am drawn to poetry, first, because there is just so much of it.

I am not, however, arguing that these particular authors deserve placement in the American literary canon. That argument will need detailed, extensive scrutiny for what we mean by "American," "literary," and "canon." My primary purpose is not argumentative but archival. Much of this work has been forgotten, books that have gone out of print and authors who are no longer with us. Some are still active writers whether in poetry or other genres, and some are living lives doing other things. My desire here is remembrance: first, to remember these authors and their texts, and, second, to remember the time, the constant dread, and the flickers of light.

Poetry is a genre of imagination fueled by creative uses of words and phrases, sound and imagery. Gregory Orr, prolific poet and longtime professor, has recently developed a framework that enables writers and readers of poetry to scrutinize, as he puts it, "language use in poetry" (155), with the following categories of such "language use" including: naming, singing, saying, and imagining (Orr 155). Generally, naming and saying lean toward more expository purposes, and singing and imagining are potentially more whimsical. Orr continues, "These four kinds of language use are layered or mixed into poems in varying proportions depending on the poet and the poem, so that what results is the rich complexity of meaning and sound that we recognize as a poem" (157). He follows with a caveat: "[T]hese qualities can be roughly distinguished from one another; yet in actual language use they aren't distinct but mingle and braid and overlap in the rich flow of speech or writing" (Orr 158). I highlight these points not to insert a formative taxonomy into my analysis but as a reminder that a lot about language is up for grabs when it comes to poetry. Playfulness arises alongside earnest serious-mindedness. Words embody simultaneous—and sometimes ironic—multiple meanings and purposes.

Playfulness and shifting word meanings do not seem to align with prevailing approaches toward representing illness from the time. Susan Sontag quite famously cautioned against using metaphor—in poetry and elsewhere—to represent the realities of living in a world (or body) surrounded by illness. In 1978, Sontag published *Illness as Metaphor*, stating explicitly on the opening page, "My point is that illness is *not* a metaphor, and that the most truthful way of regarding illness—and the healthiest way of being ill—is one most purified of, most resistant to, metaphoric thinking" (3). In 1989, Sontag updated her thinking in *AIDS and Its Metaphors* by stating clearly on the first page, "Of course, one cannot think without metaphors. But that does not mean there aren't some metaphors we might well abstain from or try to retire" (93). Sontag is right on both counts. Basic thinking requires relying on metaphor, simile, or simple comparison, but all figures of speech can be interpreted in ways that lead to ill effects.

None of this is to say that poets writing about AIDS in the years before protease did not have the same goal as the theorists writing at the same time: to represent AIDS when it was destroying life faster than seemed possible. Metaphoric writing? Factual data? At a certain level, no one really cared what language was used if it could play a role in promoting social change and raising the voices crying out. As much as academics were immersed in postmodern and poststructural theories of language, there were scholars fighting—and I use that metaphoric verb intentionally—to find a way to represent reality while simultaneously trying to find out what was real about this virus. The October 19, 1994, issue of the *Chronicle of Higher Education* focused deeply on the effects of HIV on academia. One article, with the unmistakable title of "AIDS as Metaphor," rightfully anointed four scholars as leaders in meeting the challenges of conducting deep analytical thought at what felt like lightning speed: Douglas Crimp, Cindy Patton, Paula A. Treichler, and Simon Watney (McMillen A18). In terms of academic discipline, these scholars represent great diversity, having been trained in art history, sociology, linguistics, and medicine.

Still, they each argued for greater awareness of how the language used to depict HIV/AIDS affects public policy, medical procedures, and individual life decisions. In my mind, poetry before 1996 plays a significant role in these other domains. In 1987, Douglas Crimp edited *AIDS: Cultural Analysis Cultural Activism*, a special issue of the academic journal *October* that was subsequently published as a separate book and immediately became one of the most foundational texts in the sociopolitical analysis of HIV/AIDS. Crimp argues in the introduction, "AIDS intersects with and requires a critical rethinking of all culture: of language and representation, of science and medicine, of health and illness, of sex and death, of the public and private realms" (15). Treichler concurs in her chapter, reprinted in her 1999 collection, *How to Have Theory in an Epidemic: Cultural Chronicles of AIDS*: "the very nature of AIDS is constructed through language and in particular the discourses of medicine and science" (11). But Treichler clarifies that analysis of the language of medicine and science should not be privileged over the analysis of other rhetorical situations. As she spells out, "the AIDS epidemic is simultaneously an epidemic of a transmissible lethal disease and an epidemic of meanings or signification. Both epidemics are equally crucial for us to understand" (11). One of Patton's earliest contributions to the discussion appears in 1990's *Inventing AIDS*: "Representations of AIDS seem inadequate, even sinister, carriers of the deep, unconscious political anxieties that inhabit the terrain which those who engage with the epidemic must negotiate daily. And yet we *must* speak about our experience, participate in public debate, make experiences out of which broader scientific and pedagogical strategies may be created" (2). Of course, some may claim that it is much easier to argue for the kind of work to be done than to do the work itself.

Watney takes on the challenge of doing this almost microscopic level of work directly in his contribution to the collection, *Taking Liberties: AIDS and Cultural Politics*, published in 1989 (and a revision of a leaflet Watney created for British journalists). Like many poets of the time, Watney zeroes in on the specificity of how individual words shape understandings of HIV/AIDS. Watney worries that "careless" and "ill-informed" writing detracts from the knowledge gained through the actions of scientists and activists (184). For example, he notes that HIV is *infectious* but not *contagious*. Infectious diseases are caused by distinct bacteria or viruses in limited and particular situations. Contagious diseases transfer from one person to another through various forms of physical interaction or encounters with microbes traveling in the air. HIV, he notes, "cannot be 'caught' like the common cold. All terms which imply contagion, such as 'spreading' or 'catching' should be rejected" (184). Watney was also among the first writers to challenge the notion of "high-risk groups" who were more vulnerable to contracting HIV than those from other identity categories. As he clearly states, "With HIV it cannot be sufficiently emphasized that risk comes from what you do, not how you label yourself" (Watney 185).

The principal distinction Watney makes is that between HIV and AIDS itself. "AIDS is not a disease as such," he writes, "but a collection of many different medical conditions including infections, cancers, and tumors, which may emerge as a result of damage to the body's immunological defenses caused by the Human Immunodeficiency Virus" (Watney 184). Watney was challenging those, especially the educated professionals, who would use "AIDS" and "HIV" interchangeably and create the impression that they were one and the same. Watney separates the viral agent we recognize today as HIV from the syndrome of AIDS, which is a collection of distinct medical issues that demand specific treatments.

The poetry written about AIDS at the time delved deeply into these distinctions between identities and actions, syndromes and disease. Joseph Cady presents a full analytical framework he developed in the midst of these chaotic years that focuses on delineating how writers approach representing HIV and AIDS in his 1993 chapter, "Immersive and Counterimmersive Writing about AIDS: The Achievement of Paul Monette's *Love Alone*," included in the formative collection, *Writing AIDS: Gay Literature, Language, and Analysis*. Essentially, for Cady, immersive writing features "prolonged moments when the reader is thrust into a direct imaginative confrontation with the special horrors of AIDS and is required to deal with them with no relief or buffer provided by the writer" (Cady 244). On the other hand, "counterimmersive AIDS writing typically focuses on characters or speakers who are in various degrees of denial about AIDS themselves, and it customarily treats its readers the way its characters handle their disturbing contact with AIDS, protecting them from too jarring a confrontation with the subject through a variety of distancing devices" (Cady 244). Cady uses Paul Monette's collection *Love Alone* as his primary example of "the fullest and finest example so far of immersive AIDS writing" (247).

Monette published *Love Alone: Eighteen Elegies for Rog* in 1988. Rog refers to Roger Horowitz, Monette's longtime partner, who died of complications due to HIV in 1986. Monette says in the book's preface, "These elegies were written during the five months after he died, one right after the other, with hardly a half day's pause between" (xii). It makes perfect sense Cady would see these poems as immersive considering Monette wrote them while, in fact, immersed in the pain, anger, and sorrow of grief. As Cady states, "*Love Alone* is dominated by explicit, intense, and unembarrassed statements of painful personal feeling" (247). Stylistically, the collection embodies an "immersive" approach in that there is little to no punctuation throughout. There is the occasional backslash in a date or an apostrophe to show possession, but no periods, exclamation points, or question marks signal the ends of sentences, and there are no stanza breaks anywhere. Though each poem is clearly titled, all words slide from one to the other to the next without pause. This is a true display of the spontaneous overflow of powerful emotion said to characterize the poetry of the self that evolved throughout Romanticism; these emotions just tend to be painful, negative, and the kinds most people try to avoid at all costs.

The immersive aspect of Monette's poetry can also be found in his presentation of the literal medical realities Monette, Rog, and others in their immediate community had to face. For example, "Current Status 1/22/87" chronicles one of Monette's visits to his own doctor to address HIV's destruction of his own body. Monette's T4 cells, the parts of the human immune system that detect and fight foreign invaders (and that HIV obliterates), number 465, fifteen fewer than the previous August and thirty-five more than the previous June (34). The size of his swelling lymph nodes—just under a centimeter in his neck but over a centimeter in his armpit—is notable but "not suggestive / unless they harden or start to throb" (Monette 34). His bowels are normal, though, he notes, "I peer at each specimen / in the bowl like an oracle poking entrails" (Monette 34). He lists the amounts of drugs coursing through his system: 400 milligrams of Ribavirin, an "equal dose" of Acyclovir, twenty milligrams of Sinequan, and fifteen milligrams of Dalmane (Monette 34–35). He sweats. He cries. Still, he does not suffer as Rog did. Monette remembers Rog suffering through "six / spinals" and the way his bone marrow was "sipped by / a ten-inch needle" (35) while a milliliter of Xylocaine turned Rog's larynx to "slush," quelling his voice "to a strangle / for two three hours" (36). These immersive details exemplify Watney's call to understand HIV as a virus that leads to the syndrome of conditions that have come to define AIDS. The specifics Monette details are unique to his body, but they represent the kinds of things HIV-positive patients worry about and that most who are not HIV-positive can routinely ignore.

Cady presents the idea of counterimmersive texts primarily to criticize them for allowing audiences to maintain their passive ignorance and active denial. Interestingly, Cady finds his examples of counterimmersive writing in fiction written by gay white men such as Andrew Holleran, David B. Feinberg, Edmund White, and others who, in Cady's view, create characters who distance themselves from the disease and the syndrome even while living in the midst of them. To those who would posit that these characters are meant to represent denial but not encourage it, Cady asserts, "any critique of character in counterimmersive AIDS writing ordinarily does not go beyond muted implication, and counterimmersive writing typically does not include in its texts any forceful alternative to its characters' detachment" (257). Therefore, this kind of writing "exempts its audience from too close a contact with the horrors of AIDS and makes no compelling demands on the denying reader to change" (Cady 257).

Counterimmersive approaches should be recognized as such and challenged, but I posit that some of these distancing techniques can actually represent an everyday way of living in a world with AIDS in it, and poetry acknowledges such realities. In 1992, acclaimed British poet Thom Gunn, who had received fellowships from the Guggenheim Foundation and the MacArthur Foundation, published *The Man with Night Sweats*. One of the book's most recognized poems, "Lament," details the death of an unnamed man addressed directly in the second person. The first line says, "Your dying was a difficult enterprise" (Gunn 61). Right away, the language embodies its own figures of speech but is primarily formal and almost banal. He describes the "cough's dry rhetoric" as an "irritant" (Gunn 61). Several lines down, the "cough grew thick and rich" (Gunn 61). At the end, Gunn returns to the image of the cough at the moment of life's end: "Nothing remained / But death by drowning on an inland sea / Of your own fluids" (63).

Obviously, Gunn's work is distinct from Monette. Compared directly, Gunn seems distant. Beret E. Strong, in her 1994 article entitled "The Aesthetics of Rage and Civility in Poetry about AIDS" in the *Indiana Review*, suggests, "Such language operates largely outside the hospital room, making us less witness to what is actually happening to the man than imaginary witnesses of a drama borrowed from the traditional *topos* of the missionary or saint lost in a storm" (101). The final lines of the poem remain reserved as Gunn writes of the body's "blood hospitable to those guests who / Too over by betraying it into / The greatest of its inconsistencies / This difficult, tedious, painful enterprise" (64). Strong argues, "In the terms of its polite metaphor, this is a poem about a gullible host who too generously allowed evil, trickster guests into his party/body. Death is the result of throwing a very bad party, of giving opportunity to opportunistic infection" (102). I read these lines and this poem differently. "Lament" does represent a counterimmersive perspective, but it uses that distance to convey the shields and walls many caregivers build around themselves as a means of survival. This poem may depict the observation of a dying man, but that does not mean it is a poem of witness. It is a poem where a man watches the steady, relentless deterioration of a man he loves; to be available to the dying, he has to toughen his emotions.

None of this sociopolitical analysis is to say scholars in the early 1990s did not examine this poetry through literary lenses. Of particular interest for many scholars of the time is how the poetry of AIDS fits into the longstanding history of the elegy. In 1992, Gregory Woods chooses this focus in his contribution to the collection, *AIDS: The Literary Response*, "AIDS to Remembrance: The Uses of Elegy." He highlights a historical approach to the elegiac tradition and notes, "By speaking of elegy, we invoke at once, a classic sequence of sentimental friendships, which some would call love affairs, cut short by loss" (Woods 159). The following year, Ed Madden publishes "Against Transcendence: AIDS and the Elegy" in the *Borderlands: Texas Poetry Review* and expands on contemporary approaches to the elegy: "Emphatically personal and often emphatically political, the AIDS elegy, in an attempt to recover the social contexts of death, resists the poetic urge to universalize" (81). They each use Monette and Gunn as examples for analysis, but I want to focus on a forgotten text that functions in the same ways.

Just as Paul Monette eulogizes his lover, Rog, by recording his last days in 1988's *Love Alone*, Ron Schreiber eulogizes his lover John W. MacDonald, Jr., in 1989's *John*. Most of these poems are titled with dates from throughout 1986, the last year of John's life. Schreiber includes a few prose poems at various points, but most poems consist of unrhymed couplets. These short stanzas replicate the fleeting moments that fuel the final memories of this last year. There is the sparse but poignant, "'happy birthday' (6-10-86)," which states, in its entirety, "a month ago I didn't know / I'd get to say that, but now // you're here. you're home. / you're 35. // you're living" (Schreiber 45). There is more punctuation in Schreiber's poems than in Monette's, but the lack of capital letters at the start of sentences provides a stylistic connection. Schreiber's use of lowercase portrays exhaustion. He pays constant attention to John's illness, getting up in the middle of the night to give John oxygen during coughing fits or carrying John to bed before picking shards from a broken glass of water off of the floor. These elegies do not accentuate the universal, just as Madden describes, and to connect to Woods, these poems certainly reflect a love cut short.

Reading all of these poems together, I fixate on a question that needs more recent theories to begin answering: Is the proliferation of HIV a trauma? As Lauren Berlant argues in 2011's *Cruel Optimism*, "[I]n critical theory and mass society generally, 'trauma' has become the primary genre of the last eighty years for describing the historical present as the scene of an exception that has just shattered some ongoing, uneventful ordinary life that was supposed just to keep going on and with respect to which people felt solid and confident" (9). She continues, "My claim is that most such happenings that force people to adapt to an unfolding change are better described by a notion of systemic crisis or 'crisis ordinariness' and followed out with an eye to seeing how the affective impact takes form, becomes mediated" (Berlant 10). As we face the fourth decade in which people die from exposure to HIV, the notion of "systemic crisis" makes a lot of sense. The identities of the populations who die of the disease have shifted over time. The medical interventions created for those living with HIV have produced the possibility for those with access to live into the foreseeable future. AIDS is not an event that altered our realities. It is a crisis that continues to transform our world.

That will continue to be the case into the foreseeable future. In 2009's *Cruising Utopia: The Then and There of Queer Futurity*, José Esteban Muñoz envisions a queer future that is utopian because of the ways queerness promotes a sense of possibility by challenging heteronormative, misogynistic, and white supremacist narratives of how humans form relationships with each other. Most important for my project is the emphasis Muñoz places on the role of the past in creating such a future. In a close reading of Elizabeth Bishop's exquisite villanelle, "One Art," he notes, "This command to write is a command to save the ephemeral thing by committing it to memory, to word, to language. The poet instructs us to retain the last thing through a documentation of our loss, a retelling of our relationship to it" (Muñoz 71). Though he is speaking specifically of Bishop, any poet who has written about HIV/AIDS could be substituted in as "the poet." From the start, I have emphasized this chapter's archival impetus, the need to remember who was writing in the midst of chaos. These texts do not substitute for the lives lost, but they do play a role in the creation of historical memory. As Muñoz puts it, "And although we cannot simply conserve a person or a performance through documentation, we can perhaps begin to summon up, through the auspices of memory, the acts and gestures that meant so much to us" (71–72).

While I write of history and memory, I do not mean to pretend that HIV/AIDS is a problem of the past, but the problems of the past are not the problems of the present. Poetry before protease represents different experiences with the disease and the syndrome than poetry after PrEP does. Danez Smith, a genderqueer poet who goes by they/them, published *Don't Call Us Dead* in 2017, and it immediately garnered attention and awards such as the British Forward Award. They see their HIV diagnosis as part of a larger context that places black lives in jeopardy. In "recklessly," Smith connects HIV and mass incarceration to each other, a place where men live in a "bloodprison" (41). Smith's speaker states, "I got the cellblock blues," followed a few lines later with "I got the cell count blues" (41). The context in which Smith lives with HIV is vastly different than the ones mentioned throughout this chapter and included on the following reading list. Growing economic inequity paired with a lack of adequate healthcare creates a chasm between those who have access to PrEP and those who do not. Align that with the white supremacist ideologies fueling ongoing precarity of brown and black bodies, and the world is a different place than it was in the early years of HIV/AIDS. Well, the world may actually be the same in many ways, but how we talk about it is different. The call to use language carefully that fueled the earliest scholars and poets in the first years of what came to be known as AIDS is vital because there is still no cure, and people are still living with HIV and still fighting to be seen and heard. We need to respond to the present, but we can do so while remembering the past.

POETRY BEFORE PROTEASE: A READING LIST

In keeping with Visser's renewed focus on "storage memory," below is a comprehensize list of poetry collections with a central focus on HIV/AIDS. I chose 1996 as the cutoff because it was the first full year of the existence of protease inhibitors. I hope it leads to further examination of these texts as historical documents and literature. There must be gaps, and I look forward to the list's growth.

1985
Boucheron, Robert. *Epitaphs for the Plague Dead*. Ursus Press, 1985.

1988
Almond, Marc. *The Angel of Death in the Adonis Lounge*. Gay Men's Press, 1988.
Monette, Paul. *Love Alone*. St. Martin's Press, 1988.

1989
Lynch, Michael. *These Waves of Dying Friends*. Contact II Publications, 1989.
Schreiber, Ron. *John*. Hanging Loose Press and Calamus Books, 1989.

1990
Fries, Kenny. *The Healing Notebooks*. Open Books, 1990.
Lassell, Michael. *Decade Dance*. Alyson Publications, 1990.
Reed, Jeremy. *Nineties*. Jonathan Cape, 1990.

1991
Claire, Thomas. *Songs of Surrender*. Fithian Press, 1991.
Doty, Mark. *Bethlehem in Broad Daylight*. David R. Godine, 1991.

1992
Ciscel, Dennis. *Tiny Stories*. Plain View Press, 1992.
Gunn, Thom. *The Man with Night Sweats*. Noonday Press, 1992.
Holland, Walter. *A Journal of the Plague Year*. Magic City Press, 1992.
Woolverton, Terry. *Black Slip*. Clothespin Fever Press, 1992.

1993
Ciscel, Dennis. *Patting the Air*. Plain View Press, 1993.
Dent, Tony. *What Silence Equals*. Persea Books, 1993
Doty, Mark. *My Alexandria*. University of Illinois Press, 1993.
Johnson, Greg. *AID and Comfort*. University Press of Florida, 1993.
Kikel, Rudy. *Long Division*. Writers Block Publishing Company, 1993.

1994

    Campo, Rafael. *The Other Man Was Me: A Voyage to the New World.* Arte Público Press, 1994.

    McCann, Richard. *Ghost Letters.* Alice James Books, 1994.

    Monette, Paul. *West of Yesterday, East of Summer.* St. Martin's Press, 1994.

1996

    Campo, Rafael. *What the Body Told.* Duke University Press, 1996.

This is a list of anthologies of poetry that include multiple authors writing about HIV, especially its intersection with race as in the Hemphill and Hunter collections. Some include prose along with poetry.

1989

    Klein, Michael, editor. *Poets for Life: Seventy-Six Poets Respond to AIDS.* Crown, 1989.

1991

    Hadas, Rachel, editor. *Unending Dialogue: Voices from an AIDS Poetry Workshop.* Farber and Farber, 1991.

1992

    Hemphill, Essex, editor. *Brother to Brother: New Writings by Black Gay Men.* Alyson Publications, 1992.

    Miller, Andrew, editor. *Don't Hang Up: An Anthology of Poems about AIDS.* University of South Dakota Press, 1992.

1993

    Harold, John, editor. *How Can You Write a Poem When You're Dying of AIDS?* Cassell, 1993.

    Hunter, B. Michael, editor. *Sojourner: Black Gay Voices in the Age of AIDS.* Other Countries, 1993.

1995

    Newman, Lesléa, editor. *A Loving Testimony: Remembering Loved Ones Lost to AIDS.* Crossing Press, 1995.

1996

    Borger, Irene, editor. *From a Burning House: The AIDS Project Los Angeles Writers Workshop Collection.* Washington Square Press, 1996.

There remain, of course, poems published individually in literary journals of the time, especially those created by and for LGBTQ readers such as *The James White Review, Christopher Street, Bay Windows, The Evergreen Chronicles*, and others.

WORKS CITED

Berlant, Lauren. *Cruel Optimism*. Duke University Press, 2011.
Cady, Joseph. "Immersive and Counterimmersive Writing about AIDS: The Achievement of Paul Monette's *Love Alone*." *Writing AIDS: Gay Literature, Language, and Analysis*, edited by Timothy F. Murphy and Suzanne Poirier. Columbia University Press, 1993, pp. 244–264.
Crimp, Douglas, editor. *AIDS: Cultural Analysis, Cultural Activism*. MIT Press, 1987.
Gunn, Thom. *The Man with Night Sweats*. Noonday Press, 1992.
Madden, Ed. "Against Transcendence: AIDS and the Elegy." *Borderlands: Texas Poetry Review*, vol. 3, 1993, pp. 81–93.
McCann, Richard. *Ghost Letters*. Alice James Books, 1994
McMillen, Liz. "AIDS as Metaphor." *The Chronicle of Higher Education*, October 19, 1994, pp. A18–A20.
Monette, Paul. *Love Alone: Eighteen Elegies for Rog*. St. Martin's Press, 1988.
Muñoz, José Esteban. *Cruising Utopia: The Then and There of Queer Futurity*. NYU Press, 2009.
Orr, Gregory. *A Primer for Poets and Readers of Poetry*. Norton, 2018.
Patton, Cindy. *Inventing AIDS*. Routledge, 1990.
Schreiber, Ron. *John*. Hanging Loose Press, 1989.
Smith, Danez. *Don't Call Us Dead*. Graywolf Press, 2017.
Sontag, Susan. *Illness as Metaphor and AIDS and Its Metaphors*. Doubleday, 1989.
Strong, Beret E. "The Aesthetics of Rage and Civility in Poetry about AIDS." *Indiana Review*, vol. 17, 1994, pp. 99–114.
Treichler, Paula A. *How to Have Theory in an Epidemic: Cultural Chronicles of AIDS*. Duke University Press, 1999.
Watney, Simon. "AIDS, Language, and the Third World." *Taking Liberties: AIDS and Cultural Politics*, edited by Erica Carter and Simon Watney. Serpent's Tail, 1989, pp. 183–192.
Woods, Gregory. "AIDS to Remembrance: The Uses of Elegy." *AIDS: The Literary Response*, edited by Emmanuel S. Nelson. Twayne Publishers, 1992, pp. 155–166.

Chapter Four

Early Representations of IT

AIDS, the American Canon, and Robert Ferro's Second Son

Ryan Calabretta-Sajder

This chapter questions the avoidance of the term "AIDS" in early AIDS fiction and simultaneously explores the motifs of space and place. I argue that the importance of Robert Ferro's final novel, *Second Son* (1988)—an exemplary case of literature that refers only to IT in its exploration of AIDS—solidifies its place as the "first" AIDS novel in the American canon. Although Ferro's *Second Son* illustrates the difficulty of the historical moment for those diagnosed with IT, it also offers a unique sense of hope and a message of possibility lacking in most works of the period. Through not naming AIDS directly within the text, Ferro succeeds in constructing a novel permeated with hope, especially through the creation of the protagonist's Cape May home as its own character, which represents a reconstitution of the family unit.

THE NOMENCLATURE OF AIDS IN THE 1980S

The acronym AIDS was not popular with the white urban homosexual community in the United States of the 1980s. In fact, numerous authors and activists rejected the name; it distracted emotion from the individual and community and created a "scientific" or "sterile" sensation. Those active in the community tried to offer a message which resonated with those most intimately involved. Robert Ferro, for example, argued against using the word in several interviews towards the end of his own life: "I hate the acronym. [AIDS is] the ugliest sound in the English language right now"

(Hoctel 17). When interviewed regarding the theme of his most famous novel, *Second Son,* he claimed, "I did not set out to write a novel about AIDS. *Second Son* is not *about* anything. It's a story, a love story actually, in which a life-threatening disease, never specified or even named, is a complicating factor" ("Unidentified Interviewer"). Ferro's insistence that *Second Son* is not an AIDS novel, even though he was adamant about publishing the first AIDS novel, proves challenging to accept at face value, particularly because he pressured Crown Publishers to release *Second Son* before Christopher Davis's *Valley of the Shadow*, another novel representing AIDS (Bergman 228–229). Furthermore, in other interviews, Ferro argued that the community was well aware of what the antecedent of IT was; therefore, it was unnecessary to remind the audience of its significance. In this period, naming the disease AIDS was equated with a death sentence for those associated with the queer community.

Another noted author during the AIDS epidemic, Adam Mars-Jones, replaced the word "AIDS" with "Slim" in his 1986 short story with the same title. Even though the narrator of "Slim" chooses to reject using the word "AIDS," his tale remains tragic. As his protagonist proclaims, "I don't use that word. I've heard it enough. So, I've taken it out of circulation, just at home. I say Slim instead, and Buddy understands. I have got Slim" (Mars-Jones and White 3).[1] Adam Mars-Jones's perspective is similar to Ferro's, yet it remains singular at the same time. In his short story, "Slim," Mars-Jones made a conscious decision to rename the illness, which demonstrates an action of ownership over the disease; ownership produces a sense of power. In the short story, the narrator, who has been diagnosed with Slim, or AIDS, recounts his relationship with the disease by sharing his experience with Buddy, the name the narrator assigns to his caregiver. The story offers the narrator's reflection of his current state of affairs, both physical and emotional, as the tale closes with the narrator observing Buddy continuing his daily routine from his window, blocked from reentering society and forced to remain a lonely onlooker. Although Buddy prevails as a positive influence in the story, the final message ceases to be happy. Buddy maintains his freedom, while the narrator endures a prison sentence, ill and confined to his home awaiting his own immortality, barely able to observe Buddy come and go from his window. Being unnamed himself, the narrator clearly represents anyone diagnosed with AIDS.

The tale is noteworthy because nothing is truly named, yet the message is straightforward: "Slim is what they call it in Uganda, and it's a perfectly sensible name. You lose more weight than you thought was possible. You lose more weight than you could carry" (Mars-Jones and White 3). The author underscores two points in adopting "Slim": the globalization of the disease and its physical side effects. This story was originally published in 1986, a time when little was understood about AIDS or its impact both on the micro- and macrocosms. By making this connection between the United States and Uganda, Mars-Jones purposely acknowledges the global reach of the epidemic; AIDS does not attack only homosexual men from the United States. This aspect of the story is significant, but having been published in primarily gay venues, contemporary readers outside of the LGBTQIAA+ audience remain ignorant to the fact that AIDS has never been solely a gay illness.

The second aspect of the word "Slim" refers to visual connotations (i.e., to one of the side effects of the disease—weight loss). In the story, the narrator discusses at length the physical symptoms of the disease: loss of appetite, extreme wasting, and, of course, the appearance of lesions on the body. The protagonist maintains an ironic sense of humor throughout the short story, so much so that he jokes with "Buddy," which refers to a charitable organization the Trust (short for the Terrence Higgins Trust, a British charity that supports HIV and sexual health services): "He [Buddy] doesn't flinch if I talk about my chances of making Slimmer of the Year" (Mars-Jones and White 4). The narrator even resolves the issue of directly referring to his lesions too, telling Buddy to substitute the word: "He's learned to say *blackcurrants*. He said 'lesions' just the once, but I told him it wasn't a very vivid use of language, and if he wasn't a doctor he had no business with it" (Mars-Jones and White 4). Though satiric in tone, these linguistic examples are a direct play with semiotics; both newly assigned nouns already possess connotations which encompass the meanings of the original words, particularly from a stance of physical interpretation. In this fashion, the stigma of those terms is avoided even if the understanding remains clear to the contemporary reader.

Unlike Mars-Jones's story, Robert Ferro's *Second Son* rather distinctly exhibits a possibility of hopeful change for the protagonists. The imposing difference, however, between both authors' lack of nomenclature materializes from the tone. When Mars-Jones's substitutes "Slim" for "AIDS" and "blackcurrants" for "lesions," he creates a satirical commentary regarding the culture around the AIDS epidemic, while Ferro's lack of naming the disease seems to be deliberately different, aimed at minimizing the gravity of the epidemic, as will be further demonstrated. Even though this chapter will focus on Robert Ferro's *Second Son,* it is important to note similar, and diverse, themes and motifs can be examined in other texts of the same period in order to grasp the ways this literary subgenre is politically motivated. Naming gives perception, as author Stanley Fish has argued, "language is not a handmaiden to perception; it is perception; it gives shape to what would otherwise be inert and dead. The shaping power of language cannot be avoided" (Fish 42). While both Mars-Jones and Ferro refuse to name the disease AIDS in their works in order to refrain from aligning with the contemporary "perception" of the period, the final message of each work differs greatly, most noticeable for the contemporary reader.

Although brief and simple, these blatant modes of circumventing language are significant not only from a semiotic point of view, but also—and maybe more pertinent today—from a sociocultural perspective. Before I delve further, it is necessary to take a step backwards and consider spectatorship, a concept which was mentioned in early 1990s criticism and seems to be afforded less attention recently. In "AIDS Writing and the Creation of a Gay Culture," Michael Denneny questions the spectatorship of such literature on AIDS and suggests that the audience was rather small and focused. Noted Violet Quill author Andrew Holleran says, "I really don't know who read them [AIDS books/literature] for pleasure" (12). Both citations evidence the idea that, at least originally, most of what is coined "AIDS literature" was aimed primarily at readers who were HIV-positive or people somehow directly affected by the epidemic; this was not a genre read by the masses. Even today, AIDS literature is not a genre that audiences engage with for entertainment or relaxation. Rather, it holds a certain place within academic and/or activist communities. These works are critical because they serve as a platform for academics and activists to unify rather than divide. However, a few texts from this subgenre and period have become canonical due to the thematic nature. One distinguished example is Paul Monette's *Borrowed Time,* a noted work often studied within the genre of memoir.

Thus, the lack of nomenclature has effects in cultural discourse and creates political ramifications. When critics study the opus of early US AIDS literature (1985–1995), the scholarly approach needs to shift from that of the contemporary scholarship and readership of the late 1980s and early 1990s, as a majority of millennials are removed from the gravity of the AIDS epidemic having only a historical, rather than an empirical understanding. In this vein, new critical lenses need to examine these understudied texts.

During the height of the epidemic, various critics attempted to analyze the absence of the term "AIDS" in literature when the "first" novels on the topic hit the shelves. Susan Sontag, in *Illness as Metaphor* and more precisely with *AIDS and Its Metaphors,* argues that disease is *not* metaphoric—and that certain illnesses acquire direct connotations (3).[2] She argues that the AIDS epidemic breaks the mold, since "AIDS is understood in a premodern way, as a disease incurred by people both as individuals and as members of a 'risk group'—that neutral-sounding, bureaucratic category which also revives the archaic idea of a tainted community that illness has judged" (Sontag 134). In this manner, AIDS has been and even to a certain level is currently, viewed negatively as a disease that a community of people *deserve* to contract. This perspective of both the disease and the community solidifies another motive to abstain from naming AIDS in literature—it immediately ghettoized the author, protagonists, and work itself; literature's task as art form is to liberate those connotations from the text. As Sontag begins to conclude her argument, she claims,

> Fear of sexuality is the new, disease-sponsored register of the universe of fear in which everyone now lives. . . . Not only does AIDS have the unhappy effect of reinforcing American moralism about sex; it further strengthens the culture of self-interest, which is much of what is usually praised as "individualism." (161)

Sontag's point is quite powerful—the metaphor of AIDS as gay death offers no hope for the homosexual community, a concept Leo Bersani and Lee Edelman have both discussed at length. Not only will the community be ostracized from the larger society, but they will also be forced backwards in time and be afraid to be themselves (i.e., partaking in gay sex which will again be seen as a complete demasculinization of the homosexual man, both individualistically and societally). This fear thus attempted to force the homosexual male back into the closet, a metaphor in itself that is built on shame and guilt. Once the sexual liberation movement had occurred, and succeeded, homosexual males found a place and a space to call their own along with a time that they could finally own. Once the AIDS epidemic broke out and they were told to metaphorically "return to the closet," some were unable to do so, and others flat out refused. These options, albeit, sociopolitical ramifications of oppression instituted by the dominant society, meant for many to retreat back to the closet.

To this effect, the question of nomenclature is not original and justly significant; it has been discussed by the various authors of the day and by some scholars. To bring the concept of AIDS as metaphor to the forefront, it is necessary to consider the linguistic choice to refrain from using the acronym AIDS in the early texts. James W. Jones eloquently broaches this question in "Refusing the Name: The Absence of AIDS in Recent American Gay Male Fiction." He describes American society's need to compartmentalize blame and punish groups for nonnormative behaviors, affecting AIDS patients directly. Because AIDS mostly affected the socially marginalized—gay men, drug users, and prostitutes, among others—these groups were stereotyped the most. As such, AIDS patients were grouped into two categories: "innocent victims" and those "deserving of the disease" (Jones 226). Sontag argues, "AIDS has become the metaphor for the *sin* of homosexuality and, more generally I think, the *sin* of sexual pleasure" (Sontag 82–83, qtd. in Jones 226); Jones creates an entire equation for the connotations revolving around AIDS: "AIDS=homosexuality; HIV=AIDS=death . . . sin=sexual pleasure, and thus for homosexuals, homosexuality=HIV=AIDS-death" (Jones).

In the second part of his essay, however, Jones questions the feasability of breaking his equation of AIDS=homosexuality=general moral decay=death (228). The answer, he proposes, is accessible through literature. First and foremost, Jones claims that even if the narrators never overtly state the name of the illness, it is "clear that the unnamed disease is AIDS" through the side effects and symptoms (weight loss, diarrhea, night sweats, cytomegalovirus, and dementia) along with treatments described in relationship to the illness (228). Secondly,

> The name *AIDS* evokes certain images that circumscribe the ability to transcend the limits they impose. By refusing to utter or write the name *AIDS* in these stories, as in the case of *Second Son*, the author pushes the disease to the edge of fiction; it is the effects upon the lives of individuals and the life of the community that form the centers of these stories, rather than the disease itself and its public mythology. (Jones 228)

Jones's point is worthy of a second glance. He claims that through marginalizing the term, AIDS no longer assumes the role of protagonist in the story; instead IT serves as supporting actor. Indeed, this approach is definitely evidenced in Ferro's *Second Son* where hope plays the star role: "The major point I had in writing this book is often missed. And that's that hope *has* to be injected into this situation, hope has to be injected into the epidemic" (Hoctel 17). Moreover, as previously mentioned by the author himself, "it's a story, a love story actually, in which a life-threatening disease, never specified or even named, is a complicating factor" ("Unidentified Interviewer"). Arguably an overstatement, the distinguishing element from the citation is the fact that first and foremost, the novel is a love story (i.e., love wins over death).

Ferro's longing for hope calls into mind Michael Bronski's argument reflecting upon the AIDS epidemic—"It is impossible to be a gay male today and not think of AIDS all the time"—which clearly reflects the sociocultural aspect of the day, one that cannot be re-created for the contemporary reader (60). Bronski's outlook paints a grim picture for gay literature of the time; those associated with the queer community were concerned with contracting the virus. Therefore, the literature of the period needed to fundamentally change. Therefore, Jones concludes his argument by stating that:

> Not naming AIDS represents a process of empowerment for these gay authors. By refusing to succumb to AIDS they are able to define death *and* life ... most of the other stories and novels reflect attempts to define death on gay men's terms, that is, not as the end of gay identity or gay community but as leading both in new directions. (239)

Jones's appeal exemplifies the importance of Robert Ferro's *Second Son* in so much as the novel maintains a confident tone for a fruitful future. The medical field has done wonders to alleviate many of the symptoms and side effects HIV/AIDS has caused and currently causes; therefore, some of the arguments Jones makes would not resonate anymore with an uninformed audience. Moreover, many of these texts are not readily available and most are only commonly presented within academia, which truly limits the knowledge along with the sociocultural importance these works intended to provide. None of them are "solely" about AIDS. Markedly, these texts are substantially more important as they discuss the human condition. As such, I urge a newfound reading of these early AIDS novels, and texts in general, but via new critical tools available to the field. Despite the noteworthy contributions scholars and critics of the 1990s provided the field, as queer theory has developed, maybe adversely, as scholar Teresa de Lauretis argued in 1999, we are better equipped to more thoughtfully consider these critical texts both within the sociohistorical context of the epidemic but, maybe more importantly, as critical works that have influenced generations to delve deeper into the self and its place in community and society at large.

ROBERT FERRO'S BACKGROUND

Ferro's *Second Son* succeeds at forcing the reader out of his/her/their comfort zone to seriously consider two options available to the two main characters of the novel: stay on Earth and try an experimental drug sequence or escape to the planet Splendora and be exiled with a community of people living with AIDS.[3] This challenge, as fantastical as it may be, re-creates for the reader both a reality and a dream desire, laced in hope.

Both an activist and author, Ferro is most notably remembered as one of the members of the Violet Quill, a group of seven homosexual male authors who met eight times formally from March 31, 1980 until March 3, 1981. As an author, Ferro's background and pedigree informed and influenced his writing overtly. Ferro, originally born in Cranford, New Jersey, on October 21, 1941 to an upper-class, conservative, Italian American, Catholic family, realized his passion for storytelling in his youth, and although not a huge surprise, his family, his father in particular, was never overly enthusiastic when Ferro attended Rutgers University to earn a BA in English in 1963. Immediately after, Ferro traveled Europe extensively, spending time in Italy before returning to the United States to complete an MFA in creative writing from the prestigious University of Iowa program in 1967, where he studied under the noted Chilean author José Donoso, who remained supportive, maybe even a bit jealous at times, of Ferro throughout his career.

During his lifetime, Robert Ferro was not only a familiar name in gay literature and in the New York City writing scene, but by the end of his lifetime also a powerful person in the publishing world. The first of five novels, *Atlantis* (1970), co-authored with Michael Grumley, his lifelong partner, explores the search for the lost city of Atlantis. In his second novel, *The Others* (1977), young Peter Conrad accepts an invitation on a Mediterranean yacht of a family friend, and while aboard, the present replicates some of his fantasies, which offers a parabolic reading. *The Family of Max Desir* (1983) is a gay bildungsroman of Max Desir, an Italian American gay young male, as he embarks on his coming out with Nick. In *The Blue Star* (1985), Peter and Chase first meet through homosexual friends in Florence, and over the next twenty years, their lives intertwine as they grow up and pursue their lives. Ferro's writing is crisp and full of layered interpretations.

Building on such themes as illness, coming out of the closet, and familiar relations, Ferro's *Second Son* is considered the first AIDS novel in the American canon.[4] Due to Ferro's connections in the publishing world, he learned that Christopher Davis's *Valley of the Shadow* was due out before his own work and successfully pressured Crown to release his novel first (Bergman 228–229). *Second Son* discusses the life of Mark Valerian, a homosexual male who is still grieving the death of his mother in the house where she passed. The family, particularly the father, would like to sell the house for both emotional and financial motives and move on. Thanks to a friend with whom Mark communicates through letters, he is introduced to Bill Mackey while both are traveling in Italy; they are set up by Matthew, a common friend and pen pal of Mark, because they both have been diagnosed with IT. Upon returning to the United States, Mark and Bill become a serious couple, and the reader experiences the difficult scenarios present for those who were infected with the disease. The novel addresses the themes of death, mourning, survival, and family relations all amidst an Italian cultural background, and even though autobiographical notes are sprinkled throughout, the mixing of genres in *Second Son* blurs the autobiographical lines and figuratively frees the author's work from a memoir reading.

SECOND SON: HOPE DELIVERED
THROUGH LANGUAGE AND CHARACTER

Second Son works in simpatico with Ferro's previous three novels, *The Others, The Family of Max Desir,* and *The Blue Star,* all somewhat autobiographical in nature—though none of the four could be considered a memoir because they contain fictional characters along with creative, nonlinear story lines; none can be characterized as a memoir, which differs from most AIDS literature of the period. Although there is no true overlap in these four novels, and each novel stands completely on its own, certain characters nonetheless flow from one work to another; consequently *Second Son* has been described as the "culmination of a four-novel cycle. . . . All four novels develop themes of family, sexuality, illness, coping with death, and the thin line between fantasy and reality" (Reed 25). In fact, *Second Son* is dedicated to Bill Whitehead, a friend and editor of Ferro who died of AIDS complications in 1987.

Before even entering the text, the reader finds an epigraph from Voltaire's *Candide*: "You are looking very well. / Weren't you clever, dear, to survive? / I've a sorry tale to tell. / I escaped more dead than alive" (Ferro, *Second Son*). *Candide*'s citation immediately introduces the reader to the concepts of life and death, but in a playful, satirical manner. Even if the epigraph provides negative imagery, the overall tone suggests survival. Survival is brought to the immediate forefront of the discourse, even though the reader does not understand what threatens the protagonist's survival. Therefore, the epigraph itself maintains a lack of nomenclature of illness/disease, as Ferro himself will subscribe in the novel. In this manner, *Candide*'s epigraph foreshadows *Second Son*'s ending.

Second Son is divided into four "Parts," and there are no formal chapters. From the opening of "Part One," the reader is introduced to Mark Valerian's world: he lives in the family's beach house, where his mother had died one year earlier. The initial scene sets the novel up to be a historical novel, mentioning the history of the house including the previous owners and how their presence still lurks in the rooms. As soon as we are introduced to Mark, we learn that he is dying from an illness, which is never overtly named throughout the novel, even though he quickly adopts the word "IT" to describe AIDS. "Part Two" focuses on Mark's relationship with his good friend Matthew, with whom he maintains an epistolary communication. Additionally in "Part Two," Matthew indirectly introduces Bill to Mark while both are in Italy, and the book shows them falling in love. "Part Three" brings the couple back to the United States and the reader observes the various conflicts that arise between Mark's family, Bill's past, and their current illness. "Part Four" brings the novel to a close, focusing on Mark and Bill's illness and their decision regarding treatment.

This fantastical tone present from the very first page until the absolute last truly sets and continues to establish the novel's influence. The motif is most heightened throughout his epistolary exchanges with Matthew, a homosexual friend who has also been diagnosed with IT and learns of a Lambda Project, which is a group of gay males searching for a haven and learning about the planet Sirius, which the Sirians call "Splendora." When Mark informs his father that he is moving far away, he refers to the option of leaving Earth for Splendora with Bill.

Mark is a *mammone*, or a mommy's boy. The English translation does not do justice to the role it plays in Italian society. Mark and his mother's loving connection is underscored by the fact that Mark—and not his sisters, for example—renounces his life to live and care for her while ill, an act which is not considered masculine for an Italian male, nor is it in line with the traditional division of labor. Moreover, Mrs. Valerian's illness is never named in *Second Son*.[5] The lack of nomenclature in *Second Son* creates a shared experience amongst mother and son, which is intensified through the character of the house. In this regard, the reader can delve into Mark's character.

Mark loves the Cape May beach home from an aesthetic point of view, but, more importantly, he holds an emotional connection to the physical space because he cared for his mother, Margaret, there until her death one year prior. Mark continues to inhabit the home after his mother's death, and even takes over her room, sleeping in the same bed where she died. Despite the intensity of that action, this intentional choice physically reunites him with his mother and is noteworthy for the development of Mark's character. For Mark, and many of Ferro's homosexual characters, the mother figure is central to understanding the protagonist himself. The fact that both suffer from an unnamed illness in the same physical space invokes a shared emotional intimacy.

The symbolism contained within sharing the bed pushes the analysis much deeper—Mark and his mother have a shared experience, which is illness=death. But his death is not typical, nor was hers. Mark's return to the "womb," or his mother's deathbed, symbolizes a shared struggle of suffering before death. The connection shared by Mark and Margaret is strong, stronger than with any of his siblings, and is heightened by the fact that the family is Italian American and by this nature their bond is twofold, not only through family/culture but also through illness.

The house itself morphs into another foundational symbol for the text as it remains a point of discontent throughout the entire novel. The initial struggle regarding the house begins in the opening pages of the work. The Valerian family, particularly Mark's father and brother, want to sell the house but Mark attempts to convince his sister, Vita, that their mother would not have supported that decision. Margaret's last grand act before dying was

> an extensive restoration of the house—two processes sharing themes and schedules along similar though reversed lines: an Egyptian way of death, in which a place for the abiding comfort of the spirit is prepared. Mrs. Valerian had theorized that the house would bind its occupants—her family—to her after she was gone. She had concluded that she herself would be bound, an intention to be evoked with her name and memory by whoever entered the house. (Ferro, *Second Son* 5–6)

The house preparations indirectly represent Margaret Valerian's preparations before death in her attempt to keep the family united. Her intentions seem clear—updating the house so that it remains a focal point for the family. It is the only space where illness "has its place" in as much as Mark can feel comfortable there: "The *house* is the legacy. . . . He felt that nothing was more important to him than this house. . . . But the others did not love the house in these terms; why should he care so? Its beauty, no doubt; its canopic aspects regarding his mother, and now, being ill, regarding him; the memory of thirty years together" (Ferro, *Second Son* 10–11). One can imagine therefore the significance the house offers our protagonist: protection, emotional connection, and to a certain extent motivation, as he later continues to keep the house in its wonderful condition.

Until the final pages of the novel, the Valerians struggle with selling the family beach house. Mark insists that his mother had bequeathed the house to him and his siblings, not his father; thus Mark would never agree to sell. The Valerian family business however is in peril and desperately needs liquid cash, and the home becomes the only means to keep the business afloat; for the Valerian males, except Mark, the house only assumes a capitalistic nature. In an intense, emotional scene between father and son, Mr. Valerian and Mark blow up about the current situation, particularly about Mark being gay and dying of IT. During the argument, Mark informs his father that he and Bill will soon be moving far away and the family will not have to worry about him anymore. At this, his father becomes even more upset and declares his love for his son and asks for forgiveness.

The Valerian family, however, is unable to grasp the importance of place and space for the sick, homosexual couple. It is noteworthy that Mark and Bill do not meet in the United States, but in Italy—first in Rome and later consummating their relationship in Venice. This use of Italy as idyllic space is not a new motif for Ferro as he uses Italy and the Mediterranean throughout most of his works. Particularly, his homosexual characters often encounter their initial gay experience in Italy. Italy therefore serves as an exotic place, one where homosexuality and bisexuality has been accepted since the beginning of time. The scene in Venice allows Mark and Bill to embark figuratively on a rebirth, as Mark had not had any sexual experiences in two years. After meeting Bill in Rome, Mark openly declares his homosexuality to friends and colleagues, celebrating his newfound love. Being outside of the United States then, away from family and a homophobic society, love is able to flourish.

In the beginning of "Part Three" for example, Mark worries about Bill's relationship with the beach house. Mark claims that he would happily live anywhere with Bill, as he makes him so happy, but "I am thoroughly blessed by his reaction to the house—and, I must admit, by the house's reaction to him. How dotty darling to think a house cares" (Ferro, *Second Son* 104). For Mark, the house is in fact its own character, with a personality of sorts and a memory which will outlive the two of them. Moreover, this citation underscores a solidification of the house creating a new sense of family and their relationship morphing into a home. This seems to be one of the reasons why he refuses to sell the beach house because it will contain memories of the entire Valerian family, particularly that of him and his mother, and now him and Bill. Mark claims that the house is always filled with people, even when it is not. Bill questions, "But what's the difference between this and your memory," to which Mark states, "It's the house's memory, not mine." "What's the difference?" "Well, the difference," Mark replied, "is that it will still be here when we're gone" (Ferro, *Second Son* 109). This brief discussion between protagonists captures the importance of family, comfort, and memory. Although time passes and death is inevitable for all, Mark argues that certain places remain forever sacred; Mark's safe queer space is the house, and his memories serve as his happy place.

Mark and Bill face adversity from the Valerian family in diverse ways due to their illness. One of Mark's most overt arguments with the family is that they do not understand the current situation, from both physical and emotional perspectives. Mark is bound to the Valerian beach house for numerous reasons, the connection with his mother being just one. For Mark, the beach house is a safe place in which he controls both the concepts of space and time. This is critical because when Mark and Bill return from Rome and become a couple, they attend a family party where they are mistreated. In a conversation with his own brother, George, Mark realizes just how ignorant and selfish his brother actually is:

> "I feel fine," Mark replied, "other than fatigue in the afternoon and headaches."
> "And Bill?" George asked.
> Mark hesitated.
> "I assume he's gay."
> "Yes, as a matter of fact."
> "Is he okay?"
> The question meant was Bill sick. "Why do you ask?"
> "Because he's gay, Mark. It's a natural question." (Ferro, *Second Son* 124)

The previous conversation clearly highlights Jones's theoretical construction: AIDS=homosexuality; HIV=AIDS=death. Here, however, the situation is worse because the first part of the equation is reversed: *Homosexuality=AIDS*; HIV=AIDS=death. Flipping the first part of the equation becomes dangerous, even though plenty of folks in the late 1980s and early 1990s did so. This mentality further ghettoizes the homosexual and did not, nor does it now, properly reflect the reality many homosexuals faced during that era. In fact, even LGBTQIAA+ literature includes works from this moment in which the protagonist becomes consciously aware of the gravity of HIV/AIDS and makes choices based on his knowledge of this disease.[6] What is worse, Mark's own family does this to him and his partner. This aspect of the conversation underscores the importance of the safety net of both the house in the novel and also the queer community at large for the individuals diagnosed. Mark and his partner cannot even feel safe, not to mention welcome, within the confines of the Italian family.

The conversation continues, however, and the argument accelerates, bringing their sister, Vita, into the situation:

> So George looked up. "It's Sarah's—it's my daughter's right to know, *to protect her baby*." He spoke in legal italics. Vita sat down beside Mark. "Bill's got it, too," George added.
> "So I understand," Vita replied. "I'm sorry . . . But I don't see how that affects you or Sarah." (Ferro, *Second Son* 125)

This second part of the conversation demonstrates both sympathy and empathy for the protagonists. First and foremost, it solidifies, which is clear earlier on in the novel, that Vita is the closest living family member in Mark's life and the only one who even attempts to understand him and his reality without judgment, rather with compassion. Vita, meaning life in Italian, promotes the life and happiness of her brother. Additionally, the importance of a female presence for Mark can also be interpreted; in a certain manner, Vita assumes a motherly role in Mark's life.

Second, this conversation demonstrates one facet of living with a chronic illness, like AIDS; people are always assuming not only that one has it but that he/she/they either pass it on to his/her/their partner or infect others with the illness. In this regard, Ferro's novels in general, but particularly *Second Son*, evidence the difficulty of being homosexual in contemporary society and—with this novel—the challenges of living with AIDS. This is one of many examples in the novel where Mark and Bill are ostracized, or at the very least made to feel unwelcome at a social gathering. Unfortunately, many uncomfortable moments occur within a familial setting.

From a more social stance, Mark and his father partake in an earlier debate about AIDS from a societal perspective. Mr. Valerian inquires about Mark's health and he asks what the doctors actually know about IT. Mark states, "'The bottom line is that there's no cure.' And his father retorts, 'that's where you're wrong. It's not the bottom line. You mustn't think that way. They'll find a cure. They're all looking.'" And Mark's response is extremely important for the novel's progression: "'Utter bullshit,' Mark interrupted. 'It's not a cure they're looking for, it's a vaccine. Protect the healthy, let the sick die off'" (Ferro, *Second Son* 28). This exchange is paramount to explore because it returns to the sociopolitical aspect of the novel. The outsider, here the heterosexual, believes in the fairy tale ending: all those infected will soon be saved. This savior complex of Mr. Valerian represents that of so many who attempted to be hopeful. Even though Mr.

Valerian's character could be defined as "hopeful," traditionally he has not been, which may be surprising. This focus on this dialogue however comes from Ferro's protagonist's voice; he openly criticizes the research being conducted around AIDS, particularly the focus of the research. His point of "protecting the healthy" underscores the drastic change in addressing the epidemic, particularly when Ryan White was diagnosed with AIDS in December 1984, and suddenly AIDS was a disease that could *also* affect heterosexuals.[7] In short, hope can only be created from within the community; as such, Mr. Valerian's encouraging outlook is viewed as an uneducated person's fantasy world, or that of an overly hopeful parent, to a certain extent one in the same.

On the flip side, once Mark and Bill become close, Mark learns that Bill had a partner, Fred, who recently died of AIDS complications. During a conversation regarding home and NYC, the couple discusses the following:

> "Is there someone in New York?" Mark asked.
> "There was. He got It first . . . Fred was a few years older than me." Bill looked away, over rooftops. "I couldn't go through that again."
> "You won't have to," Mark said. "I have no intention of dying."
> "I'm sorry. That sounded odd."
> "I know. But I'm not going to die, not from this anyway. Everyone expects it. It's automatic. But you can't let yourself. You just say no."
> "No."
> "That's right."
> "No, no, and no." (Ferro, *Second Son* 87)

In opposition to Mr. Valerian's false sense of hope, this dialogue ironically attempts to offer a truer version. Although not based in scientific fact, the discourse stresses the importance of a positive outlook concerning life and being infected with IT. As noted in the final lines, both Mark and Bill become the support the other needs.

Another sense of hope arrives from the epistolary communications from Mark and Matthew. In a letter to Matthew sent after Mark and Bill cohabitate, Mark states,

> The great irony is that this romance is suitable only because of It. If it were not in both of us, or even neither of us, fear would have prevented everything outright. Perhaps this is not mere irony. To be ill in his company, in his arms (forgive me) is to be well in relation to each other. . . . We are ill but It does not mean what it did, day to day. All depression gone. Not so frightening, not so real. (Ferro, *Second Son* 99)

Once again, the concept of hope comes from within the community. Mark notes the reality of his happiness; ironically, he and Bill would not be together if it were not for IT. Yet, at the same time, the love which stems from their shared situation changes their lives for the better, making life at the very least livable. Here the reader can begin to understand the importance of a shared experience and how even if HIV=AIDS=death may be inevitable for most, being part of a community with hope makes all the difference for the journey.

In addition to moving to Splendora, Mark offers another option to Bill. Mark is presented with an experimental treatment by Dr. Thompson. The procedure requires extensive blood from familial matches. In the end, it is suggestive that the two will attempt this trial procedure with Dr. Thompson; however, the novel concludes on the same fantastic note in which it began:

> They sat atop the tower in the afternoons, and often late at night before bed paced the deck over the porch, waiting as if for the ship to Splendora. For it seemed that what they would do together—what would be done to them in the hospital—was a kind of trip, a voyage home. As with Matthew, the ship had become their metaphor, something to look for by day over the horizon, by night among the stars. (Ferro, *Second Son* 214–215)

This beautiful conclusion of *Second Son* demonstrates how much Mark and Bill love each other and how dedicated they are to being together, whether on Earth in pain or on planet Splendora. In either situation, the novel ends with a positive tone full of hope. As they sit together and look towards the sky, the metaphor of the stars suggests the hope they live by. Consequently, this novel stands out from many others written contemporaneously due to its sense of promise for those suffering from AIDS symptoms. The novel realistically provides a sense of the difficulty of living with the illness but simultaneously demonstrates that it can only eliminate individual power if allowed. Hope can still prevail.

The framing of the text begins and ends the novel with strong development of character; the end remains ambiguous exactly for that motive—the protagonist has grown and is still contemplating his future. What is concluded by the end of the novel is the fact that two men with AIDS can still fall in love and be committed to each other. Ferro's novel is foundational because it is one of the earliest true "novels" to be published by a mainstream press in which AIDS is the focal point, and through all the turmoil, the characters still find the possibility of living. Ferro's character negates the opening epigraph of this piece: death *does not* prevail over them. In fact, Ferro claims the message of *Second Son* is that "belief in the healing power of love is a proper response to catastrophe, and that there can be no survival without hope and an underlying belief in survival" (Ferro, qtd. in Reed 45). By the end of the novel, the Cape May house remains, but the couple themselves have created a home together, whether on Earth or on the planet Splendora. And together they will continue to fight IT and succeed.

SUGGESTED AIDS NOVELS, 1987–1988

Bishop, Michael. *Unicorn Mountain*. Arbor House, 1988.
Borgman, C. F. *River Road*. Plume, 1988.
Bram, Christopher. *In Memory of Angel Claire*. Fine, 1988.
Bryan, Jed A. *A Cry Is the Desert*. Banned Books, 1987.
Champagne, John. *The Blue Lady's Hand*. Stuart, 1988.
Davis, Christopher. *Valley of the Shadow*. St. Martin's Press, 1988.
Diaman, N. A. *Castro Street Memories*. Persona, 1988.
Dunne, Dominick. *People like Us*. Crown, 1988.
Fast, Howard. *Dinner Party*. Houghton Mifflin, 1987.
Ferro, Robert. *Second Son*. Crown, 1988; Plume, 1989.
Mayes, Susan. *Immune*. New Rivers, 1987.
McBain, Ed. *The House That Jack Built*. Holt, 1988.
Micklowitz, Gloria D. *Good-Bye, Tomorrow*. Delacorte, 1987.
Mitchell, Larry. *My Life as a Mole*. Calamus, 1988.
Puccia, Joseph. *The Holy Spirit Dance Club*. Liberty, 1988.
Redon, Joel. *Bloodstream*. Knights, 1988.
Reed, Paul. *Longing*. Celestial Arts, 1988.
Rubin, Martin. *The Boiled Frog Syndrome*. Alyson, 1987.
Turnbull, Peter. *Two Way Cut*. St. Martin's Press, 1988.
Wolfe, Tom. *The Bonfire of the Vanities*. Farrar, Straus, and Giroux, 1987.

NOTES

For a complete annotated bibliography on AIDS literature from 1982–1991 across genres, see Franklin Brooks and Timothy F. Murphy, "Annotated Bibliography of AIDS Literature, 1982–1991" in *Writing AIDS: Gay Literature, Language, and Analysis*, Timothy F. Murphy and Suzanne Poirier, eds., Columbia University Press, 1993.

1. Adam Mars-Jones, "Slim," pg. 3 in *The Darker Proof: Stories from a Crisis*. "Slim" was first published in *Granta* and later appeared in *Mae West Is Dead* (1986, 1987).
2. Sontag's argument begins with the stigma revolving around tuberculosis and cancer. Then she adopts her theoretical foundation to consider AIDS.
3. It is important to note that this aspect of the novel is autobiographical. Robert Ferro did in fact try an experimental drug sequence towards the end of his life, which proved unsuccessful. This treatment, from what I understand from all my research on Ferro and having been through all the documentation in the archives, was not known to many, nor was the fact that he and Michael Grumley had AIDS. Documentation of his treatment is available at the Beinecke Rare Book and Manuscript Library, Yale University, New Haven, Connecticut.
4. All research points to Ferro's *Second Son* as the first official AIDS novel even though some do exist pre-1988. See the bibliography for more information. See also Bergman's *The Violet Quill*.
5. In Robert Ferro's previous novels, it is understood that the protagonist's mother had cancer; however, in this novel, it remains rather unclear. Moreover, this aspect of his novels reflects the autobiographical death of Ferro's own mother, from cancer.

6. See John Champagne's *The Blue Lady's Hands.*
7. In addition to the Ryan White story, it is important to recall the numerous blood transfusions which occurred internationally with HIV-infected blood. This series of events added attention to the disease because it was attacking heterosexual people.

WORKS CITED

Bergman, David. *The Violet Quill: The Violet Quill and the Making of Gay Culture.* Columbia Universtiy Press, 2004.
Bersani, Leo. *Is the Rectum a Grave? and Other Essays.* University of Chicago Press, 2010.
Bronski, Michael. "Death and the Erotic Imagination." *Radical America*, vol. 21, no. 2–3, Mar.–Apr. 1987, pp. 59–65.
Brooks, Franklin and Timothy F. Murphy. "Annotated Bibliography of AIDS Literature, 1982–91." *Writing AIDS: Gay Literature, Language, and Analysis*, edited by Timothy F. Murphy and Suzanne Poirier. Columbia University Press, 1993, pp. 321–339.
Champagne, John. *The Blue Lady's Hands.* Lyle Stuart Inc., 1988.
Davis, Christopher. *Valley of the Shadow.* St. Martin's Press, 1988.
De Lauretis, Teresa. "Gender Symptoms, or, Peeing like a Man." *Social Semiotics*, vol. 9, no. 2, 1999, pp. 257–270.
Denneny, Michael. "AIDS Writing and the Creation of a Gay Culture." *Confronting AIDS through Literature: The Responsibilities of Representation*, edited by Judith Laurence Pastore. University of Illinois Press, 1993, pp. 36–54.
Ferro, Robert. *The Blue Star.* Dutton, 1985.
———. *The Family of Max Desir.* Dutton, 1983.
———. *The Others.* Scribner, 1977.
———. *Second Son.* Crown Publishers, Inc., 1988.
Ferro, Robert, and Michael Grumley. *Atlantis.* Doubleday, 1970.
Fish, Stanley. *How to Write Sentences: And How to Read One.* Harper, 2011.
Hoctel, Patrick. "A Talk with Novelist Robert Ferro." *San Francisco Sentinel*, March 25, 1988, pp. 17, 20, 28.
Holleran, Andrew. *Ground Zero.* William Morrow and Company, Inc., 1988.
Jones, James W. "Refusing the Name: The Absence of AIDS in Recent American Gay Male Fiction." *Writing AIDS: Gay Literature, Language, and Analysis*, edited by Timothy F. Murphy and Suzanne Poirier. Columbia University Press, 1993. pp. 225–243.
Kramer, Larry. *The Normal Heart.* Samuel French, 1985.
Mars-Jones, Adam and Edmund White. *The Darker Proof: Stories from a Crisis.* Faber and Faber Limited, 1987.
Monette, Paul. *Borrowed Time: An AIDS Memoir.* Harcourt, Inc., 1988.
Pastore, Judith Laurence. *Confronting AIDS through Literature: The Responsibilities of Representation.* University of Illinois Press, 1993.
Reed, Paul. "To Find through Fear and Horror: Author Robert Ferro Tells Why He Wrote 'Second Son.'" *Bay Area Reporter*, vol. 18, no. 10, March 10, 1988, pp. 25, 45.
Sontag, Susan. *Illness as Metaphor and AIDS and Its Metaphors.* Picador, 1988.
Stambolian, George. *Men on Men.* Plume, 1986.
"Unidentified Interviewer. Questions and Answers, [1988]." Box 10, Folder 235. Robert Ferro Papers. Beinecke Rare Book and Manuscript Library, Yale University, New Haven, CT, May 2015.

Chapter Five

Borrowed Time, Body Counts, and The Nearness of Others

Three Approaches to AIDS Memoirs

Jennifer J. Lavoie

When critics discuss Paul Monette's *Borrowed Time* (1988), they are often divided on how to handle the memoir. Douglas Eisner suggests that it is melodramatic, while David Jarraway suggests Monette's "rhetoric sustains the homophobic myth of contagion." In contrast, Bertram Cohler argues that *Borrowed Time* "is an indictment of a government refusing to acknowledge the presence of a mysterious killer stalking a generation" (365). Analyzing gay memoirs more generally, Felice Picano suggests that they "will not only show how many of us [gay men] there are, but how brave, how clever, how determined, how unafraid many of us were" (24). While there has been discussion of early gay memoirs, including AIDS memoirs such as Monette's *Borrowed Time* (1988), little has been done with more contemporary memoirs, such as Sean Strub's *Body Counts* (2014) or David Caron's *The Nearness of Others* (2014). Though the three texts are considered AIDS memoirs and all three authors spend a large majority of the books discussing AIDS, I have noticed a shift in method between the earliest memoirs and those published within the last decade. Drawing on Monette, Strub, and Caron as my examples, I will discuss the change from AIDS consuming all aspects of the author's life to AIDS being just one part of it due to the change in politics and biomedical realities, and that this change is reflected in both the chronological format and content of the books.

Early memoirist Paul Monette finds his life controlled by the diagnosis of Roger, whom he calls "friend" but readers will recognize as his partner, and later his own diagnosis; this is unlike contemporary memoirist Sean Strub, who has moved beyond his diagnosis, and David Caron who reflects on his diagnosis after the height of the AIDS crisis and whose writing is caught between the emotional writing of Monette and straightforward writing of Strub. For Monette, the politics focus on the Reagan administration and their lack of response to the AIDS crisis, which shifts in focus for Strub who becomes heavily involved in politics himself, to Caron who lives during the Obama administration where gay rights have come to the center of the nation's attention. Furthermore, the biomedical realities have changed in the sense that while Monette had no access to effective treatments, Strub nearly died before effective treatments were developed, and Caron has dozens of treatment options available to him in order to maintain his health and manage HIV. Reading the changes in AIDS memoirs is crucial to the white gay male community because it reveals not only how desperate the crisis was at the onset, but how far AIDS research has come in the years following as well as how far it still needs to go. Focusing attention on *Borrowed Time*, *Body Counts*, and *The Nearness of Others* gives insight into the initial experiences of white gay men with AIDS and those who survived to enjoy full, meaningful lives and continue to thrive even today.

As Ann Jurecic states in *Illness as Narrative*, "narratives about suffering sustain individuals and communities. [Medical humanists] observe how autobiographical illness narratives reclaim patients' voices from the biomedical narratives imposed upon them by modern medicine" (3). While she argues that this approach is "out of step" with what she calls "mainstream literary criticism" (3), she acknowledges that the split between the two approaches must be recognized. The position of the medical humanists has been echoed by several other critics, including Lisa Diedrich in "'Without Us All Told': Paul Monette's Vigilant Witnessing to the AIDS Crisis" in a section on "vigilance," where she argues: "Monette demonstrates this peculiar and perplexing experience of survival in his vigilant witness to all those who did not survive" (118). As a member of the gay community, Monette knew many victims as friends and lovers, but he also recognized "countless others . . . whose voices—unlike his own—are now lost to us" (118). Bearing witness is a theme that comes up often in theories on trauma and illness narratives, as well as reviews of works that involve a disease such as AIDS. Diedrich relates this even earlier in her article when she discusses how Monette can be read "in relation to theories of witnessing that have developed roughly concurrently with the AIDS crisis" (114). Though Monette was a writer in his own right at the time of the AIDS crisis, Diedrich argues that AIDS, ironically, "both gave Monette his voice and mortally wounded him" (112) and that the voice he gains and AIDS are bound to each other; to tell his story without AIDS would be an impossibility since it colors all aspects of his life.

This idea of bearing witness, however, changes in style as the focus shifts in AIDS memoirs. In a review of *Body Counts*, Walter Armstrong uses the term twice, saying first, "[b]earing witness to the AIDS catastrophe of the 1980s is not for sissies. Still, we survivors now recognize, in our last decades of life, that our firsthand testimony may have historical meaning or, at least, save our dead from oblivion." Later, he says: "as a PWA, Sean has always rejected the label of victim. Now, as a survivor bearing witness, he rejects what he views as the equally offensive label of hero."

This refusal of the categories of both victim and hero is evident in Strub's writing as he takes a less emotional approach to documenting his experience with AIDS. Instead, Strub is a survivor and moves beyond his diagnosis to bear witness to events outside of AIDS such as in political and activist movements. It seems that no matter what argument they support, many critics and reviewers can agree that AIDS memoirs serve to bear witness to the events at the height of the crisis in order to preserve an identity that is destroying a generation of gay men. Caron, on the other hand, takes a middle ground. He survives, yes, and has treatments available to him, but at the cost of contact with those who are HIV-negative. His biomedical reality allows for him to live without the complications of HIV/AIDS on a medical level, but it greatly impacts his life on a personal level that Monette did not face and Strub does not mention in his memoir.

Borrowed Time takes place during a relatively short span of time in Paul Monette's life. It was published during 1988 and covers the time of Roger's diagnosis of AIDS up until his death, although the memoir also includes some references to earlier times. As for why Monette decides to write about his experiences with AIDS, several times he mentions the call from others to write, including the immunologist Gottlieb who, upon discovering he is a writer, says, "'Why don't you write about this? Nobody else does'" (Monette 80). John M. Clum writes about the importance of Monette's memoir in "'The Time before the War': AIDS, Memory, and Desire": "Monette's memoir is not just of him and Rog: it is a memoir of AIDS itself and the way it is decimating a culture" (649). Clum's observation calls to mind my theory that early AIDS memoirs are written by people who are consumed by the disease: people who find their lives taken over by it in every way and need a way to respond. A close reading of *Borrowed Time* suggests the centrality of AIDS in the author's life through the language Monette uses and his frequent references to time, the moon, and even the necessity of the AIDS underground.

In "Borrowing Time: Writing and Resisting Viral Narratives in Novels about AIDS," Lisa Garmire suggests that the depiction of the disease becomes temporal, and that this temporality is problematic. Garmire argues that "[t]his representation of AIDS as a temporal sequencing has lethal consequences for the people who live with AIDS, because, as Sontag writes, AIDS becomes '. . . only a matter of time, like any death sentence.'" Temporal sequencing is evident throughout *Borrowed Time*, and it is significant to the text in that it reveals the moments of Monette's life in relation to AIDS. It controls all aspects of his life, which presents itself in the memoir. Furthermore, as Monette counts down the death of friends and tracks the health of Roger, there are moments of displacement after Roger's second bout of PCP. Of the months that follow this second scare, Monette writes:

> I have virtually no record of the next three months. Except for a few doctors' appointments, Roger's calendar is completely blank for the rest of the year, he wouldn't even bother with a calendar for '86. Between then and the end of January there is a single five-line entry in my journal, and my daily calendar is as empty as Roger's, because I ceased to write my appointments down. I kept the ones I could remember. Indeed, we both went on working as long as we could, struggling into November, but it was as if the whole idea of calendars had become a horrible mockery. (192)

Why does Monette frequently relate his life to time and calendars if temporal sequencing "has lethal consequences" as Garmire suggests?

One reason could be the fact that early AIDS patients at the height of the crisis had no answers and everything was "only a matter of time," as is suggested in the previous passage. Why should they keep track of appointments in the future when their future is so uncertain? Diedrich may argue against this temporal sequencing, but given the limitations of understanding and medication at the time, when they "were part of the nether world of the sick, trying to get some control, taking risks the government wouldn't sanction" (Monette 175), Monette and other AIDS memoir writers have limited time with which to work. With such an uncertain future, it is difficult to write about hopes and dreams that may not include a loved one. They are also writing against time itself. For authors at the height of the AIDS crisis, especially for those whose books are the first of their kind, they write against time as events occur, or the order in which they occurred, offering little distance between them and the events in the battle against time that early diagnoses of the disease impose.

The opening lines of *Borrowed Time* reflect Monette's uncertainty about his own status in real time when he writes, "I don't know if I will live to finish this" (1). It is important to note that Monette is concerned with finishing the memoir, not that he will live long enough to finish anything else, or reach a certain age. Unlike later memoirists, especially those who survive beyond the mid-1990s, writers living with AIDS during the early years of the epidemic are unable to reflect back on times from a great distance because they write while sick with a virus that has no effective treatment. Temporal sequencing helps to frame their work from the span of prediagnosis to the conclusion of the memoir, which may, as in the case of Monette, end with the death of a loved one.

Even prior to writing *Borrowed Time*, Monette was conscious of time, as seen in journals written during Roger's illness. After talking to Craig, a friend who also has contracted AIDS, about Dose 5 of suramin, he writes in his journal:

> A dozen times a day, a hundred times, I think about Rog and what it would mean to lose him and I go to pieces inside. We had a supper delivered from J. Spector and a lovely quiet talk. But where am I going? All I want is what we have to go on and on. The world out there, I don't understand what they want, how do they bear the matter of time? (Monette 140)

The uncertainty of the efficacy of Roger's medication drives Monette to think about his potential death constantly. The awareness of time lends a sense of urgency to the memoir because readers know that Roger *will* die, but it is not clear exactly when Monette will write about Roger's death. This uncertainty comes through in the Cinderella-like moments where Monette says, "[w]e'd always have to be back by ten-thirty or eleven, when the night nurse would be coming by, so there was a Cinderella clock ticking behind every foray now" (287). Though it occurs much later in the memoir and further into Roger's illness, this choice of language is important; just as Cinderella had a limited amount of time at the ball, so Roger has a limited amount of time left in his life, and the clock is ticking for Monette's readers. By including the allusion to Cinderella, Monette again makes connections to the temporality that is the AIDS diagnosis.

A second element that frequently shows up in *Borrowed Time*, and no less than ten times, are references to the moon. These references to the moon are directly connected to the temporal sequencing as Monette has seemingly placed himself in a world with Roger where the temporality of AIDS drives their battle for life. Several examples bring this to mind, notably when Monette, in the opening pages, invites readers to experience the isolation he and Roger feel when he writes, "[u]ntil that long night in October, it didn't seem possible that any day could supplant the brute equinox of March 12—the day of Roger's diagnosis in 1985, the day we began to live on the moon" (2). Why would Monette choose to use the imagery of the moon in this manner? The moon is a cold, dead place that is isolated from Earth and is connected to temporal sequencing, as are the phases of the moon. A diagnosis of AIDS in 1985, the early years of the epidemic, *was* a death sentence due to the lack of effective medical interventions, and those diagnosed were stigmatized by society and ignored by the Reagan administration. Another significant passage in which Monette mentions the moon shows just how clearly it relates to isolation: "I have oceans of unresolved rage at those who ran from us, but I also see that plague and panic are inseparable. And nothing compares. That is something very important to understand about those on the moon of AIDS"

(83). The emotion Monette most strongly experiences is rage because friends, family, and the general population have abandoned "us," who are left alone to battle this disease. The moon in this case is such a strong symbol because of how far it is from Earth and, therefore, contact with humanity. However, it is not Paul and Roger who have placed themselves in isolation; it is society's fear and misunderstanding of AIDS that have put them in such a position.

Further evidence that suggests how AIDS is the central concern for Monette are the references to the AIDS underground. While this does not relate to temporal sequencing, the focus in this instance shifts to the biomedical realities of Monette's time period. This group of AIDS victims and their friends and lovers form a community they can rely on for information when the government and medical community fail to come through for them. Monette writes about one particular moment during a visit to Mexico where the US government fails them and countless others:

> [w]e bought all the ribavirin and Isoprinosine they had, chatting amiably with a couple from San Francisco who were buying cancer drugs. I realized then we weren't the only ones being driven underground by the FDA. We were part of the nether world of the sick, trying to get some control, taking risks the government wouldn't sanction, and all in the same boat. (175)

This mention of the underground, a community of resistant, organized people supported by illegal methods of gaining medication that ultimately failed in treating AIDS, highlights the reality of life prior to the biomedical response of the mid-1990s and invention of effective medication. It also shows just how embedded Monette and Roger were in regard to the illness. It consumed their lives in a way that had also consumed all others, creating a new society of people who were desperate for answers. This desperation shows later in the memoir when Monette writes more of this underground community of people, saying, "It wasn't until a week or two later that reports began to filter in through the AIDS underground that four suramin patients out of a hundred had lost adrenal function" (208). It is important to note that this information does not come from doctors, but from this underground society. Monette and Roger were incapable of waiting for information from the medical establishment—they needed to take matters into their own hands just as the others did. At this time, the biomedical response to AIDS was lacking and leading to the deaths of thousands of gay men. Not only that, but the drugs that were tested had often disastrous effects on the already precarious health of already ill patients such as Roger. Of the time they were at UCLA, Monette writes, "[t]he whole AIDS underground cocked its ear to the tenth floor at UCLA, as a hundred skeptical doctors wandered in and out to get the scoop on the latest magic bullet. Just call us Command Central"

(211). Once members of the underground, Paul and Roger have access to information before others not involved, including many doctors, and as such have the ability to dispense the information to the men whose lives are also consumed by the disease. This ability to dispense the information puts them in a position to possibly help others if the drug turns out to have the desired effectiveness in treating AIDS.

Body Counts by Sean Strub is different from *Borrowed Time* not only in when it was published, but the topics on which the texts focus, as well as the format of the book itself. Though they are both memoirs by men with AIDS and have some similar elements such as a discussion of the AIDS underground, a focus on health and gaining weight, war as metaphor, listing friends and acquaintances who have died, and references to smuggling drugs from other countries, they are also vastly different. Paul Monette lived on the West Coast during the AIDS crisis while Sean Strub lived on the East Coast. This difference in location put Strub directly at the hub of activity in research and activism. Strub was also largely indifferent to learning more about AIDS until it benefited not only himself but others, while Monette digested everything he could, even if it was difficult to understand; Strub instead admits, beyond learning the acronyms and being able to pronounce the words they stood for, "I had never read medical journals and sometimes couldn't understand them, but it was reassuring to know that someone, somewhere, was trying to find treatments" (176). Beyond knowing that others were trying, however, is the attitude Strub has adopted about his disease not only when diagnosed, but in writing this memoir at a much later time. As I have previously suggested, Monette is consumed by AIDS while Strub is able to live beyond it due to the interval between when Monette first published his memoir and 2014, when Strub publishes his. Monette and Roger can be read as victims of not only the disease but also an apathetic government that turns a deaf ear towards the community while Strub himself has outright rejected the label of victim that is often applied to men who contracted HIV/AIDS in the early years of the epidemic. Monette writes with passion and emotion, and the memoir centers on the diagnosis of Roger while Strub's accounts are factual, often lack emotion, and move *beyond* the diagnosis to contain events from before—as far back as his arrival in Washington, DC, and his coming out to the present day.

In writing about his life before being diagnosed with HIV—or ARC (AIDS-related complex) as it was then called—Sean Strub displays his ability to move beyond his diagnosis. Though Strub initially rejects the idea that he has the virus even though he has several of the symptoms, including swollen lymph glands, he thinks "about those who had AIDS as luckless victims, a step removed from my own life. I had only just begun to experience sexual freedom, mentally as well as physically, and I resisted any scenario that would take that away from me" (120). Strub's sexual freedom and resistance to thoughts of AIDS occurs in 1982, and it is not until 1985, after he contracts shingles, that he is tested for HIV and the results come back positive. Though he has some moments of melancholy, he is overall optimistic about his diagnosis and subsequent activism after he visits the PWAC Living Room where he is given literature on AIDS. Of the information he is given, Strub writes, "[a]s I read through the literature, I realized the voice of PWAC's membership wasn't desperate and despondent; nor was it strident or didactic. It was thoughtful, practical, and often funny" (172). He goes on to read the Denver Principles, which further confirm his optimistic outlook. Strub suggests that they were an iconic text:

> [It] began with a preamble rejecting the word "victim," the walking-dead descriptor most common at that time, noting it is "a term that implies defeat." They also objected to being called "patients," which they wrote, "implies passivity, helplessness, and a dependence upon the care of others." "We are People With [sic] AIDS," they declared, staking claim to the right to control the language used to describe themselves. (142)

Of the Denver Principles, Strub also writes that "they were a guide to living in the shadow of a potentially fatal illness. The document was like a life preserver thrown my way by other people with AIDS" (Strub 172). The key idea is *living*. While Monette and Roger are living and attempting to continue their lives by keeping jobs and appointments for as long as possible, they are soon completely overshadowed by AIDS. Monette frequently checks on Roger and hovers over him to ensure his continued health. He takes his role of caregiver seriously and ensures they are home when they need to be, that Roger is well fed and rested. Strub, on the other hand, continues to live his life as he would whether he had AIDS or not; he is not limited by time. He is not the only person to reject the idea of being an AIDS victim. He also writes, "[Michael] Callen once told me, 'An AIDS victim is sad and pitied, but a person with AIDS who tries not to be defined by the disease, or, God forbid, dares criticize anything about the gay community's response to AIDS, is considered to be in denial, a threat, or an ingrate'" (Strub 172). The idea that a person with AIDS can be a threat to the gay community refers to the division between gay men in how the disease is spread and the attempts to stop the spread of the disease; those who promoted a change to sexual behaviors were often ridiculed and "called 'sex-negative' and 'self-hating' and accused of 'blaming' gay liberation for the epidemic" (Strub 130).

As with Monette, temporal sequencing is present in Strub's memoir; however because of his involvement in politics and the development of effective medication that manages HIV/AIDS, Strub's usage in the memoir does not have "lethal consequence" as previously mentioned. He has lived beyond the previous life expectancy of a gay man who has contracted AIDS and, in the writing of his memoir, has moved beyond it. Additionally, during his life, instead of being overwhelmed by the disease, Strub and those who live during the same time period are moved to act out or, as with some activists, ACT UP. Strub states, "[o]ur activism became the calendar against which we measured our lives" (199). As Strub becomes more involved in activism, such as fund-raising for ACT UP, he lives beyond his disease; that is to say he is not limited by the diagnosis of himself and reaches out to aid the community as a whole. In this way he is able to fight back, which later affects the way he presents information in his memoir. In writing, he rarely mentions how he felt during these moments, but instead focuses on bringing awareness to the community.

Though the act of writing a memoir and publishing it makes the book available to the public and, in a sense, moves beyond the individual writing, the style of writing shifts between memoirs. While *Borrowed Time* is more personal, *Body Counts* moves beyond the body of the writer and his loved ones to the well-being of the queer community. This is not to suggest that Strub's life has no difficult moments such as Monette's; however his writing and thus the reader's attention do not linger on his grief. While Monette's memoir ends with Roger's death, Strub is only on page 212 of 400 when his lover, Michael Misove, dies from AIDS-related cryptococcal meningitis. In fact, he does not even mention Michael's illness until page 209. This may be in part due to Michael's refusal to get tested. As Michael says, "I probably have it, too, but I still don't want to know. If I've got it, I've got it. There's nothing different I would do" (Strub 165). Despite not officially knowing his diagnosis, Michael and Sean are sure he must be infected, but according to his writing, do not dwell on the emotional aspect of a positive diagnosis. This attitude is what drives not only Michael, but the author as well, and when his lover dies, he feels grief but it does not prevent him from moving on with his life to give it further purpose; instead, he says "I buried my painful feelings in constant activity, including expanding the scope of ACT UP's fund-raising. I felt a deep-seated need to be in that room at the LGBT Community Center every Monday throughout 1989 with hundreds of others who understood the loss and grief I now felt more acutely than ever" (Strub 219). This is the extent to which Stub mentions his grief, and it is less palpable on the page than Monette's. Monette writes with great detail how he feels, letting the emotions linger, but Strub continues to bury his emotions behind his activism and career. By writing in this manner, with the emotions taking a backseat to the actions of his work, his writing in the memoir does not dwell on the diagnosis or even his loss.

After Strub's own brush with death just as the protease inhibitor treatment is released in conjunction with combination therapy, he begins to get his life back and discovers:

> My planning window, which for years had been steadily shrinking, started to expand. I had a renewed sense of energy and expectation. I felt confident making plans a few weeks and, soon, a few months into the future. Eventually, I could think about the following spring or summer. It was exciting but tentative. Every day I wondered, Is [sic] this the day my treatment will stop working? (363)

The temporal sequencing that is a problem for many AIDS patients ceases to carry a grim reminder of mortality as new drug therapies are introduced, work, and continue to work beyond the ability of their predecessors. This is a revelation to Strub, and he states, "[l]ike a lot of people with AIDS who expected to die, I had to spend time putting my life back together and trying to figure out what to do next. But I could never have put AIDS behind me, even if I had wanted to" (368). This inability to put AIDS in his past is not due to Strub allowing the disease to consume him; rather, it is because he has accepted that he has it, like Michael, and accepts his life for what it is and moves forward.

In contrast to *Borrowed Time* and *Body Counts*, it is important to note other contemporary memoirs such as *The Nearness of Others* by David Caron. Though it was also published in 2014, the same year as *Body Counts*, it is written by a man from a very different perspective; Caron was not diagnosed with HIV until 2006, ten years after effective treatments for HIV had been produced. As a result, his writing reflects the view of a man for whom HIV is no longer a literal death sentence due to biomedical advances. Just as with *Body Counts*, it is difficult to find critical reviews of *The Nearness of Others*. Most come in the form of short book reviews often found on review sites and in journals such as *Library Journal* and *French Studies*. The most significant and extensive review comes from David Herkt in "Degrees of Proximity in the Age of HIV," published in *Cultural Studies Review*. Of Caron's memoir he writes, "*The Nearness of Others* is an attempt to examine, for the early twenty-first century, the liminal spaces that exist between individuals with HIV and their social environment. The book delineates a relationship with the virus that would have been unimaginable twenty years before its publication" (Herkt 299). This relationship exists due to the biomedical advancements that have created effective drug regimens. Additionally, Herkt's use of the word "liminal" in this case is fitting. According to the *Oxford English Dictionary* there are three possible definitions of the word, but for Herkt, the most fitting are the second and third: "characterized by being on a boundary or threshold, esp. by being transitional or intermediate between two states, situations, etc.," and from cultural anthropology, "of or relating to a transitional or intermediate state between culturally defined states of a person's life, esp. as marked by a ritual or rite of passage" ("liminal"). Herkt is suggesting that Caron examines the transitional state between a person who is being diagnosed with HIV and the world around him, but also the boundary that the HIV-positive body finds itself against after diagnosis.

Just as with the previous two memoirs discussed, there are some similarities between the two; the aforementioned liminal space can also be found in Monette when he describes the moon, and in Strub when he finds the LGBT community withdrawing from those with HIV. However, Herkt agrees that there *has* been a drastic change in how early AIDS memoirs were written compared to Caron's when he writes, "unlike the first-person works by other writers of the early years of HIV/AIDS, such as those by Paul Monette, . . . Caron's recounting is vastly more distanced. Where these earlier writers often focused on the circumstances of infection as crucial moments in a definition of being, Caron refuses this reading. He deals, instead, with the aftermath" (301). It is crucial to look at this difference in order to not only discuss the importance of Caron's work in the body of HIV/AIDS literature, but also understand how, and why, HIV/AIDS memoirs have changed. As Herkt suggests, Caron is not interested in *how* he has become infected, but what comes next, or the life *beyond* the diagnosis, those liminal moments that exist beyond contracting the virus, which Strub also embraces. This aftermath is what defines the liminal spaces for those gay men living with HIV, as up until that point, they are considered part of the LGBT community. The aftermath of diagnosis brings them into new contact with their communities, and it is not always a positive, progressive experience. Monette touches upon this new relationship to society, as previously discussed, when he and Roger find themselves secluded and "on the moon" away from those not in the direct line of AIDS.

While Sean Strub's *Body Counts* does separate the book into sections, they are unnamed, but they follow a mostly linear sequence. Caron's *The Nearness of Others*, however, rejects this linear timeline; it is divided into six distinct sections, each focusing on a theme with titled chapters within each section. These sections—diagnosis, others, disclosure, taste, tact, contact—allow Caron to explore different elements of being HIV-positive today. They also help to create a nonlinear timeline as Caron is able to focus on the specific topic of the section without regards to chronology. Furthermore, the narrative is decidedly postmodern in its disjointed narrative style and discussion of disclosure as a forced act. As such, there is a dual reading embedded within the structure: it is hopeful with regards to the advancement of biomedicine, but then pivots to the act of disclosure and how this has forced many HIV-positive men back "into the closet." The narrator anticipates hope and progress but doubles back. While the majority of the population seems to have moved on and "forgotten" about AIDS, unlike in *Borrowed Time* where AIDS is frighteningly new, the queer community, particularly those diagnosed with HIV, has found itself combating the stigma against those who contract HIV/AIDS, a stigma that comes from within the gay community itself. Furthermore, Caron introduces the idea of juxtaposing HIV/AIDS with other traumatic events in his section on tact, which puts these historical and present-day events in context. While controversial, Caron suggests reading these events with tact allows for a better understanding of new events, such as AIDS, where the audience may not fully understand the import of the tragedy. This is unlike the writing in *Borrowed Time* because Monette is unable to relate to events outside of AIDS due to his limited time and focus on Roger. Nonlinear structure makes possible putting together events and people that would not have previously existed together. As a man who has contracted HIV after the development of effective drugs, Caron is in that position to be able to create a nonlinear style; he does not need to be limited by temporal sequencing.

Caron begins his memoir by disclosing his HIV-positive status and how he discovered his status from his doctor. What follows is Caron's spiral into depression and frenzy of trying to make himself fit and healthy, which ends up having the opposite effect as his friends begin to question his health. In each of the memoir's six parts, Caron dedicates a significant amount of time to discussing his diagnosis, the act of disclosure, and changes in contact and tact. By separating his book in this way, he utilizes a nonchronological approach because he focuses on one particular theme per section, which might traverse time in a nonlinear manner. What makes this memoir different from the previous two is that Caron also brings in the "other," or people who are not necessarily HIV-positive, but who share similar experiences at the hands of the majority population. As an academic, Caron often discusses literature, popular culture, and literary theorists in his attempt to analyze HIV in the context of his life, and this life along with the topics explain his postmodernist approach.

Prior to learning how to disclose his status, Caron initially falls into a depression after his diagnosis, much like Monette with Roger's diagnosis, which he discusses in conjunction with disclosure of another kind. As he states, "For an academic to admit to being clinically depressed can be tricky, because to disclose that your mind isn't functioning as it should is to disqualify yourself, to risk rendering irrelevant everything you do or say as a professional thinker" (Caron 12). For Caron to be an academic, he believes that he must have a strong mind, and that depression negates this strong mind and, as such, disqualifies him from being an academic. His use of the term "disclose" is interesting in this case because disclosure is one of the key topics in his book, as it was in Monette's and Strub's. In this instance, however, he is talking about the disclosure of depression rather than the disclosure of HIV-positive status. He does have to disclose his HIV-positive status, but there are times when that is not necessarily the most important type of disclosure in his world. Caron also uses the word "disqualify," which further echoes the way in which gay, positive men are "disqualified" from sexual and nonsexual contact with HIV-negative gay men. "Risk" is also used, which is also a word he closely associates with being HIV-positive, as to risk disclosure of positive status disqualifies the gay man from participating in the HIV-negative community. Furthermore, discussing risk in another way, one can risk disclosure of depression, and this disclosure has the potential to disqualify a scholar from his field. These risks can lead to depression, and Caron goes on to say that "[d]epression doesn't make you a different person exactly, it makes you disappear little by little until nothing of you remains. . . . you feel yourself gradually cease to exist, the force of the madness—this complete lack of discernment—overcomes your body" (Caron 12). As Caron suggests, a person with depression is not inherently different from their pre-depression self; however, as they contend with depression, they lose energy, and with it, little pieces of themselves until they are a shell of their former self. Once vibrant people are quiet and withdrawn. As a scholar, this is particularly worrisome as Caron fears he will lose credibility to admit he is depressed. Not only that, but he fears that he will lose himself entirely as he "gradually cease[s] to exist" (Caron 12).

Caron's awareness of his own depression grants the narrative a kind of credibility, despite his belief that it disqualifies him from communities such as academia. What is interesting about this is the paradox that if, in fact, depression disqualifies him in the world of academia, then how is he able to narrate his memoir? I argue that his admission of depression actually gives his narrative credibility because of his self-awareness and ability to elucidate his position within the world. Furthermore, this discussion of depression ties directly to what—in the past—has physically and mentally occurred within people living with AIDS. Before protease inhibitor treatments, those with AIDS would gradually experience a decline in their physical and mental health. As Monette noticed with Roger, it happened slowly over time with a cough that they hardly noticed, until that cough was diagnosed as pneumocystis pneumonia; with Strub it was the headache Michael developed until it was cryptococcal meningitis. Caron goes on to say, "[t]he fact that from such a disruption depression emerged signaled to me that HIV means disorder in many senses of the term but also that there may be something interesting in the opportunity it offered me to reassess everything" (17). This eventual insight appears crucial, especially in considering biomedical advancements. Prior to effective treatments, would Caron have been able to say the same thing? As his doctor tells him at the initial disclosure from doctor to patient, "HIV no longer meant an automatic death sentence" (Caron 3).

Though it has been more than thirty-five years since the initial epidemic began, and more than twenty years have passed since the first truly effective treatments, stigma still faces those who have been diagnosed with HIV/AIDS. This stigma becomes clear to Caron when he attempts to find physical—and many times sexual—contact with men who are seronegative. A shift occurs, he notices, through HIV-positive status. Caron notes with irony, "Funny how a gay man's hand resting heavily on your shoulder used to say let's fuck but now means let's not. Funny how ostensible nearness really betrays distance sometimes" (26). Herein lies a paradox; to be near is to be distant. The codes in the body language of gay men change when the serostatus of one of the potential partners changes. Even though contact physically remains at that moment, any offered exchange is withdrawn, and yet the touch remains not to invite, but to ground the seropositive person and hold them at bay, as if to push him away and keep both the man and HIV at bay. This change in touch is significant for those seeking contact despite their positive status, and for Caron he admits that it has made him "touchy," and, since contact is one of the primary motifs of the book with an entire section dedicated to it, the change in touch and contact further emphasizes the disruption of HIV. Caron is able to step back to analyze this, however, and discusses the change in state when he writes:

> What defines the uncontaminated isn't its current status but the capacity to lose it, its susceptibility to infection. As an HIV-positive person, the fact of my contamination will never change. . . . An HIV-negative person, however, cannot make a parallel claim to permanence, and if an HIV vaccine ever comes along, there are other viruses out there. To think of oneself as clean presupposes that one identifies in relation to dirt—a negative relation, to be sure, but a relation nonetheless. (Caron 27)

Caron does suggest that there is the possibility in the future for a cure given the rapid changes in biomedicine; however he feels that even if he were to be cured of HIV, he would not feel that he was uncontaminated because the virus had at one point been in his system. As such, those who remain negative have more to "lose" in this sense were they to contract the virus. The idea of losing one's negative status, as Caron suggests, is related to being "dirty" or "unclean," as those who are negative have—at least in the past—referred to themselves as "clean." This idea that the blood is therefore somehow dirty puts the positive person into the position of the "other," making them untouchable, which circles back to the idea of contact. To keep the positive person away is to keep the "dirt" away and to remain negative and clean, reinforcing the stigma and separation which result in keeping those who are HIV-positive on the "moon" where their predecessors had been placed by political administrations and the heterosexual majority of the past.

There is a remarkable shift in the way AIDS memoirs were first written in 1988 to the contemporary memoirs of the twenty-first century. *Borrowed Time* by Paul Monette is frequently hailed as the first of its kind, and as such, there is nothing for Monette to build on. Instead, he sets the precedent by talking about his experience with AIDS through Roger's diagnosis and death.

Monette is trapped as an AIDS victim as are many of the men of that era; they have been ignored by the government and medical community, friends and family, and even other members of the gay community. A shift occurs, however, in those memoirs such as *Body Counts* by Sean Strub, that were written after combination therapy was introduced and began saving lives. It is this, perhaps more than anything, that helps shape Strub's narrative. Rather than become emotional over events, Strub is able to distance himself from his diagnosis and discuss events beyond AIDS. He writes about coming out, starting new ventures, and living beyond—and even despite—his disease. Similarly, *The Nearness of Others* collects the work of David Caron who is diagnosed at a time when HIV is manageable. Due to the change in stigmatization and distance from the past, the gay community has abandoned some of its own and holds them at arm's length; this same distancing is comparable to what Monette faced in the 1980s. While Monette writes a work that is heavily influenced by temporal sequencing, that is to say presenting events with relation to time, Strub is able to step beyond the restriction of time because, unlike Monette, he has a nearly unlimited amount of it left. With greater access to information and medication, Strub is able to weave in events from earlier and even later into his narrative because he has seemingly conquered the time restriction placed on many people with AIDS, especially those with Kaposi's sarcoma. He has lived beyond the "90 in Nine" or the "90 percent of those diagnosed with KS in their lungs [who] died within nine months" that Michael Callen revealed (Strub 321). Caron, an academic, ignores temporal sequencing and events strictly within his own life to bring greater meaning to his memoir, using it to highlight not only the loss of contact for the present-day HIV-positive gay man despite the new biomedical realities, but also the struggles of the "other" in many senses of the word, adding even more to the political aspect of HIV/AIDS.

WORKS CITED

Armstrong, Walter. "Body Counts: POZ Founder Sean Strub Tells All." *POZ*, January 8, 2014.

Caron, David. *The Nearness of Others: Searching for Tact and Contact in the Age of HIV*. University of Minnesota Press, 2014.

Clum, J. M. "'The Time Before the War': AIDS, Memory, and Desire." *American Literature*, vol. 62, no. 4, Dec. 1990, p. 648, EBSCO*host*, search.ebscohost.com/login.aspx?direct=true&db=aph&AN=9101281162&site=ehost-live&scope=site. Accessed February 10, 2018.

Cohler, Bertram J. "Life Stories and Storied Lives: Genre and Reports of Lived Experience in Gay Personal Literature." *Journal of Homosexuality*, vol. 54, no. 4, 2008, pp. 362–380, EBSCO*host*, search.ebscohost.com/login.aspx?direct=true&db=mzh&AN=2008393583&site=ehost-live&scope=site. Accessed January 15, 2018.

Diedrich, L. "'Without Us All Told': Paul Monette's Vigilant Witnessing to the AIDS Crisis." *Literature and Medicine*, vol. 23 no. 1, 2004, pp. 112–127, *Project MUSE*, doi:10.1353/lm.2004.0002. Accessed February 10, 2018.

Eisner, Douglas. "Liberating Narrative: AIDS and the Limits of Melodrama in Monette and Weir." *College Literature*, vol. 24, no. 1, Feb. 1997, pp. 213–226, EBSCO*host*, search.ebscohost.com/login.aspx?direct=true&db=mzh&AN=1998072075&site=ehost-live&scope=site. Accessed February 10, 2018.

Garmire, Lisa. "Borrowing Time: Writing and Resisting Viral Narratives in Novels about AIDS." *Thresholds: Viewing Culture*, vol. 9, 1995, pp. 136–139, EBSCO*host*, search.ebscohost.com/login.aspx?direct=true&db=mzh&AN=2000071098&site=ehost-live&scope=site. Accessed January 15, 2018.

Herkt, David. "Degrees of Proximity in the Age of HIV." *Cultural Studies Review*, vol. 21, no. 1, 2015, pp. 298–303, doi: http://dx.doi.org/10.5130/csr.v21i1.4336. Accessed March 16, 2018.

Jarraway, David R. "From Spectacular to Speculative: The Shifting Rhetoric in Recent Gay AIDS Memoirs." *Mosaic: A Journal for the Interdisciplinary Study of Literature*, vol. 33, no. 4, Dec. 2000, pp. 115–128, EBSCO*host*, search.ebscohost.com/login.aspx?direct=true&db=mzh&AN=2000072187&site=ehost-live&scope=site. Accessed February 10, 2018.

Jurecic, Ann. *Illness as Narrative*. University of Pittsburgh Press, 2012.

"Liminal, adj." *OED Online*, Oxford University Press, March 2018, www.oed.com/view/Entry/108471. Accessed April 10, 2018.

Monette, Paul. *Borrowed Time: An AIDS Memoir*. Harcourt Brace, 1988.

Picano, Felice. "In the Age of the Gay Memoir." *Gay and Lesbian Review Worldwide*. Mar. 2016, pp. 22-24.

Strub, Sean. *Body Counts: A Memoir of Activism, Sex, and Survival*. Scribner, 2014.

Chapter Six

Guibert before Guibert

AIDS and Literary Creation

Mariarosa Loddo

Anyone seeking information about Hervé Guibert (1955–1991) in 2018 will probably start with an online search. Soon she will notice the number of sources relating the author to AIDS. Eventually, she will find out how eclectic, prolific, and atypical was the career of this *enfant terrible* of French contemporary literature, a writer who gained wide popularity just before his death, only to be recently rediscovered after a period of oblivion.[1] In the 90s, those who got to know Guibert through his most famous work (*To the Friend Who Did Not Save My Life, À l'ami qui ne m'a pas sauvé la vie*) used to associate him with his fragile and emaciated appearance, since he was already ill when he took part in *Apostrophes*, the French cultural television program where he was interviewed for the launch of his book in 1990. Although his career as a writer had begun long before, through his interview on *Apostrophes* he became "the 'young writer' in vogue, even though [he] was sick and probably condemned" (Guibert, *The Man in the Red Hat* 46).[2]

Admittedly, addressing Guibert's AIDS writing and his impending death means to focus on just one part of his extensive literary production, namely those texts in which illness plays a significant role.[3] In choosing to embrace this partial perspective, I seek to assess and discuss the author's particular contribution to representing the disease. However, I will consider two works that are not Guibert's best known works: *Incognito* (*L'incognito*, 1989) and *The Man in the Red Hat* (*L'homme au chapeau rouge*, 1992). This selection is justified by their special position within the whole work of the French author: *Incognito* is the first novel in which the presence of the disease starts to emerge as a steady thread in his writing, and *The Man in the Red Hat* is his last, romanticized, autofictional text, where already AIDS appears as a fact. I will focus on these texts in order to cast light on the formation of the progressive and articulate writing process that led Guibert to fully express and expose his AIDS experience in his most famous (and perhaps finest) works. In order to do so, I will take into account specific narrative aspects, such as paratextual elements, plot structure, and use of the first person.[4] Moreover, I will refer to biographical material, since I believe it helps to better understand the circumstances in which Guibert conceived his works. Based on these premises and theoretical tools, my analysis aims to outline the trajectory that characterized Guibert's different approaches to AIDS. I will highlight how illness is for the first time integrated in the narrative fabric with difficulty (in *Incognito*), and eventually I will focus on the later text (*The Man in the Red Hat*), in which the narrator feels he had enough with the AIDS theme but still cannot avoid writing about it.

Before I evaluate the selected works in depth, they need to be briefly distinguished from Guibert's other works in which AIDS is the main topic and its disclosure is more explicit, such as *To the Friend Who Did Not Save My Life*, *The Compassion Protocol* (*Le protocole compassionnel*, 1991), and *Cytomegalovirus* (*Cytomégalovirus*, 1992). If Guibert came to be known as an AIDS writer, it was through the publication of *To the Friend Who Did Not Save My Life*, in which he revealed that he was suffering from the same syndrome that had caused the death of one of his dearest friends, philosopher Michel Foucault. In addition, Guibert wrote a sequel to his bestseller, *The Compassion Protocol*, and a short journal from the hospital, *Cytomegalovirus* (posthumous). These three works constitute the portion of Guibert's production that was largely and explicitly concerned with the everyday struggle with his illness. Both *To the Friend Who Did Not Save My Life* and *The Compassion Protocol* were labelled as novels ("*romans*"), a term that appears on the cover of the two books and that was consciously used by the author to refer less to their content and more to their structure.[5] Nevertheless, thanks to the use of the autodiegetic narrator, as well as the public exposure of the author confirming that the illness was really consuming him, the books were received as nonfictional writings.[6]

Although *Incognito* and *The Man in the Red Hat* were composed when AIDS was already part of Guibert's life, they should be set apart from the other works I have just mentioned.[7] What distinguishes these works is the fact that AIDS is not *the* subject of the narrative, but a secondary, sometimes collateral or disguised element in it. This different approach to the topic of illness signals a shift in Guibert's way of coping with his personal condition as well as the evolution of his voice as a writer. As will be clear through my analysis, *Incognito* initiated this process, which however can be identified only if we follow the traces of an AIDS discourse that unfolds under the surface of the main plot.

The paratextual frame of *Incognito* points to a fictional crime story (the label novel, "*roman*," appears on the cover) as the content of the book: the title provokes a sense of mystery that the blurb on the back cover amplifies, in a list of the events that occurred in the night that the body of a professor, Guido Jallo, was found. The readers are then supposed to find out more, but the narrator and protagonist of the novel, Hector Lenoir, mostly tells facts that are not related to the murder of Jallo, whose death is mentioned only towards the end of the book.

Lenoir, Guibert's alter ego, is a young writer who, in 1987, begins his residency at the Académie Espagnole in Rome. Later in the text, *L'incognito* turns out to be the name of Lenoir's favorite gay bar in the Italian city, but only a few scenes take place in it. Instead, the academy provides from the beginning the center stage for the plot.[8] Readers become witnesses to encounters, skirmishes, and dinners between writers and artists who gravitate around the academy; these episodes are told in a fragmented way and follow one another with none standing out as pivotal for the evolution of the plot. Among the countless characters who surround Lenoir or have a role in his life, only a few are described in detail, while most are just identified by a name or their profession ("the painter," "the *cameriere*").[9] As a result, the narrative is chaotic and often incoherent. It looks like all the characters, including Lenoir, care solely about the practicalities of their life at the *académie* (getting a bigger room, acceptable furniture, a fair telephone rate, etc.). If we consider all of these characteristics, we may be tempted to judge *Incognito* as a failed novel. However, knowing the biographical material on which Guibert's work is based can lead to a more accurate interpretation. Like his alter ego Lenoir, Guibert won a scholarship for the Villa Medici, the French Academy in Rome, where he stayed from 1987 to 1989 and which provided the setting for *Incognito*. During his residency in January 1988, the author found out he had AIDS; nonetheless, this fact is not mentioned in the fictionalized narrative. Guibert does not transfer his diagnosed syndrome to Lenoir. Instead, he lets Lenoir face the possibility, but not the certitude, of being doomed. However, Lenoir's struggle to write his new book corresponds to Guibert's creative crisis related to his reluctance to integrate AIDS into his own writing. As we shall see, the conflict between the factual AIDS threat and its reformulation in literature results in *Incognito* in recurring metanarrative fragments and allusions to illness in terms of fears and assumptions. *Incognito* can certainly be defined as a "deception-novel" as Marie Darrieussecq calls it, since it presents itself as a detective story but soon breaks the conventions of the crime plot (Darrieussecq 83). Still, even if an investigation does not take place in the novel, the reader needs to perform one in order to identify the AIDS story latent in its plot. There are, indeed, many hints about the disease throughout the narrative.

Right from the first page, we learn that Lenoir had visited the academy four years before: "I had stopped working. I was convinced I had AIDS, I didn't want to write any old thing before dying. It's already been four years; AIDS leaves you a little time to die."[10] Although the narrator is describing a past situation, it looks like things have not changed from that time: Lenoir is still having some troubles with writing and keeps thinking he has contracted AIDS, even if no medical test is carried out to corroborate this conviction. Lenoir's difficulties in carrying out the project that justifies his two-year stay at the academy—a work telling the story of his life—recur as a metanarrative leitmotiv through the whole text: "For months, I have been mentally grinding my first paragraph, so it doesn't want to come, I make myself write, everything I put on the paper disgusts me, I tear it up, I start again, I tear and tear it up, it had never happened to me before, I don't trust myself anymore."[11] In fact, Lenoir basically spends his time in Rome doing anything except writing, and he lets us know that he cannot focus on his book more than two hours a day. Moreover, it is unclear whether the infamous first paragraph, whose topic is untold, has finally been written or not.

Guibert provides the novel with a harrowing setting that works as a pretext for Lenoir's unproductivity, since the hostile environment is presented as the cause of the writer's uneasiness. In fact, Lenoir blames the academy for bringing him bad luck and making him paranoid. A painter who used to stay there confirms the narrator's feeling and describes the awful effect that this place had on him: "A permanent terror. It's there exactly that I stopped painting. It's a place that makes you paranoid."[12] We see Lenoir obsessed with keeping the doors and windows of his room always shut and wandering with suspicion the hallways that connect the different parts of the academy: danger is lurking everywhere, and it looks like something bad is going to happen at any moment. However, it is not clear if there is really someone or something threatening Lenoir and his colleagues.

We recognize the same vagueness implied in Lenoir's only supposed illness. The narrator cannot help but mention AIDS only through delimited and scattered remarks, which are, however, too sporadic to suggest that the syndrome is a theme in the heart of the novel. Instead, its reiteration is enough to deem it as a subtle leitmotiv. As some examples will highlight, what is described is less the reality of the infection but rather the fear of it.

Any sexual activity, and sometimes any simple physical contact that concerns the narrator, seem to be denied, rejected as if the virus was undoubtedly inside Lenoir's body. The narrator acts as if he had already been diagnosed positive, an attitude that functions as a catharsis aiming to invoke the virus in order to banish it: "I threw away a yellow angora scarf against which I used to rub myself, it smelled bad, it contained such a significant amount of AIDS that I should have given it as a donation to the Pasteur Institute."[13] While sharing the bed with his friend Mateovitch, the narrator feels compelled to tell him that he probably has AIDS and that the virus is the reason why he refuses to sleep with another friend of his, Matou (see *L'incognito* 12, 98). In addition, the threat of AIDS establishes tacit forms of recognition, as with Bisserier, Lenoir's fellow at the academy, as both men's eyes are marked by red blisters, which the narrator believes to be possible signs of the disease: "I say to Matou that it may be shingles, or herpes, that it must be a manifestation of AIDS, he doesn't reply anything";[14] "Anyway, Bisserier and me understood each other immediately."[15] It is not known to the reader, whether the hypothesis of Lenoir is correct; also, there is no response, confirmation, or any serious comment following his confession to his friends, although they are the only people with whom he can share the word "AIDS" (see Guibert, *L'incognito* 12, 98). The syndrome is not a subject for dialogue: Lenoir is the only one to speak about it, and his hesitant considerations are followed by silence, which seems to express a widespread and shared fear.

What leads to any choice, judgment, and action is highlighted by the dubitative tone: "If we have AIDS, we're not going to fuck this guy";[16] "If they prove that my saliva is infected, I'm done, they'll expel me from the Academy";[17] and, in reference to Bisserier alluding to a sword of Damocles hanging above his own head, "I didn't understand whether he was talking about the virus or about the case of Guido Jallo."[18]

The doubt, embodied in the fear of certainty, spreads even to the medical experts, as if the physician could not detect the disease, making thus the narrator worried about his persistent cough and distrustful of the diagnostic skills of his doctor, as Lenoir's ironic comment shows: "Doctor Cursus excels in making diagnosis: he hasn't detected Gustave's hepatitis B."[19]

The strategy of omissions and red herrings that I have disclosed here hint at an unreliable narrator. While the insistence on the gloomy influence of the academy seemingly is to blame for Lenoir's state of mind, the opposite seems plausible. In other words, Lenoir's anguish about his fate distorts his perspective and makes everything look insidious and upsetting. In particular, the way AIDS discourse is developed—or rather undeveloped—suggests an inability to face the possibility of infection. All the deviations, digressions, and rambling about the trivial hassles at the academy are the performative reproduction of the impasse Guibert himself experienced when writing the novel. The *"incognito,"* then, seems to be the disease itself, invisible and acting without being identifiable, its presence infiltrating the text without the author being able to control it, neither making AIDS a fully active and recognized element, nor keeping it out of the plot.

To support my reading of *Incognito*, I will make use of the intertextual and epitextual hints highlighted by Jean-Pierre Boulé in *Hervé Guibert: Voices of the Self*. When related to other works by Guibert as well as to his interviews, the inconclusive stance of the novel finds both meaning and justification. *Incognito* is the work that chronologically precedes the publication of *To the Friend Who Did Not Save My Life*, where its narrative begins with a paradoxical and concise sentence: "I had AIDS for three months" (1).[20] Here, AIDS is openly the main subject of the text, with the author now brave enough to speak out about his condition and willing to preserve his writing project from the destructive power of the disease. In *To the Friend Who Did Not Save My Life*, Guibert confesses his difficulty in creating a book that ignores his pathological condition:

> I had this big, tedious, labored book right in front of me, and even before I'd begun working on it, I'd known it would turn out bastardized and incomplete in any case, because I didn't have the courage to confront its real first sentence, the one that kept springing to mind and that I fended off each time like a true curse, trying to forget it because it was the most unjust premonition in the world, because I was afraid to validate it through writing: "Disaster had to strike us." It had to happen—it's awful—for my book to see the light of day. (202–203)[21]

The first sentence that Guibert (disguised as Lenoir) was not ready to embrace in *Incognito* is the one finally accepted later in *To the Friend Who Did Not Save My Life*, the work that eventually replaced the autobiographical book which, according to *Incognito*, the author had in mind to write. It is another, unexpected work that the disease makes urgent: a *true* story about AIDS, told in the first person that overtly corresponds to the author. In fact, in *To the Friend Who Did Not Save My Life*, Guibert does not opt for a pseudonym, a choice that suggests a shift in his acceptance of the syndrome and, simultaneously, a less fictionalized mode of writing. Later, Guibert himself will describe *L'incognito* as "a slip-up, I did not keep it quite in check, it is the only one of my books that I feel no affection for" (Boulé, *Hervé Guibert* 179).[22] Here is the problem with *Incognito*: the author was not able to exercise effective control of the material. He lets it branch off in various directions and adopts an incoherent fictive frame. Nevertheless, as Boulé notes, *Incognito* proved to be a necessary step that would lead him to conceive *To the Friend Who Did Not Save My Life*: "Guibert learnt that the illness was swamping the text whether he had resolved to let it or not, so he might as well control it by deciding himself to write it" (Boulé, *Hervé Guibert* 189).

The difficulty Guibert encountered trying to include AIDS in *Incognito* should also be related to the relatively new topic he had selected for his literary work. In the late 1980s, French authors were making the first attempts in search of a language and a form that could address AIDS, which was an unprecedented subject at that time. Hence, before becoming the writer everyone would recognize on the newspapers, Guibert was painfully searching for the courage and the right words to tell his experience. His choice to opt for a fictional narrative and to count on the protection offered by the pseudonym (*Incognito*), before moving towards autobiography (*To the Friend Who Did Not Save My Life*), was part of the initial steps taken by AIDS writers who were inaugurating, if not a genre, a characteristic expressive form. Guibert learned both from his own mistakes (such as the controversial *Incognito*) and from his predecessors as well:

> Perhaps the raw authenticity of testimonial writing contributed to the general public holding back in the mid-1980s. . . . Hence Guibert had learned from the pioneers in the field to stay clear of traditional novels, testimonial writing or autobiographies, or at least to fictionalise the autobiography (the act of writing is a fictionalisation *per se*, but there are different *degrees* of "fictionalising" a text) in deciding to write about AIDS. (Boulé, *HIV Stories* 147)

To the Friend Who Did Not Save My Life and *The Compassion Protocol* came out in 1990 and 1991. Guibert died at the end of 1991, and *The Man in the Red Hat* was published posthumously in January 1992. This work is particularly meaningful since it shows the further progress Guibert made in his exploration of the ways AIDS could become part of his writing. *The Man in the Red Hat* has some features in common with *Incognito*: the crime story in form of the disappearance of an antique dealer who denounced a counterfeit painting trade, the paranoid and ominous atmosphere that dominates the events, and the fictionalized mode the author chose to make himself the hero of his narrative. In fact, even if the protagonist of *The Man in the Red Hat* is Guibert himself, the events that involve him in the narrative are implausible, making this text a clear *autofiction*. However, between *Incognito* and *The Man in the Red Hat*, Guibert had already publicly disclosed his illness and had found his own way to deal with the topic.

The first pages of *The Man in the Red Hat* focus on the writer's biopsy to ascertain the possible presence of a tumor and the spread of his disease. Nonetheless, Guibert decides to take part in some trips out of France, not giving up his passion for the paintings he tracks down in the antiquarian shops in Paris. In the novel, Guibert meets Lena, an expert in identifying counterfeit works of art and the sister of the antiquarian who disappeared in Russia, and joins her in Moscow so as to find out more about what happened to her brother. Moreover, the writer goes to Corfu to visit the painter Yannis and later poses for one of his portraits. The plot follows these two trajectories where its protagonists are well defined and restricted in number: there is no question that the dispersion and vagueness of *Incognito* are gone and that Guibert, as an author, seems definitely more confident in controlling the narrative. He has come to a point where he can openly disclose himself in his writing and make AIDS a part of it, without the disease determining his work. Through *The Man in the Red Hat*, Guibert wanted to distance himself from the topic he had profoundly explored in his previous two books (*To the Friend Who Did Not Save My Life* and *The Compassion Protocol*); hence he consciously chose to focus on painting and on the fictional spy story. Guibert tried his best to conceive his illness as a condition of which he could take advantage:

> Certainly, I've had to love it, otherwise my life would have become unliveable, it has inevitably been a fundamental, crucial experience, but now that I've been through it all, I can't go any further, after that road towards wisdom a revolt is stirring in me for the first time. I now can't bear any talk of Aids [sic], I hate my Aids [sic]. I want to have done with it, it's served its time in me. (*The Man in the Red Hat* 42)[23]

He was forced to learn to accept AIDS in his life, but it was still his choice to make something out of this experience: literature and an opportunity for personal growth. If we go back to *Incognito*, disorientation and uncertainty haunt both the writing and the existence of the author, whose agency seems to be dominated by fear: "I thought: I'm not experiencing anything anymore, fear has triumphed. I was there, ready for danger, but in retreat from danger, at the border, as a voyeur, as a passive being of experiences."[24]

With *The Man in the Red Hat* Guibert is expressing his desire of existing beyond AIDS: if he cannot be saved, he then wishes that he would be able to at least write a story in which the disease is absent. This seems to be the project behind the novel, albeit merely a wishful thought. Since AIDS cannot be expelled from Guibert's life, then it must be present in his work, which is fed by his existence, even and especially when it takes a turn for the worse. Hence, in spite of his dangerous travels and his exciting encounters, the narrator remains an ill person who cannot lift heavy objects, too thin and recognizable as the "skeleton in the red hat" (*The Man in the Red Hat* 85).[25] To write about AIDS remains inevitable and to do it on the author's own terms seems to be his only weapon against his destructive actions.

Through the reading of *Incognito* and the comparison with *The Man in the Red Hat*, I attempted to measure how far Hervé Guibert went in his literary duel with AIDS. Although the subject remains the same, Guibert never stops searching for different literary forms which could reflect his changing perception of the syndrome. Conventions of genres, narrator's posture, distancing and fictionalizing strategies were variously combined in Guibert's original AIDS corpus. However, whatever forms he chose to give to his works, Guibert kept writing to resist the virus, and constantly engaged in a battle against time:

> The joy of writing has been followed by the terror of being interrupted. This book threatens my mind. Maybe I've already lost my mind or I'm losing it, it scatters and shatters between the pages which devour it. They say the virus hides in the brain and undermines the nervous system. I feel like I'm going to

fall in a coma. It looks like that through the book I am erasing time, gradually, faster and faster, until no distance is left between the time of consciousness and the lost time of death.[26]

NOTES

1. See Arnaud Genon, "Hervé Guibert en 2004: état des lieux des études guibertiennes."
2. "le 'jeune écrivain' en vogue, bien que je fusse malade et probablement condamné" (Guibert, *L'homme au chapeau rouge* 70).
From now on, the quotes through the text will refer to the English editions of Guibert's works. Original French quotes will be provided in footnotes.
3. Before *To the Friend Who Did Not Save My Life*, Guibert had written at least sixteen books. While his literary debut took place in 1977 (*La mort propaganda* [*Propaganda Death*]), it was only in 1988 that he found out he had contracted the disease.
4. My references to paratext are based on French first editions of Guibert's works.
5. During the interview in the television program *Apostrophes* Guibert says that he considers *To the Friend Who Did Not Save My Life* a novel because of the way it is written, even if "everything in it is true."
6. After the success of *To the Friend Who Did Not Save My Life*, Guibert received numerous letters from his readers who were worried for his health and his decision to stop writing books. *The Compassion Protocol*, which contains a dedication to the people who reached out to him, was the result of Guibert feeling encouraged to change his mind and let the public know, through one more confessional work, about his ongoing battle with AIDS.
7. While *Incognito* is usually not included by critics and the general public in Guibert's "AIDS corpus," *The Man in the Red Hat* is commonly considered as part of a trilogy completed by *To the Friend Who Did Not Save My Life* and *The Compassion Protocol*. However, while *The Compassion Protocol* was intended by Guibert himself as a sequel to his best-seller, *The Man in the Red Hat* was not written as a third "chapter." The trilogy frame appears to be an editorial move aimed at promoting the posthumous work by Guibert by leaning on his best-seller (*The Man in the Red Hat* was released a few months after the author's death by Gallimard, the same publisher of *To the Friend Who Did Not Save My Life* and *The Compassion Protocol*). See Jean-Pierre Boulé, *Hervé Guibert: Voices of the Self*, for a contestation of the trilogy label (234, 302), and Vincent Kaufmann, *Ménage à trois*, for an endorsement of the label (212).
8. *Incognito* is mentioned for the first time only at page 118.
9. "*Cameriere*" is the Italian word for waiter.
10. "J'avais arrêté de travailler, J'étais persuadé d'avoir le sida, je ne voulais pas écrire n'importe quoi avant de mourir. Il y a quatre ans déjà; le sida vous laisse un peu de temps pour crever" (Guibert, *L'incognito* 11).
An English translation of *L'incognito* was published by Broadwater House in 1999, but it is currently out of print. Therefore, all translations from *L'incognito* are mine. French original quotes will be provided in footnotes.
11. "Cela fait plusieurs mois que je triture mentalement mon premier paragraphe, du coup il ne veut pas sortir, je me force, tout ce que je pose sur le papier me répugne, je déchire, je recommence, je déchire, déchire, ça ne m'était jamais arrivé, je n'ai plus aucune confiance en moi." (Guibert, *L'incognito* 52–53).
12. "Une terreur permanente. C'est là justement que j'ai arrêté de peindre. C'est un endroit qui rend parano" (Guibert, *L'incognito* 68).
13. "J'ai jeté une écharpe angora jaune contre laquelle je me frottais, elle puait, il y avait là-dedans une telle concentration de sida que j'aurais dû en faire don à l'institut Pasteur" (Guibert, *L'incognito* 76).
14. "Je dis à Matou que c'est peut-être un zona, ou un herpès, et que ce doit être une manifestation du sida, il ne réplique rien" (Guibert, *L'incognito* 97–98).

15. "Quoi qu'il en soit, Bisserier et moi, au premier regard, on s'est compris" (Guibert, *L'incognito* 70).
16. "Si on a le sida, on va tout de même pas saloper ce garçon" (Guibert, *L'incognito* 121).
17. "S'ils prouvent que ma salive est infectée, je suis cuit, ils me chasseront de l'Académie" (Guibert, *L'incognito* 129).
18. "Je n'ai pas compris s'il parlait du virus, ou de l'affaire Guido Jallo" (Guibert, *L'incognito* 185).
19. "Le docteur Cursus a un excellent diagnostic: il n'a pas décelé l'hépatite B de Gustave" (Guibert, *L'incognito* 52).
20. "J'ai eu le sida pendant trois mois" (Guibert, *À l'ami qui ne m'a pas sauvé la vie* 9).
21. "J'avais ce gros livre plat et laborieux sous la main, et, avant même de l'avoir commencé, je savais qu'il serait de toute façon incomplet et bâtard, car je n'avais pas le courage d'affronter sa vraie première phrase, qui me venait aux lèvres, et que je repoussais chaque fois le plus loin possible de moi comme une vraie malédiction, tâchant de l'oublier car elle était la prémonition la plus injuste du monde, car je craignais de la valider par l'écriture: «Il fallait que le malheur nous tombe dessus.» Il le fallait, quelle horreur, pour que mon livre voie le jour" (Guibert, *À l'ami qui ne m'a pas sauvé la vie* 221).
22. "un dérapage, je ne l'ai pas tout à fait contrôlé, c'est le seul de mes livres pour lequel je n'ai pas d'affection" (Boulé, *Hervé Guibert* 179).
23. "Certainement, j'ai bien été forcée l'aimer, sinon ma vie serait devenue invivable, il a été inévitablement une expérience fondamentale, cruciale, mais maintenant j'en ai fait le tour, et je n'en peux plus, après ce chemin vers la sagesse pour la première fois c'est la révolte qui pointe. Je ne peux plus entendre parler de sida. Je hais le sida. Je ne veux plus l'avoir, il a fait son temps en moi" (Guibert, *L'homme au chapeau rouge* 64).
24. "J'ai pensé: je ne vis plus rien, la peur a gagné de toute part. J'étais là, prête à un certain danger, mais en retrait du danger, à sa lisière, en voyeur, en être passif des expériences" (Guibert, *L'incognito* 169).
25. "squelette avec son chapeau rouge" (Guibert, *L'homme au chapeau rouge* 121).
26. "A la joie d'écrire a succédé la terreur d'en être interrompu. Ce livre menace ma raison. Peut-être l'ai-je déjà perdue tout à fait, ou suis-je en train de la perdre, elle s'égrène et se brise entre chaque page qui l'engloutit. On dit que le virus se tapit dans le cerveau et épuise le système nerveux. Je me sens à la veille d'un coma. Avec le livre j'ai l'impression d'effacer le temps, au fur et à mesure, de plus en plus vite, pour laisser le moins de marge possible entre le temps conscient et le temps perdu de la mort" (Guibert, *L'incognito* 180–181).

WORKS CITED

Boulé, Jean-Pierre. *Hervé Guibert: Voices of the Self.* Liverpool University Press, 1999.
———. *HIV Stories: The Archaeology of AIDS Writing in France, 1985–1988.* Liverpool University Press, 2002.
Darrieussecq, Marie. "La notion de leurre chez Herve Guibert." *Nottingham French Studies*, vol. 34, no.1, 1995, pp. 82–88.
Genon, Arnaud. "Hervé Guibert en 2004: état des lieux des études guibertiennes." *Acta fabula*, vol. 5, no. 1, 2004. www.fabula.org/acta/document232.php.
Guibert, Hervé. *À l'ami qui ne m'a pas sauvé la vie.* Gallimard, 1990.
———. *The Compassion Protocol*, translated by James Kirkup and George Braziller, 1994.
———. *Cytomégalovirus: Journal d'hospitalisation.* Seuil, 1992.
———. *Cytomegalovirus: A Hospitalization Diary*, translated by Clara Orban. Fordham University Press, 2015.
———. *L'homme au chapeau rouge.* Gallimard, 1992
———. *L'incognito.* Gallimard, 1989
———. *Incognito*, translated by Patricia Roseberry. Broadwater House, 1999.
———. *The Man in the Red Hat*, translated by James Kirkup. Quartet Books, 1993
———. *La mort propagande [Propaganda Death].* Régine Deforges, 1977.
———. *Le protocole compassionnel.* Gallimard, 1991.

———. *To the Friend Who Did Not Save My Life*, translated by Linda Coverdale. Atheneum, 1991.
Kaufmann, Vincent. *Ménage à trois: Littérature, médecine, religion.* Lille, Les Presses Universitaires du Septentrion, 2007.
Pivot, Bernard. "Le sexe homicide." *Apostrophes,* Antenne 2, March 16, 1990.

Chapter Seven

The Dream, the Disease, and the Disaster

On Yan Lianke's Dream of Ding Village

Shelley W. Chan

Born in 1958, Yan Lianke, a nationally and internationally known Chinese writer, has published fifteen novels and several dozens of novellas, short stories, and essays to date. He has been the recipient of major awards in China and abroad, including the 2000 Lu Xun Literary Prize, 2004 Lao She Literature Award (third place, novel category), 2011 Man Asian Literary Prize, 2014 Franz Kafka Prize, and 2016 Dream of the Red Chamber Award. Nevertheless, this award-winning writer has been very controversial and, in fact, banned for a period of time in China, primarily because of the sensitive topics of his fiction. As observed by a research fellow of *Yazhou Zhoukan* (*YZZK*, the Chinese version of *Asiaweek* published in Hong Kong):

> There has never been a writer like Yan Lianke, who has been labeled "the most controversial writer with the most banned books" besides the titles of "Master of Absurd Realism" and "China's most likely Nobel Prize winner." Such a label, neither an honor nor a criticism, makes Yan Lianke feel helpless. Indeed, no publishers in Mainland China have published any of his books in the past five years. (Yuan; my trans.)

Yan Lianke is known for using illness to signify reality. Since the establishment of the new government in 1949 on the mainland, especially with the open-door policy that brings rapid economic growth after the Great Proletarian Cultural Revolution (1966–1976), China has developed tremendously over the past four decades. Its recent achievements, including the 2008 Beijing Olympic Games, the 2010 Shanghai Expo, its rapid developments in space technology, its overtaking Japan to become the second-largest economic power, and its ambitious development strategies, such as the Belt and Road Initiative seen as an attempt toward Chinese dominance in world affairs, all in all have caught much attention from the rest of the world. As a result, many Chinese people believe that their country has shaken off its humiliating image as the "Sick Man of East Asia," which was the collective anxiety of the Chinese intellectuals in the late-nineteenth and early-twentieth centuries. Nevertheless, this anxiety is still troubling some Chinese who see present-day China as an unhealthy and even morbid world wherein people are spiritually sick. Among them is Yan Lianke. For instance, *The New York Times* published his article "On China's State-Sponsored Amnesia" on April 1, 2013, which was about how today's twenty- and thirty-year-olds had no memories of important events such as the June 4 Tiananmen Incident of 1989. Yan Lianke has also published novels of disease, such as *Streams of Light and Time* (*Riguang liunian*, 1998), *Pleasure* (*Shouhuo*, 2003),[1] and *Dream of Ding Village* (*Dingzhuang meng*, 2006). These novels are about cancer sufferers, physical disabilities, and HIV patients, respectively.

This essay focuses on *Dream of Ding Village* and discusses how the daring novel shows concern for the biopolitical situation of the Chinese people, and how it spearheads its criticism on the "blood economy" (*xuejiang jingji*) in central China in the 1990s. Through studying the unconventional narrative voice and the experimental structure of the novel, this chapter examines the thanatopolitics characteristic of the story and the possibility of the author's self-censorship; it also demonstrates how the novel makes parts of the real illusory and imaginary, and how this technique serves to create a wider and deeper blurred space between reality and unreality to highlight the irrational and crazy materialistic desire of human beings, which leads to an absurd and ill-practiced modernization.

Set in Henan province in China, *Dream of Ding Village* is about how the local people engage in the infamous "blood economy" and get infected with AIDS. Henan province in central China, believed to be the birthplace of the Chinese civilization, is a relatively less developed province where the per capita GDP is significantly lower than that of the more developed coastal or central areas. In Yan Lianke's own words, "some of the most memorable events in history happened here, but, during my lifetime, it's become one of the poorest places in the country. . . . There is no dignity left, and because of that the people of Henan have felt a deep sense of loss and bitterness" (Fan). In the early to mid-1990s, the provincial government promoted a policy to "shake off poverty and attain prosperity" (*tuopin zhifu*) and urged poor people to make money by selling their blood. The authority called this the "blood economy" (or "plasma economy") and believed that this policy would make "the people rich and the nation strong" (*min fu guo qiang*). To achieve the goal of the sovereign's administration by manipulating people's bodies fits the term "biopower" coined by Michel Foucault (1926–1984), who points out that

> [d]uring the classical period, there was a rapid development of various disciplines—universities, secondary schools, barracks, workshops; there was also the emergence, in the field of political practices and economic observation, of the problems of birthrate, longevity, public health, housing, and migration. Hence there was an explosion of the numerous and diverse techniques for achieving the subjugation of bodies and the control of populations, marking the beginning of an era of "biopower." (Foucault 140)

Perhaps this biopower in the context of China, which still claims to be a socialist country but in fact is more capitalist than many other countries that practice capitalism, is what Foucault calls "an indispensable element in the development of capitalism" (Foucault 140–141), as we have seen similar practices in Yan Lianke's other works (such as selling skin and bodies in the above-mentioned novels of disease) as well as productions of other authors/artists, such as Yu Hua's 1995 novel *Chronicle of a Blood Merchant* and Zhou Xiaowen's 1994 film *Ermo*. As Carlos Rojas, who has translated several novels of Yan Lianke, points out when he discusses the novel *Dream of Ding Village*,

> residents of remote central Chinese villages are encouraged to join contemporary capitalist systems not by integrating their labor into those systems but rather by literally commoditizing their own bodies. The result is a process wherein the individual's relationship to the economic order is fundamentally transformed, as the subject's own body becomes a commodity in its own right. (Rojas 189)

Ironically, the blood economy that aimed at increasing the provincial government's revenue and improving people's well-being proved to be the most absurd joke and the main reason of a terrible outbreak. According to Dr. Gao Yaojie, China's most outspoken AIDS activist, this "blood economy" was a "blood disaster" (*xuehuo*) and "national calamity" (*guonan*) (177).

Dream of Ding Village has eight volumes with irregular length. For instance, volume 1 has only one page and volume 8 has a little more than four pages, while other volumes have over thirty, forty, or fifty pages. The longer volumes are further divided into chapters and sections. Like many of Yan Lianke's novels, the structure of this book is highly experimental, which is a mixture of reality and dreams of the narrator's grandfather. "Dream" appears in the title and is also the full content of the one-page volume 1, which consists of three short dreams: "The Cupbearer's Dream," "The Baker's Dream," and "The Pharaoh's Dream" (Yan, *Dream* 3). In fact, the dreams are part of and yet more eye catching than the reality parts when they are printed in boldface and in a different font. To be precise, the narrative is often boldfaced and set in a special font throughout the entire book, mostly for Grandpa's dreams. Interestingly, Grandpa is often more clear minded in his dreams than when he is awake in the daytime; when he dreams of something, he can always confirm it in reality, as if he has an extrasensory perception. When the reader discovers that what is in Grandpa's dream is actually real, including the fact he is the one who is forced by the director of education to convince the villagers to sell their blood, they will gradually ignore the boundary between dreams and reality and wonder why the author chooses to present reality in the form of dream.

A Chinese version of *The Plague*, *Dream of Ding Village* is a macabre story filled with depictions of death:

> *They died like falling leaves.*
> *Their light extinguished, gone from this world.*
> ... [f]or the past two years, people in the village had been dying. Not a month went by without at least one death, and nearly every family had lost someone. After more than forty deaths in the space of two years, the graves in the village cemetery were as dense as sheaves of wheat in a farmer's field. ...
> *Died like falling leaves, their light gone from the world.* (Yan, *Dream* 9)

The story is narrated by a twelve-year-old dead boy. His father, Ding Hui, is a blood head who collects blood from his fellow villagers and sells it to blood stations. After the outbreak of AIDS and people in almost every household die for selling blood, the villagers get revenge on Ding Hui by poisoning his chicken, then his pig, and eventually his son:

> I was only twelve, in my fifth year at the school, when I died. I died from eating a poisoned tomato I found on the way home from school. ...
> I died not from the fever, not from AIDS, but because my dad had run a blood-collection station in Ding Village ten years earlier. He bought blood from the villagers and resold it for a profit. I died because my dad was the biggest blood merchant not just in Ding Village but in Two-Li Village, Willow Hamlet, Yellow Creek and dozens of other villages for miles around. He wasn't just a blood merchant: he was a blood kingpin. (Yan, *Dream* 10)

The narrator is right: his father is a merchant, a person who deals with buying and selling commodities for profit. His business is one that trades death, and everything he does is related to death. He is powerful among the villagers since he has the capital regardless of how he collected it, and the power obtained from his wealth allows him to become the top predator. He gains profit by collecting and reselling blood of his villagers at the expense of the lives of his own son and younger brother, who is also a blood seller and is, unfortunately, later infected with AIDS and dies. When more and more villagers die, the county government provides coffins to the families of the dead for free. The bloodsucker Ding Hui grabs the opportunity to make a fortune by controlling the distribution of the coffins and selling them:

> No longer did my father have to do all the work himself. He had a crew of young men to unload coffins from the trucks and help villagers fill out their paperwork, while he sat at a separate table, sipping water and calling up the villagers one by one to collect their completed forms and payments. After he had counted the cash and stuffed it in his black leather case, he would issue a receipt and direct the person to the trucks to collect his or her coffin. (Yan, *Dream* 176)

Even worse, this blood head who will do anything to make money starts a new business—arranging marriages, not between living people but between the dead. He even sells the remains of his own son—the twelve-year-old boy—to the dead daughter of a local leader. This way he becomes a relative of the leader, directly connecting himself to the authority and power. When questioned by Grandpa why he has found a dead girl who was a lot older than the boy, and who was physically handicapped, Ding Hui argues, "How could I have possibly found a better match? . . . Don't you know her father is moving up in the world? They just promoted him to mayor of Kaifeng!" (Yan, *Dream* 328). The dead first-person narrator, the innocent young boy who is saddled with his own father's sin and the villagers' hatred, serves to turn the entire novel into a death narrative. Although Yan Lianke is not the first Chinese writer to use a dead first-person narrator—Fang Fang's 1987 novella *Landscape (fengjing)* is narrated by a dead child—the novel is greatly enriched by such an absurd element. On the one hand, the dead narrator creates one kind of alienation effect, better catching the reader's attention by providing a nonconventional reading experience. On the other hand, by having a dead person tell the stories of the living, the boundary between the Netherworld and the human world is erased. That the Netherworld invades and eventually exercises control over the human world well fits the death theme of the novel. Furthermore, the binary opposition between the real and the unreal is also blurred, making the impossible possible.

In the beginning, the villagers of Ding Village are hesitant about selling blood. Grandpa sees/recollects clearly how Ding Village starts selling blood in one of his dreams. The county director of education urges the highly regarded Grandpa to organize people to pay a visit to Cai county, the richest county of Henan province. The reason Cai county is able to get rid of dire poverty and become rich is through its people selling blood. The trip to Cai county is a great shock to the people of Ding Village:

> Crossing the county line was like driving into some sort of paradise. The villagers were startled to see both sides of the main road lined by modern, two-

storey homes of red brick and tile. . . . There were flowers in every doorway, trees in every courtyard and broad avenues of poured concrete. . . .

Inside the houses, even the household appliances and furnishings seemed standardized: refrigerators were to the left of the entry hall, televisions in the living room opposite the sofa, and washing machines in the bathroom opposite the kitchen. Door and window frames were shiny new aluminum alloy; chests, wardrobes and cabinets were red lacquer adorned with gold leaf. The beds were heaped with silk and satin quilts and woolen blankets, and every room smelled nice. (Yan, *Dream* 34–35)

The following descriptions remind the reader of the rosy pictures of communism:

Outside on the street, they ran into a group of laughing, chattering village women loaded down with bundles of fresh vegetables and bags of fish and meat. When the villagers asked the women if they'd been out shopping, the women answered that there was no need to shop, because the village committee gave away food for free. All you had to do was go to the committee headquarters and collect what you needed for the day. (Yan, *Dream* 35–36)

This is the "model blood-selling village for the whole county, for the whole province" in which "everyone . . . sells blood" (Yan, *Dream* 36). This wealthy model village "had been made possible by selling blood" (Yan, *Dream* 37). The rosy pictures are also reminiscent of an economic and social campaign that occurred in the late 1950s to early 1960s: the Great Leap Forward. Launched and led by Mao Zedong (1893–1976), the campaign had its goal to rapidly construct the socialist China so as to catch up and surpass the Western developed countries, such as the United Kingdom and the United States. The people's communes were a product of the campaign: the agricultural collectivization and institutionalization that prohibited private farming. Private kitchens were abandoned; all people ate for free at the communal canteens where everyone ate as they wished—an illusion of communism—the distribution principle of socialism is to distribute according to work, and that of communism is to distribute according to need. It was enjoyable for a short period of time, but very soon the canteens experienced a lack of supply, and eventually had to be dissolved. The Great Leap Forward has been regarded as a failure that resulted in a great famine and millions of deaths.[2] The practice of the communal canteens during the Great Leap Forward and that in the model village in Cai county of *Dream of Ding Village*, both based on the communist principle of distribution, are both ironically turned into deadly disasters that took away thousands and even millions of lives. What Carlos Rojas pinpoints can be a good summary of these disasters:

As Michel Foucault and others have argued, the modern state derives its authority and legitimacy from its biopolitical relationship to its citizens—a relationship that is predicated on the state's ability to nurture life. Embedded within this biopolitical logic, however, is an inverse necropolitical one, in that the state's ability to provide the conditions for nurturing life is inextricably intertwined with its parallel ability to withhold those same conditions. (Rojas 188)

Michel Foucault points out: "For millennia, man remained what he was for Aristotle: a living animal with the additional capacity for a political existence; modern man is an animal whose politics places his existence as a living being in question" (143). Interestingly, the relation between the novel and the societal reality is similar to that of dreams and the fictional reality in the novel. Despite the title, the story of *Dream of Ding Village* is a realistic reflection of the tragedy that occurred in China. The "blood economy" best exemplifies the postrevolutionary China as a wonderful setting for the sovereignty and biopolitics to be related: "the culmination of a politics of life generated a lethal power that contradicts the productive impulse" (Esposito 39). With the death of Mao Zedong and the official close of the Great Proletarian Cultural Revolution he launched that was later labeled as "ten years of disaster," China's socialism experienced a drastic change, gradually moving toward capitalism, which had been denounced in China during the revolutionary period of time. Mao's theory and practice of class struggle had led the Chinese people to believe that the poorer the better, as rich people would be categorized as class enemies and punished. After Mao's death, Deng Xiaoping's (1904–1997) open-door policy and economic reform not only unlocked the door of China, but also changed the mind-set of the Chinese people, whose materialistic desire that had been suppressed for decades was revived, and honor was given to those who were able to accumulate capital. On discussing politics over life, Roberto Esposito asks: "How is it possible that a power of life is exercised against life itself? . . . Why does a power that functions by insuring, protecting, and augmenting life express such a potential for death? . . . Why does biopolitics continually threaten to be reversed into thanatopolitics?" (39). He quotes Foucault when he uses wars and the Beveridge Plan as examples:

> Foucault accents the direct and proportional relation that runs between the development of biopower and the incremental growth in homicidal capacity. There have never been so many bloody and genocidal wars as have occurred in the last two centuries, which is to say in a completely biopolitical period. It is enough to recall that the maximum international effort for organizing health, the so-called Beveridge Plan, was elaborated in the middle of a war that produced 50 million dead: "One could symbolize such a coincidence by a slogan: go get slaughtered and we promise you a long and pleasant life. Life insurance is connected with a death command." (Esposito 39)

In the 1990s' China, with the increase of blood sellers, more and more public and private blood stations mushroomed, and the hygienic standards in the process of blood drawing and plasma production were not strictly controlled, leading to the outbreak of an AIDS epidemic, exactly the same situation as described in *Dream of Ding Village*.[3] First of all, the post-Mao China appeared to have a posttraumatic symptom of the extreme shortage of supplies in the past decades: when the previous suppression of human materialist desire by communist doctrines was relaxed, planned economy was loosened up, and market economy was practiced, people seemed to be driven into a frenzy for materialism and consumerism by fair means or foul, as if the Pandora's box was opened. In the past, it was the sovereignty that imposed the suppression, and later it was still the sovereignty that lifted the suppression and encouraged people to pursue wealth by making use of their own biological bodies; the relation of sovereignty and biopolitics was thus created. Secondly, the extreme monetary worship has turned China into a place wherein money is God and everything, equating money with power. In other words, those who have a bigger accumulation of wealth have a bigger voice and power in the hierarchized society. In the case of the AIDS epidemic outbreak, in both the fictional and the realistic worlds, the HIV patients contribute their own blood and even lives to the blood heads' accumulation of money. Behind the blood heads is an even bigger social apparatus, which has stronger destructive power once it has malfunctioned. May the intension of the blood selling policy be "in the name of a politics of power" or "in the name of the survival itself of populations that are involved," "it is precisely what reinforces the tragic aporia of a death that is necessary to preserve life, of a life nourished by the deaths of others." (Esposito 39)

People in the West used to believe that AIDS often comes from homosexual communities. As Susan Sontag indicates,

> Indeed, to get AIDS is precisely to be revealed . . . as a member of certain "risk group," a community of pariahs. The illness flushes out an identity that might have remained hidden from neighbors, job-mates, family, friends. It also confirms an identity and, among the risk group in the United States most severely affected in the beginning, homosexual men, has been a creator of community as well as an experience that isolates the ill and exposes them to harassment and persecution. (112–113)

However, the identity is different in Yan's writing of AIDS in the Chinese context, though gay people in China are also treated as a "risk group." Yan's novel discloses a fact that the authorities would rather not face, and that is why *Dream of Ding Village* was banned in China. Scholars believe that "not only is AIDS writing a literary act involving conscious decisions about what to say or what not to say and how to couch what is said, but that writing about that writing is also a political act" (Poirier 5). The novelist visited the AIDS village in his hometown in Henan seven times, and he also communicated with Dr. Gao. As a matter of fact, it was in Dr. Gao's home where Yan Lianke first met with two HIV patients and learned about the absurd ways of blood collecting of the local blood heads and blood stations. He was driven by an impulse to write something for the victims of the "blood economy," in spite of the fact that many Chinese are misled to think that AIDS is always related to homosexuality and sexual promiscuity; in other words, AIDS has been turned into a metaphor for (im)morality. As Gao points out, "people generally believe that AIDS is one kind of 'moral disease' (*daodebing*) as a result of the immoral lifestyle of the patients. They [believe that AIDS sufferers] have only themselves to blame; other people, including the government, have no responsibility for it" (Gao 342). Yan's literary writing, however, boldly discloses the fact that in China many HIV patients, at least in the 1990s' central China, are victims of the "blood economy," for which the authority must take responsibility.

Critics compare *Dream of Ding Village* with Camus's *The Plague*. Yet Yan's work is darker than that of Camus because Camus's characters are not as hopeless as those created by Yan. As mentioned above, the blood head Ding Hui is a ruthless villain. When it comes to the characters inside the quarantine, the patients are equally hopeless, displaying the dark side of human nature: they steal, they cheat, they lie, they fight for power, and they publicly humiliate adulterers. It is not so much the illness as their evil human nature that makes these people ugly and repulsive. Yan Lianke once said: "*Dream of Ding Village* is more about AIDS, cancer, hepatitis, . . . in people's heart" ("Renwu zhuanfang"). The entire Ding Village is physically and spiritually ill. While the quarantined town in Camus's *The Plague* is finally opened again and people are able to reunite with their loved ones, Ding Village becomes a dead world, and the neighboring villages are also deserted; no humans or animals are seen, and no trees or wooden furniture are left—all are used for making caskets. Interestingly, the word "AIDS" (*aizibing*) is not as frequently mentioned as the term "fever disease" (*rebing*) throughout the novel. *Rebing* not only refers to the fever associated with AIDS, but also signifies people's irrational and crazy materialistic desire. One of the basic goals of the Chinese Communist Party was to overthrow (bureaucratic) capitalism. Ironically, the postrevolutionary ruling party continues the unfinished cause of capitalism in China in the high fever of materialistic modernization through a market blood economy.

Starting his writing career in the military, Yan Lianke was known for writing realistic fiction about the lives of soldiers and peasants in his early stage of literary creation. However, the 2001 novel *Hard as Water* marked the turning point of his writing style from realism to one that has become more and more experimental and absurd, resulting in his novels being labeled as absurdism, magical realism, or surrealism by critics. Nevertheless, Yan

Lianke seems to believe that none of the existing labels would best represent the essence of his writing. As a result, he coins a term for his Kafkaesque writing style: "mythorealism" (*shenshi zhuyi*), which, according to him,

> abandons external logical relation of the existing truth, and explores a "non-existing" truth, an unseen truth, and a truth concealed by truth.... Its connection with reality is not a direct cause and effect of life; rather it more relies on human soul and spirit ... and the author's subjective vision on the basis of reality.... By no means mythorealism would reject realism, but it tries hard to create and transcend reality.... It seeks an internal truth and relies on an internal causality with which it reaches the interior of human, society, and the world so as to write about and create truth. (Yan, *Faxian xiaoshuo* 181–182; my trans.)

When he was awarded the Franz Kafka Prize, he delivered a speech at the award ceremony entitled "The Man Chosen by Heaven and Life to Feel the Darkness."[4] Obviously, he is that man who sees "a nation that is thriving yet distorted, developing yet mutated," who also sees "corruption, absurdity, disorder and chaos" (Yan, "Shangtian"). "An enormous sheet of darkness gradually approached" this man, who "developed a keen appreciation for the somber side of ... existence" and "came to understand that darkness is not the mere absence of light, but rather it is life itself. Darkness is the Chinese people's fate" (Yan, "Shangtian"). In other words, the absurdity and seeming impossibility in his fiction are in fact the internal truth of reality. Perhaps only an absurd way of writing would be able to fully describe the absurd reality and express the love-and-hate complex of the novelist. In his own words, "the reality of China is so outrageous that it defies belief and renders realism inert" (Fan).

Indeed, the reality is so outrageous that it renders realism inert and impossible, and makes a more unrealistic style necessary. When the magical realistic fiction of the postcolonial Latin America could be seen as implicit social and cultural criticism, Yan Lianke's mythorealism, which, according to some critics, is a Chinese version of magical realism, also has its complexity of being subversive and submissive simultaneously. To take the first-person narrator and the dreams as an example, a dead narrator is doubtlessly an unreliable narrator, whose omnipresent point of view is questionable, setting a thanatopolitical tone for the story. Together with Grandpa's dreams, this unreliable narrator also adds a layer of uncertainty to the mythorealistic fiction. By making parts of the real illusory and imaginary, the author inserts an artistic dimension into the story, creating a wider and deeper blurred space between reality and unreality, highlighting the absurdity of the blood economy and human greediness, and leaving the reader to question the viability of such an ill-practiced modernization. In the meantime, narrating the cruel reality in the form of a dream by a dead narrator so as to make it seem less real might be a strategy of self-censorship. As a result, they are subversive as they tactfully disclose the cruelty of the society and challenge/condemn the irresponsible policies of the authority under the disguise of unreliability and uncertainty on the one hand, and on the other hand, the use of unreliability and uncertainty can be seen as a submissive self-censorship, or an "internalization of external censorious impulses and practices" (Tsai 77).

Paralleled to the evil force represented by the blood head Ding Hui, the image of Grandpa is more interesting. As mentioned above, Grandpa, although unwillingly, is the one who actually paves the way for the villagers to sell blood. The director of education has tried very hard to mobilize the peasants to sell their blood by talking "at length about the past, the future, the development of a 'plasma economy' and the need for a 'strong and prosperous China'" (Yan, *Dream* 26), but he has not achieved much in Ding Village. Then he thinks of the educated and respected Grandpa, who is the bell ringer of the village school but has actually taught there for many years whenever the school is in need of a teacher. He hopes that Grandpa will be able to help him because villagers will listen to what he says, but the latter is too shocked to speak anything but "Sell blood, did you say?" "My God . . . you want them to sell blood?" "But good heavens, you're asking people to sell their blood?" (Yan, *Dream* 28). To his questions the director answers: "you're an educated man. Surely you must know that the body's blood is like a natural spring: the more you take, the more it flows" (Yan, *Dream* 28). Grandpa, when recollecting how he was nominated a model teacher and approved by the director so he got a cash bonus and an award certificate every year, agrees to give it a try. He rings the bell and leads the villagers to the riverbed.

Yan writes:

> When Grandpa reached the riverbed, he searched around for a moist patch of sand, rubbed it between his hands and began to dig a small hole. Before long, the hole was half-filled with water. Grandpa produced a chipped ceramic bowl and began ladling the water from the hole and pouring it on to the sand. Again and again he ladled, pouring one bowl of water after another on to the sand. Just as if it seemed that the hole had gone dry, Grandpa paused. In a matter of moments, the water began to seep in, and the hole was once again full of water. "Did you see that?" [Grandpa] asked, glancing around at the villagers. "Water never runs dry. The more you take, the more it flows." He raised his voice. "It's the same with blood. Blood always replenishes itself. The more you take, the more it flows." (*Dream* 30–31)

Then we have the above-mentioned scenes that Grandpa leads the villagers to visit Cai county. After the trip to Cai county, villagers of Ding Village are finally convinced. More importantly, Ding Hui, the son of Grandpa and father of the narrator, becomes the first blood head after he sees what happened in the riverbed and Cai county. In the novel, Grandpa, who always has a sense of guilt, eventually kills Ding Hui. The novelist means to make Grandpa to embody a sober force to counteract the shocking irrationality. From the beginning, Grandpa constantly urges his son to apologize to the villagers for selling their blood and causing the "fever disease." Interestingly, he does not consider himself the origin of blood selling although he "sees"—remembers—it clearly in his dream. When Ding Hui keeps refusing to apologize, Grandpa mobilizes all AIDS victims to move into the village school as quarantine and volunteers to take care of them. Everything he does is an attempt to redeem his son (and himself?). In the end, Grandpa's act to end Ding Hui's life suggests the author's belief that evil will not prevail over the good. This can be read as a victory of morality that Ding Hui's father wishes to uphold over the father-son bond, an important Confucian family ethic.[5] If AIDS is regarded as a moral disease implying the immoral behavior of the patients, the killing of Ding Hui by his own father is an attempt to eliminate the cause of immorality and give the reputation back to the victims of the blood economy. An ultimate hope is revealed at the end in the last dream of Grandpa, in which he sees:

> *a woman, digging in the mud with the branch of a willow tree. With each flick of the branch, each stroke of the willow she raised a small army of tiny mud people from the soil. Soon there were hundreds upon thousands of them, thousands upon millions, millions upon millions of tiny mud people leaping from the soil, dancing on the earth, blistering the plain like so many raindrops from the sky.*
>
> *Grandpa found himself gazing at a new and teeming plain.*
> *A new world danced before his eyes.* (Yan, *Dream* 341)

After the death of the old world, a freshly created new world emerges with new people dancing before the eyes of Grandpa, the representative of the positive force. Undoubtedly, such an ending brings some hope to the reader to compensate for the heaviness and darkness of the story. The woman can be related to Nüwa, the legendary Chinese goddess who created human beings. At this point, an interesting discrepancy between the original and the translation plays an important role in the understanding of the ending. While the dreams are printed in boldface and a different font in the Chinese text, they are printed in italics in the translation. The very last one-sentence paragraph is not boldfaced in the original Chinese text, but in the same font as the nondream parts of the novel. This indicates the author's belief in the certainty that a brand-new world will be created by the legendary Nüwa. In the translation, however, this last paragraph is also italicized, treating it as part of the dream and conveying a totally different message: the new world is but a dream and the reality has no redemption. Readers of the English translation will feel an implication of the author's despair, yet the more mysterious message is hidden in the original text where the font is the same as the real parts. Does it disclose the optimistic attitude of the writer who now sees China as a curable sick man? Or is it yet another example of the author's self-censorship? Yan Lianke does admit that he intentionally self-censored when he wrote *Dream of Ding Village*:

> In a rare insight, the author told the *Guardian* how he attempted [to] forestall a ban by doing the censors' work for them. Out went the novel's most ambitious features: the blood pipeline, the global trade angle and direct criticism of national politics. Instead he narrowed the focus to a single village, where blood is bought and sold with horrific consequences. "This is not the book I originally wanted to write," says Yan, who has won China's top two literary awards. "I censored myself very rigorously. I didn't mention senior leaders. I reduced the scale. I thought my self-censorship was perfect." (Watts)

Although Yan calculated much to conduct self-censorship so he could get his book published, he was not happy about it. He also told the *Guardian* that

> he still regrets self-censoring when he wrote *Dream of Ding Village*, which deals with the blood-selling scandal that led to mass HIV infections in Henan province. He wanted to ensure it was published, he said; but now his priority was reaching the highest literary standard. (Branigan)

It is not surprising that Yan Lianke regrets the self-censorship, as no matter how perfectly he thought he had self-censored himself, the book survived for three days only before it was banned. His "strategic anticipation of censorship—his internalization of external censorious impulses and practices—was ineffective," in the words of Chien-hsin Tsai (77). Ironically, the biopolitical environment is unsatisfactory not only for people in reality and fictional characters, but also for the fiction per se.

Nevertheless, the reader does find his novels being more optimistic. Take the three novels of disease as an example: the ending of each story becomes increasing positive. *Streams of Light and Time* can be read metaphorically as the efforts to prolong people's lives and can be regarded as prescriptions to heal the sick society, but the society is so incurably ill that it is beyond any redemption after all attempts failed. When it comes to *Pleasure*, the author gives the novel a little hope by healing the insanity of Chief Liu even though the character's "wholeness" is taken away by being disabled. Yet being disabled is not a bad thing in Pleasure Village, particularly when the novelist paints a rosy picture of the paradise in the last "further reading" of the novel. Finally, we see a completely fresh and new world created by the presumed goddess Nüwa dancing before Grandpa's eyes in *Dream of Ding Village*, suggesting a hopeful future. Interestingly, in his recent novels, Yan Lianke tends to create a "good man," perhaps in the hope to maintain a balance in the otherwise totally dark and absurd stories. Besides Grandpa in *Dream of*

Ding Village, another good example is the character Li Tianbao in the 2015 novel *The Day When the Sun Died*. In the novel, somnambulism hits a small town called Gaotian, and all people of the town are sleepwalking and doing all kinds of evil things. The sun does not rise at daybreak, and therefore people will not wake up. Eventually Li Tianbao burns himself to create an artificial sun to wake people up, and thus brings the nightmare to an end. Does the pessimistic novelist still wish to search for a good soul as a remedy for the irrational and morbid society? When comparing Grandpa with Li Tianbao, the reader finds an interesting similarity: both characters are meant to be moral models for the society, but neither of them is flawless. While Grandpa is not as perfect as some critics suggest due to the fact that he actually confirms and encourages Ding Village's blood-selling business, Li Tianbao used to be an informant who exposed the secrets of the families that practiced ground burial when cremation was required by the government. Their extreme behaviors (i.e., killing his own son in the case of Grandpa and sacrificing himself in the case of Li Tianbao) are seen as acts of redemptions. Does this reveal the hidden hope in the author's mind even though he appears to be pessimistic by conveying such a message: people can still be decent as long as they correct the mistakes they have made in the past, and so can a society? In the speech at the Franz Kafka Prize award ceremony, Yan Lianke claimed, "It is a writer's job to find life within this darkness" (Yan, "Shangtian"). In the same speech, Yan Lianke told a story of a seventy-year-old blind man. Every day he would look at the direction where the sun rose and said that the sunlight was dark. This same blind man had several flashlights since he was young. When he walked at night, he always turned one on and held it in his hand. This way other people could see him from afar and so they would not bump into him. At the same time, passersby also benefited from his bright flashlight. In order to express their gratitude, villagers brought various flashlights to his funeral when he passed away. The blind man's story inspired Yan Lianke: there is one kind of writing—the darker it is, the brighter it gets; the colder it is, the warmer it becomes. The entire meaning of its existence is to allow people to avoid darkness. Yan Lianke believes that he and his writing are like the blind man who turned on the light in the dark.

The reader has every reason to believe that *Dream of Ding Village* exactly belongs to this kind of writing.

NOTES

1. The title of *Shouhuo* is translated by Carlos Rojas as *Lenin's Kisses*. See Yan Lianke, *Lenin's Kisses*, translated by Carlos Rojas, Grove Press, 2012. I personally believe that "pleasure" is closer to the original meaning of the Chinese expression. As a result, I decide to not adopt Rojas's translation of the title in my discussion.

2. For more information of the Great Leap Forward and people's communes, please consult Jisheng Yang et al. (2012).
3. For a detailed description of the epidemic outbreak, see Wang Jinping (2008).
4. This is my literal translation of the original Chinese title. It is translated as "Finding Light in China's Darkness" by Carlos Rojas.
5. Deng Hanmei believes that Ding Hui's father has transcended the affection between father and son when he kills his son with the "stick of justice" (*zhengyi de gunbang*). See Deng, 224.

WORKS CITED

Branigan, Tania. "Chinese Intellectuals Avoid Key Issues amid Censorship Fears, Says Author: Award-Winning Satirist Yan Lianke Says Chinese Intellectuals and Writers Must Push Leaders to Embrace Social Reform." *The Guardian*, February 6, 2013, www.theguardian.com/world/2013/feb/06/chinese-writers-failing-censorship-concerns. Accessed October 23, 2018.

Deng Hanmei. *Zhongguo xiandangdai wenxue zhong de jibing xushi yanjiu* [A Study of Illness Narratives in Modern and Contemporary Chinese Literature]. Jiangxi renmin chubanshe, 2012.

Ermo. Created by Zhou Xiaowen, Shanghai Film Studios, 1994.

Esposito, Roberto. *Bíos: Biopolitics and Philosophy*, translated by Timothy Campbell. University of Minnesota Press, 2008.

Fan Jiayang. "Yan Lianke's Forbidden Satires of China." *The New Yorker*, October 15, 2018, www.newyorker.com/magazine/2018/10/15/yan-liankes-forbidden-satires-of-china?from=singlemessage&isappinstalled=0. Accessed October 23, 2018.

Fang Fang. "Landscape." *Contemporary Chinese Women Writers II*, translated by Gladys Yang. Panda Books, 1991, pp. 18–135.

Foucault, Michel. *The History of Sexuality: Volume 1: An Introduction*, translated by Robert Hurley, Vintage, 1990.

Gao Yaojie. *Gaojie de linghun: Gao Yaojie huiyilu* [A Noble and Unsullied Soul: Gao Yaojie's Memoirs]. Revised and enlarged ed, Ming Pao, 2010.

Poirier, Suzanne. Introduction. *Writing AIDS: Gay Literature, Language, and Analysis*, edited by Timothy F. Murphy and Suzanne Poirier. Columbia University Press, 1993.

"Renwu zhuanfang: zhuming zuojia Yan Lianke changtan xinzuo 《Dingzhuang meng》" [Special Interview: Famous Writer Yan Lianke Speaks of His New Book *Dream of Ding Village*]. *Zhengyi wang zhibo* [live.jcrb.com], live.jcrb.com/html/2006/93.htm. Accessed October 23, 2018.

Rojas, Calos. *Homesickness: Culture, Contagion, and National Transformation in Modern China*. Harvard University Press, 2015.

Sontag, Susan. *Illness as Metaphor and Aids and Its Metaphors*. Anchor Books, 1990.

Tsai, Chien-hsin. "In Sickness or in Health: Yan Lianke and the Writing of Autoimmunity." *Modern Chinese Literature and Culture*, vol. 23, no. 1, Spring 2011, pp. 77–104.

Wang Jinping, "Chongwen xuejiang jingji he aizibing de hunluan shidai—yi shi wei jian" [A Review of the Chaotic Times of the Blood Economy and AIDS: Benefit from History]. *Huanqiu shibao* [Global Times], October 31, 2008, www.haodf.com/zhuanjiaguandian/wangjinping_22943.htm. Accessed June 28, 2014.

Watts, Jonathan. "Censor Sees through Writer's Guile in Tale of China's Blood-Selling Scandal." *The Guardian*, October 8, 2006, www.theguardian.com/world/2006/oct/09/books.china. Accessed October 23, 2018.

Yan Lianke. *The Day the Sun Died*, translated by Carlos Rojas. Chatto and Windus, 2015.

———. *Dream of Ding Village*, translated by Cindy Carter. Grove Press, 2009.

———. *Faxian xiaoshuo* [Discovering Fiction]. Nankai daxue chubanshe, 2011.

———. *Jianying rushui*. [Hard as Water]. Changjiang wenyi chubanshe, 2001.

———. *Lenin's Kisses*, translated by Carlos Rojas. Grove Press, 2004.

———. "On China's State-Sponsored Amnesia." *The New York Times*, April 1, 2013, http://www.nytimes.com/2013/04/02/opinion/on-chinas-state-sponsored-amnesia.html?pagewanted=all&_r=0. Accessed June 27, 2014.

———. *Riguang liunian*. [Stream of Light and Time]. Chunfeng wenyi chubanshe. 2004.

———. "Shangtian he shenghuo xuanding nage ganshou heian de ren" [Finding Light in China's Darkness], translated by Carlos Rojas. *The New York Times,* October 23, 2014, www.nytimes.com/2014/10/23/opinion/Yan-Lianke-finding-light-in-chinas-darkness.html?smid=tw-share&_r=0. Accessed October 23, 2018.

Yang Jisheng, Edward Friedman, Roderick MacFarquhar, translated by Stacy Mosher and Jian Guo. *Tombstone: The Great Chinese Famine, 1958–1962*. Farrar, Straus, and Giroux, 2012.

Yu Hua. *Chronicle of a Blood Merchant*, translated by Andrew F. Jones. Anchor Books, 2004.

Yuan Weijing. "Yan Lianke: Wo xiang hui dao duzhe de huibao zhong" ["Yan Lianke: I Would Like to Return to My Readers"]. *Yazhou Zhoukan* [Asia Week], May 20, 2018, medium.com/@cyanyuan/閻連科-我想回到讀者的懷抱中-6a4e5e0bb922?from=singlemessage&isappinstalled=0. Accessed October 23, 2018.

Chapter Eight

Abortion and Family as HIV Prevention Strategies

Kitia Touré's Les gestes ou la vie

Christine J. Cynn

In Côte d'Ivoire, early education around HIV/AIDS represented the solutions to HIV as self-discipline and self-denial, rigor and maturity. Such messages reinforced ongoing structural adjustment programs promulgating neoliberal conceptions of free individuals who needed only to be educated to be induced to behave rationally and efficiently. As a 1989 campaign poster warned, "Say no! Protect yourself!" However, directives to self-manage were not always consistent or coherent, and not surprisingly, for certain gendered bodies, injunctions to self-manage did not always suffice. The HIV-positive pregnant woman in particular provoked intense anxieties and fears around contamination, expressed in contradictory and shifting messages.

This chapter focuses on the 1993 four-part series *Les gestes ou la vie* (*Gestures or Life*) scripted and directed by Ivoirian writer and filmmaker, Kitia Touré, with funding from the European Union, United Nations, World Health Organization, French government, and Ivoirian Ministry of Culture, and with the support of state television and the National Committee for the Struggle against AIDS (CNLS). The series broadcast on state television and also screened at film festivals where it won a number of awards, including the Promaco Prize for the Struggle against AIDS, the Telcripro Prize for Technical Quality at the Panafrican Film and Television Festival in Ouagadougou (FESPACO), and the special jury prize at the Festival of Scientific Film in Paris-Eiffel Tower. Each of the four segments urges HIV testing, explains various prevention methods, and attempts to combat stigmatization of people living with HIV. One of the twenty-six-minute-long segments titled "Raisons de la peur" ("Reasons for Fear") focuses on convincing pregnant women to test for HIV, and if they test HIV-positive, to terminate their pregnancies. Although approved by the state, these astonishing officially unofficial (or unofficially official) messages directly contravened both state and religious prohibitions of abortion. The directives further implied acceptance, even endorsement, not only of legally banned procedures but also of female sexuality not securely oriented toward reproduction.

Other segments of the series—"Au nom d'amour" ("In the Name of Love"), "Ça n'arrive qu'aux autres" ("That Happens Only to Others"), and "Mon nom est 'la vie'" ("My Name Is Life")—contained such threats through insistent incorporation of HIV-positive women into the patriarchal family, a form of normalization that, like properly disciplined heterosexuality, was proposed as in itself a mode of HIV prevention. The *Les gestes ou la vie* series produced the heterosexual family as central line of defense and, alongside the private corporation, as the primary providers of care and support for people living with HIV. Women's submission to paternalistic medical and conjugal authority over their bodies and reproductive capacities figured as safety, solution, and reward. This self-reinforcing logic continued to frame HIV prevention in the television series even after drug regimens decreasing the likelihood of mother-to-child HIV transmission became more readily available in Côte d'Ivoire.

TERMINATION OF PREGNANCY AS HIV PREVENTION

In 1992, seroprevalence among pregnant women in Abidjan, the largest city and the economic capital of Côte d'Ivoire and of the region, was estimated at 15 percent. The effectiveness of the drug zidovudine (or azidothymidine, AZT) in lowering perinatal, or mother-to-child, HIV transmission was not established until results from the AIDS Clinical Trial Group 076 were published two years later in 1994. The trial showed that AZT administered orally during pregnancy, intravenously during labor and delivery, and orally to a newborn in the six weeks after birth lowered perinatal HIV transmission by two-thirds, or from between 15 to 40 percent to about 8 percent. After the efficacy of the treatment was established, the trial was suspended and results released (Connor et al.). Produced in 1993, the *Les gestes ou la vie* series attempts to address the potential of perinatal transmission of HIV during the period when reported HIV prevalence rates among pregnant women were alarmingly high, but no protocols had yet been established to decrease the possibility of HIV transmission from mother to child. At the same time, the state, undergoing major cutbacks following the imposition of structural adjustment policies, continued to reduce healthcare spending despite the increasing needs generated by the growing epidemic. President since independence from the French in 1960, the ailing Félix Houphouët-Boigny died at the end of 1993 after a thirty-three-year dictatorship. Coping with a weakening state on the verge of major struggles for political succession, the "Raisons de la peur" segment of *Les gestes ou la vie* proposes as a solution to perinatal transmission that all pregnant women who test HIV-positive end their pregnancies.

According to the World Health Organization, in the absence of prophylactic regimens, a child born to an HIV-positive woman has about a 15–40 percent chance of becoming infected with HIV in utero, during delivery, or via breastfeeding ("HIV/AIDS"). A pregnancy is also by definition the product of shared bodily fluids, more specifically, in the absence of reproductive technologies generally unavailable in Côte d'Ivoire, of unprotected penile-vaginal heterosexual sex. According to the terms of HIV education media centering on inculcating individual responsibility for prevention, the HIV-positive pregnant woman therefore embodies a failure of HIV education and poses a double, even triple, threat to the health and well-being of individuals and of the community, to the future itself as symbolized by the child. "Raisons de la peur" directly addresses this threat.

Contrasting Muslim/Christian and rural/urban, the segment opens with the series theme song in Dioula, "Men and women, AIDS is not good. Allah help us" ("Raisons"),[1] playing over establishing shots of a ferry landing in the country's economic and political capital city, Abidjan, followed by a woman entering an office. The camera then cuts to Kouako, a physician from the interior of the country, telephoning a white nun, identified in the credits only as "Sister Catherine." Sister Catherine runs an AIDS information hotline, AIDS Direct (SIDA Direct), in Abidjan, and the segment depicts her wearing a white habit and a crucifix in an office where she is seated next to a television and telephone. The film marks her as central figure of white Christian, religious, technological, and medical authority from whom others solicit advice. The woman who has come to consult with Sister Catherine in her office listens alongside viewers of the segment as Kouako recounts his predicament to Sister Catherine on the hotline, and the scenes that he recounts play out on-screen ("Raisons").

During a prenatal visit, Kouako tells his patient, Sita, that he will conduct routine screening but does not tell her that he has added HIV to the list of tests. When she tests HIV-positive, he is unable to disclose the results to her because, as Kouako explains to his own wife, they will "shatter her entire life" ("Raisons"). After Kouako's wife suggests that he wait until after Sita delivers to inform her, or her partner, about the test, Kouako counters, "No, she cannot keep this pregnancy [*garder cette grossesse*]. The child will have every likelihood of having the AIDS virus [*l'enfant va avoir toute la chance d'avoir le virus de SIDA*], not to mention that she can contaminate her partner if it hasn't already happened" ("Raisons"). His wife encourages him to tell Sita's partner and reminds him: "You are a doctor. Your work requires that you tell your patient what they're suffering from" ("Raisons").

In the next scene, Sita's partner, Touré, comes to the clinic room where Sita lies recovering from what is clearly an abortion. Kouako takes Touré aside and confesses that he had lied: "There was no risk with Sita's pregnancy.... The truth, unfortunately, is that I did a test for the AIDS virus on your girlfriend. It is done with all pregnant women. She is seropositive.... I did not have the courage to tell her this truth" ("Raisons"). Kouako urges Touré to test but still does not inform Sita about her own test results. As Kouako later explains his actions to his supervisor (*doyen*), also a physician, he requested the HIV test and confirmed the positive result but could not tell Sita. Instead, he used the pretext (*prétexter*) of unspecified "serious complications, a pathological pregnancy, in order to advise a termination of the pregnancy [*lui conseiller une interruption de grossesse*]" ("Raisons"). For him, it was paramount "to avoid the birth of a child who could be born with the AIDS virus" ("Raisons"), since the child and Sita will confront "the anguish, the stress, the fear of the gazes of others [*des regards des autres*]" ("Raisons") that could accelerate their decline and death, especially since they live in a rural area.

In 1985, the US Centers for Disease Control recommendations stated that "[i]nfected women should be advised to consider delaying pregnancy until more is known about perinatal transmission of the virus" ("Current Trends" 721–726; 731–732). As Ronald Bayer notes, in the context of the United States, "[o]nly timidity and the bitter ideological politics of abortion precluded an open discussion" about whether the recommendations required that HIV-positive pregnant women be urged to terminate their pregnancies (Bayer 502). The *Les gestes ou la vie* segment displays no such timidity. In "Raisons de le peur," Kouako explains that he has explicitly urged Sita to terminate her pregnancy, and that she heeded his advice. Kouako's supervisor chastises Kouako for taking the risk of performing the procedure; Sita might have consulted another doctor for a second opinion. Nevertheless, the supervisor eases Kouako's faltering conscience and lingering doubts. The supervisor characterizes AIDS as instigating devastating social and medical disruptions that authorize physicians to act in violation of all previous norms and laws in order to save individuals and the community. As the supervisor says to Kouako: "Listen my friend, AIDS is a new illness that comes to turn all customs and our morphology upside down [*bouleverser toutes les moeurs et notre morphologie*]. Know only that you have a duty [*un devoir*] to your patient and to society. We must avoid contamination on a grand scale" ("Raisons").

As Kouako explains on the hotline telephone to Sister Catherine, his predicament centers on informing Sita about her HIV status, especially since Sita's partner, Touré, later also tested HIV-positive, and although Touré is full of self-recrimination about his many sexual affairs, he still has not told Sita. In contrast to Kouako's supervisor, the nun advises Kouako to inform Sita of her test results and to refer her to an HIV specialist. Significantly, however, the nun does not interrogate the assumption that pregnant women who test HIV-positive must not carry their pregnancies to term. The pregnant woman, Jeanne, who had come to consult Sister Catherine, tells the sister that she fears that she is HIV-positive but that her doctor was hiding her results from her, just as Kouako did with Sita. Recounting the story of a young man who was convinced that he was HIV-positive, when he was not in fact, the nun convinces Jeanne to test first: "Do the test and have your boyfriend do it" ("Raisons"). As Jeanne departs, she thanks the nun: "I will do it because of my baby. I am expecting a child, and I wanted to abort it. That's why I came to see you and to talk with you a little" ("Raisons"). While the nun and Jeanne both agree on the importance of testing for the sake of the child, neither expresses any doubt that if Jeanne's results are HIV-positive, she will "abort [*avorter*]" the pregnancy.

The segment insistently frames HIV prevention as the responsibility of pregnant women who must take initiative and decide to test for HIV and convince their partners to as well. However, the representation of HIV/AIDS as inaugurating a state of exception works to reinforce both existing legal prohibitions on abortion and to rationalize further assertions of paternalistic medical and conjugal authority over women, their bodies, and their reproductive capacity. In his influential theorizing of the state of exception, Giorgio Agamben considers how states of emergency that provoke and justify suspension of the law thereby strip certain bodies of human status, placing them outside the law's purview. For Agamben, the juridico-political decisions about whose lives are not worth living and who as "bare life," or *homo sacer*, can be killed with impunity, define national sovereignty as the "politicization" of biopolitics (Agamben 71–72, 142; Foucault, *The History of Sexuality* 138; Foucault, *"Society Must Be Defended"* 250). As Penelope Deutscher argues, abortion law, and women's reproductivity more generally, represent symptomatic omissions in Agamben's analyses. Deutscher notes that abortion law inverts the states of exception that Agamben examines and that he reads as epitomized by the Nazi death camps. In contrast to these examples, recent abortion laws in the Global North have not decriminalized the practice of abortion and thereby expanded techniques of state sovereignty, so much as granted certain exceptions to preexisting regulations: "The state of exception is not the state, not the nation or a country's suspended legal system; rather, it is abortion 'itself' that has frequently existed in a state of suspension or exception to its own illegality" (Deutscher 50).

Insofar as Côte d'Ivoire's abortion laws were modeled on French legislation, they too reproduce the inverted form of the state of exception, of abortion as the exception to its own illegal status. In France, the conflation of religious and legal doctrine made abortion punishable by death beginning in 1556 (Knoppers et al., "Abortion Law"; Knoppers and Brault, *La Loi et l'Avortement*). A Penal Code of 1791 granted immunity to women who procured abortion but punished those who performed them with twenty years imprisonment. Article 317 of the Napoleonic Penal Code of 1810 eliminated the granting of immunity to pregnant women who procured an abortion and imposed imprisonment on them, as well as anyone who administered or advised the administration of an abortion that took place. At the same time, the penal code did permit abortions performed to save the "gravely threatened" life of a pregnant woman. This law has become the basis for the most restrictive antiabortion laws persisting throughout Francophone sub-Saharan Africa (Knoppers and Brault 34).

A 1920 French pronatalist law that applied to Algeria and to French colonies, including Côte d'Ivoire, prohibited abortion and sterilization—as well as contraception and "propaganda" about contraception. In 1923, abortion became a civil rather than criminal offense, but penalties expanded to encompass even attempted abortions, and in 1939, to women who procured or attempted to procure an abortion whether or not they were even pregnant or actually succeeded in their attempts. In 1939, an important exception was also carved out for "therapeutic abortions" performed to save the life of a pregnant woman, although two additional physicians had to be consulted and attest that the procedure was necessary to save the life of the mother, and that no other procedure could do so, a provision that was reiterated in a 1955 law (Knoppers and Brault 94). Significantly, while in 1975 France amended their laws to permit voluntary termination of pregnancies within the first ten weeks of pregnancy, the law was explicitly framed as a state of exception to the existing prohibitions on abortions, and Article 317 of the 1810 penal code still applied to cases outside the permitted exceptions.[2]

Both Agamben and Deutscher are particularly concerned with the United States and Western Europe, and Deutscher refers to these contexts when she argues that "the repeated creation of abortion as a state of permanent exceptionality has been one of the essential workings of twentieth- and early-twenty-first-century biopolitics concerning women's reproductivity" (64–65). Deutscher reads reproductive biopolitics as a "parallel subregime" to those states of exception analyzed by Agamben. For her, the special dispensations that characterize abortion law constitute a modality of sovereignty that, through the state of exception, ensures the maintenance of the harshest forms of the rule targeting women's bodies.

In the context of postcolonial Côte d'Ivoire, the "biopolitics concerning women's reproductivity" were principally animated by postcolonial nation building. Revising French colonial legislation, Côte d'Ivoire's 1981 abortion laws reflected the single-party state's continuing emphasis on population growth as enabling economic development and as reflecting the nation's wealth (Anoh et al. 10, 691).³ The 1981 law, which as of October 2017 was still in effect in Côte d'Ivoire, rejects the French 1975 revisions and preserves the language from the earlier laws that punished not just the person who performed or tried to perform an abortion, but also the woman who procured, tried to procure, or consented to using methods that would result in the termination of her pregnancy. The Ivoirian penal code further prohibits any dissemination of information or publicity about abortion but, following the 1939 and 1955 French laws, does permit the procedure in tightly restricted cases where the mother's life is in "extreme danger," in which case the abortion has to be carried out with the consultation of two additional physicians who must certify that the woman's life can be saved only through the performance of the procedure (Le Code Pénal).⁴ Although in 1981, the July 31, 1920 law prohibiting "provocation to abortion and contraception propaganda" was abolished, the penal code imposed the death penalty for sterilization, "the act of depriving a person of procreative potential [*la faculté de procréer*]" (Le Code Pénal).

The 1981 Ivoirian law prohibiting abortion falls under the chapter "Crimes and Offenses against Children [*Enfants*] and People Incapable of Protecting Themselves by Reason of Their Physical and Mental State," and follows the section on "Infanticide." The Ivoirian law frames the banning of abortion as protecting the lives of "children" and "infants," and at the same time, of pregnant women deemed incapable of "protecting themselves." This formulation conflates "fetus" with "infants/children [*enfants*]" (and pregnancy with physical and mental incapacitation) as a life that if aborted, would be deemed outside the law and able to be killed with impunity, or Agamben's *homo sacer*. In their arguments in the state daily, opponents of abortion in Côte d'Ivoire invoked this legal understanding of abortion. An article in *Fraternité Matin* described a 1989 meeting in which Episcopal bishops condemned the widespread practice of abortion as a "plague" and a sign of "a certain decadence" that "menaces the moral order" (Ayé). Although some bishops disagreed and framed the issue as one of individual choice, the newspaper column writer countered: "Must be we then permit [*Faut-il alors se laisser aller*] a certain license, a certain licentiousness and kill unwanted children [*qu'on ne désire pas*]?" (Ayé).

Deutscher critiques such antiabortion rhetorical, legal, and political slippages as false and pernicious, casting pregnant women as merely reproductive life, a competing and threatening sovereign from whom the child must be protected (66–67). In the context of postcolonial Côte d'Ivoire, these slippages enable the assertion of a form of biopolitical postcolonial state sovereignty extended through laws that target not only women's bodies but also French laws, or rather, that target the French suspension of laws that Côte d'Ivoire insistently retains. Jan Stepan describes as a "tragic irony" that Francophone sub-Saharan African countries compelled to adopt French colonial antiabortion laws did not continue along the path of "modern legal development" after formal independence and similarly adopt the 1975 French "Veil law," which permitted more expansive exceptions (ii). In Stepan's implied narrative of progress, suspension of abortion prohibitions constitutes modern legal advancement, and Francophone sub-Saharan African countries' refusals to adopt similar measures signal their lingering backwardness and failure to attain modernity. Such a narrative does not recognize the reproductive biopolitics of the postcolonial nation aimed at producing subjects of and workers for a new nation and glosses over the extent to which women's bodies served as critical sites for definition and assertion of postcolonial national identity (Boddy; Hunt; Mikell; Thomas, *Politics of the Womb*; Thomas, "Gendered Reproduction."). The paradoxes of asserting postcolonial state sovereignty through the maintenance of prior colonial laws exemplify the paradoxes of postcolonial sovereignty and of the condition of postcoloniality more broadly.

A further paradox around abortion in Côte d'Ivoire is the extent to which, despite its illegality, it is performed in open secret. A population control program was not instituted in Côte d'Ivoire until 1997, and limited family planning services meant that although illegal, the termination of pregnancies was a common practice as a form of birth control and as a resolution for unwanted pregnancies (Guillaume and Desgrées du Loû 159–166, 159, 161; Desgrées du Loû et al. 462–468, 466). For women living with HIV, as researchers note, abortion likely "exacerbated a practice already common and admitted by this population" (Desgrées du Loû et al. 466).

In 1989, an Episcopal bishop in Côte d'Ivoire praised the country's restrictions on abortion but sharply condemned the "well-known" permanent incorporation of associations offering abortions in state Centers for Maternal and Infant Protection (Centres de protection maternelle et infantile, or PMI) ("L'état protège l'enfant"). A series of articles in the December 2–8, 1990 state weekly, *Ivoire Dimanche*, lamented the "calamity" of frequent abortions: according to the weekly, 97 percent of unmarried women have abortions as a form of birth control "very often." Another article noted that to obtain an abortion at the public hospital, "[i]t suffices to know the hours of aborters [*avorteurs*] and to have a recommendation. This confirms the rumors that our public hospitals [CHU, or Centres hospitaliers universaitaires] are veritable nests of aborters." The article reminded readers about the laws against abortion—although it also observed that the laws were rarely enforced (Ehoura and Masoso 4).[5] These paradoxes around abortion were amplified in the representations of HIV/AIDS as inaugurating a state of emergency that, rather than provoke state response, justifies its further attrition.

HIV/AIDS AS STATE OF EMERGENCY: "REASONS FOR FEAR"

In "Raisons de la peur," for Kouako's supervisor, AIDS provokes a state of emergency essentially empowering medical authorities to suspend the law and locate both physicians and women who test positive for HIV outside its purview. "Raisons de la peur" explicitly represents HIV/AIDS as *not* activating the existing legal exception that permits the termination of a pregnancy (with required confirmatory medical opinion, if applicable) if this procedure constitutes the only means to save the lives of the women. Kouako states that he has lied, that "there was no risk" ("Raisons de la peur") about the pregnancy. Similarly, Jeanne, who also consults Sister Catherine, states that she will terminate her pregnancy if her test is HIV-positive, not because of any threat to her life, but because she cannot deliver a child who might be HIV-positive. Kouako's supervisor essentially agrees that such abortions must be performed on HIV-positive pregnant women—as, presumably, did the state, which co-produced the series. The segment further depicts Sister Catherine, the embodiment of white Christian religious and medical authority, as aligned with the state in its sanctioning of the further suspension of the law in the cases of pregnant women who test HIV-positive. This suspension of abortion laws affirmed the fundamental prohibitions against abortion and rationalized expansion of medical authority over pregnant women, and at the same time, the denial of state responsibility for responding to the epidemic, or to conditions of increasing social precarity.

Deploying a zero-sum biopolitical calculus, the segment insists that, although in the absence of any prophylactic treatment perinatal HIV transmission rates are estimated at between 15 to 40 percent, an HIV-positive woman must avoid all risk of even the possibility of infecting her child. The segment implies that individuals and society would be best served if pregnant women were routinely—mandatorily—tested for HIV and insists that if the results are positive, the women must terminate their pregnancies. According to "Raisons de la peur," preventing *all* women who test HIV-positive from reproducing constitutes a necessary strategy to "avoid contamination on a grand scale."

The segment relies on and reproduces what Linda Singer identifies as "epidemic logic," one that produces HIV as a threat, to then propose the solutions to contain it (29–32). In its representation of HIV as inaugurating a state of emergency, the segment exempts pregnant women living with HIV and their physicians from the punishments outlined in state antiabortion law. The segment thereby produces HIV as the sole, or at least the most extraordinary, threat to the fetus, the overdetermined symbol for the future community in whose name pregnant women in particular must test. The series justifies the prohibition against reproduction for women who test HIV-positive through the establishment of maternal and child negative serostatus as guarantor of the safety, health, and vitality of the future and of the community. However, as UN statistics bear out, even when reported AIDS cases were relatively low, the health of the child and of the community were far from secure. Estimated mortality rates for children under five in Côte d'Ivoire, even before identification of the first AIDS cases in 1985, were about 154 out of 1,000 live births, a rate that remained consistent throughout the 1990s (UN IGME).

In its figuring of HIV as extraordinary peril justifying extraordinary interventions, the episode does not address the everyday perils resulting in the deaths of around one in five infants and young children *regardless of HIV status*. It not only elides but also naturalizes as "safe" or acceptable how many infants and young children die from preterm or intrapartum complications and from other infectious diseases like pneumonia, diarrhea, and malaria. The high rates of childhood mortality—which, not incidentally, are about equivalent to the likelihood of mother-to-child HIV transmission in the absence of prophylactic regimens—index poverty, a term that in turn indexes an array of conditions: lack of clean water, shelter, proper sewage treatment, and nutrition, as well as healthcare, education, and other services. These conditions, which have come to serve as overdetermined and racist signs of "Africa," are not natural or inevitable, but the results of specific local as well as global histories and economic policies, including structural adjustment (Useche and Cabezas 16–27, 25). The film further normalizes as acceptable the high rates of maternal mortality, estimated in 1990 at around 20 percent of all deaths of women from ages fifteen to forty-nine, with rates tripling between 1978 and 1990 (World Health Organization et al. 68). It also does not acknowledge that illegal abortions were the major cause of maternal deaths—80 percent according to one study of maternal deaths in Abidjan hospitals between 1989 to 1992 (Thonneau et al.). More broadly, the film produces the conditions in which all people with a negative serostatus live as a state to be defended against the threat of HIV, especially as embodied by the HIV-positive pregnant women. It works in the service of preservation, rather than transformation of the status quo.

While "Raisons de la peur" represents HIV as activating a state of emergency impelling direct interventions on pregnant women, the segment does not address the health of the women themselves, except insofar as it could potentially affect their children. In other words, while the threat of HIV prompts the tacit suspension of the state and Christian religious law, significantly, the terms and targets of that suspension are selective. While the segment sanctions the performance of technically illegal medical procedures on HIV-positive pregnant women, the international laws protecting pharmaceutical companies' patents, for example, remained fully enforced. In March 1987, the US Food and Drug Administration approved AZT to treat HIV infection. However, limited provision of subsidized antiretroviral treatment in Côte d'Ivoire did not begin until more than a decade later in Abidjan in August 1998 (Msellati et al. S63–S68, S64).[6] The high costs of patented drugs in large part accounted for the long delay of treatment access for most people living with HIV/AIDS in Côte d'Ivoire and almost all of the Global South.[7] I will not here rehearse the heated debates around the safety and efficacy of AZT and around the ethics of the clinical trials that led to provision of cheaper, shorter—but less effective—courses of treatment to prevent perinatal HIV transmission in the Global South. Nor will I detail the activism around treatment access that eventually led to the carving out of certain limited exceptions to international property laws so that cheaper generics could be dispensed in low-income countries. "Raisons de la peur" does not address treatment access at all. It produces the "Reasons for Fear" that it names—the threat of children becoming infected by HIV through their mothers—as well as the protection against this danger: further interventions on women and their reproductive capacities.

"Raisons de la peur" identifies HIV-positive pregnant women as the most significant hazard to the fetus and proposes as safeguard the termination of their pregnancies. The series represents medical, religious, state, and family authority as aligned in approving procedures performed with impunity on pregnant women, especially pregnant women who test positive for HIV. The exemption of HIV-positive pregnant women and of medical personnel from laws restricting abortions affirms the necessity of the regulation of female reproductive capacity and frames such interventions as critical mode of defense for the future of the community. At the same time, HIV prevention media effectively silences the state, which does not provide services or enforce—or officially suspend—its own antiabortion law. HIV prevention media financed by foreign funders themselves constitute important demonstrations of international organizations' authority over that of the postcolonial state in crisis. The foreign-funded prevention film series represents a consequence of state retrenchment—the state cannot fund its own prevention campaigns—even as they provide important legitimizing discourse for the cutbacks. Women's bodies and reproductive capacity serve as the familiar terrain for these struggles (McClintock 354–355).

HETERONORMATIVE ROMANCE, FAMILY, AND "THE HEALTHY CARRIER": "AU NOM D'AMOUR"

The "Raisons de la peur" segment seeks to persuade viewers that pregnant women, and by extension all women, who test positive for HIV, must avoid even the possibility of transmitting HIV to fetuses. Women of reproductive capacity who test positive for HIV are therefore in a bind. If they defy prevention messages, they threaten the child, the family, and society. However, if they comply with medical directives and terminate their pregnancies and never reproduce, they cannot conform to heteronormative, reproductively oriented gender roles. Further, the insistence on abortion as solution for mother-to-child transmission for all pregnant women who test positive for HIV implies that even the potential of a life with HIV must be eliminated as such a life is not worth living. The prevention messages in "Raisons de le peur" thereby risk exacerbating the stigma that the series purports to combat. Two other segments in *Les gestes ou la vie* attempt to resolve the impasses established by the series. "Au nom d'amour" and "Ça n'arrive qu'aux autres" insist that HIV-positive women can be incorporated into the family constituted as what Linda Singer describes as itself a "strategic and prudential safe sex practice" (85). The series establishes equivalences between family and corporation as responsible for the care of people living with HIV and as providing essential protection and support. In the series, both family and corporations mobilize to take responsibility for the care of people living with HIV defined as "healthy carriers." The reliance on the nuclear family for social services reproduces prior colonial and postcolonial networks defined by a centralized political administration as oriented around the nuclear family (Toungara, "Changing" 43–44, 55–57; Toungara, "Inventing" 46–49).

In attempting to combat stigmatization of people living with HIV, the aptly titled segment "Au nom d'amour" in effect delineates and enforces the terms of their reincorporation into family and workplace. "Au nom d'amour" proposes that if HIV-positive women never reproduce and always use condoms, then they can be redeemed by heterosexual romance—and the corporation. In the segment, the central character, a middle-class office worker, Angeline, is set up by a friend with Serge. Angeline insists on testing for HIV and then using condoms when she and Serge have sex while they wait for the results. A poster on her bedroom door reminds viewers of the ongoing social marketing campaign urging usage of Prudence-branded condoms: "Prudence first. Prudence condoms" ("Au nom d'amour"). As Angeline tells the friend who tries to dissuade her from testing, "I love him, so prefer to lose him than contaminate him if I am seropositive" ("Au nom d'amour"). After Angeline tests HIV-positive, she worries that Serge will abandon her but tells her friend that she "wishes him great happiness [*je lui souhaite un grand bonheur*] if he leaves me" ("Au nom d'amour"). Instead, Serge recognizes that "she spared me [*m'a épargné*] in demanding a test. She saved me. . . . Angeline needs care and help"—and marries her ("Au nom d'amour"). As Serge's friend, Alain, a doctor, explains the sudden marriage plans to Serge's baffled mother: Angeline is HIV-positive, and the family serves as critical defense for Angeline. He says, "Angeline is not sick. She is a carrier of the virus. . . . She needs love, the family's total support to help her fight" ("Au nom d'amour").

On their way to a medical consultation with an HIV specialist, Angeline, Serge, and Alain pass by emaciated patients surrounded by doctors in the infectious disease clinic. Revising the stigmatizing script of the "AIDS carrier," Angeline's doctor in the next scene defines Angeline as HIV-positive, a "carrier of HIV," but "far from being sick" ("Au nom d'amour"). The editing of the images starkly contrasts Angeline with those suffering in the hospital and implies that Angeline's conformity to the doctor's directives will enable her to avoid their suffering and deaths. Angeline must have medical checkups every two months and never have sex without condoms. She must avoid reinfection, as well as alcohol, drugs, and stress. Nevertheless, Angeline "must lead a normal family life and continue to go to work" ("Au nom d'amour"). The doctor promotes "normal family life" and "work" as analogous to condoms, as themselves modes of protection, and at the same time, challenges assumptions that "family life" by definition entails reproduction. In the next breath, the doctor warns: "No pregnancy, as you risk contaminating your spouse [*votre conjoint*] and the child" ("Au nom d'amour"). Serge agrees, insisting, "She will live with me. Everything will be watched over [*On va veiller à tout*]" ("Au nom d'amour"). Incorporation into the reconstituted family then serves as defense and support, and provides necessary surveillance for Angeline, the family, and the community.

As ordered by the doctor, Angeline continues her job. When colleagues leave an anonymous note on her desk reading, "NO AIDS AT WORK," Angeline informs her boss and offers to quit: "I know that I am not contagious, but if I pose a problem for my colleagues' peace of mind [*tranquilité*], and for that of the department [*le service*], I am ready to leave" ("Au nom d'amour"). Having heard an educational radio program, the boss has been convinced that stigmatization of people living with HIV would impede the functioning of the corporation: "I heard on the radio that one in six in urban areas are contaminated [with HIV]. If all these HIV-positive people [*séropositifs*] are fired, then there will be no one at work" ("Au nom d'amour"). Although he recognizes the pragmatic reasons not to exclude HIV-positive people from the workplace, the boss further accepts the care of HIV-positive people as the financial responsibility of the company and promises to organize an information session for the department. As he tells Angeline, "It is terrible to carry the virus, but you need money and support. If I fire you, how will you live?" ("Au nom d'amour").

The series depicts the woman living with HIV as necessarily dependent on benevolence and compassion, what Angeline's husband describes as the "love and support," of the family, as well as on what her boss affirms as the "money and support" of the private corporation. Angeline will continue to supply her necessary labor to the workplace where her colleagues, taught tolerance, shamefacedly apologize to Angeline and contribute to a collection for her care. Those unnamed and unrepresented who are excluded from sustaining love, support, and money include the pregnant woman who tests HIV-positive and the woman who is HIV-positive and becomes pregnant, and who do not terminate their pregnancies. Similarly, the HIV-positive woman who contributes neither unpaid reproductive nor paid labor and who cannot be incorporated into heteronormative romance and the corporation as a "healthy carrier," and as worthy beneficiary of charity—humble, grateful, self-sacrificing—is cast aside. Like the woman who resists assimilation into heteronormative "family life," with the significant exception of the nun, they are the constitutive exclusions enabling the production of the heterosexual family and the corporation as primary sources of support and care, and at the same time, this method of protection against the danger of HIV.

THE GOOD WIFE AND THE CORPORATION AS SOLUTIONS: "ÇA N'ARRIVE QU'AUX AUTRES"

The *Les gestes ou la vie* series attempts to counter stigmatization by carefully differentiating "healthy carriers" or "carriers of HIV" from those manifesting symptoms of AIDS-related illnesses. In an interview, director Kitia Touré stated that he had sought through the series to show that "being seropositive doesn't mean being sick. [*(q)uand on est séropositif, on n'est pas malade*]" (Touré, "SIDA" 81–87). In particular, he wanted to shoot in "a big corporation to show how you can be seropositive and work [*on peut être séropositif et travailler*]" (Touré, "SIDA" 81–87).[8] In attempting to challenge the stigma around HIV/AIDS, the series affirms the bodies able to work as worthy of reintegration—they demonstrate their worth through that reintegration into family and workplace—in contrast to those suffering from illness and who in the logic of the narrative are abandoned and left to die.

Another segment, "Ça n'arrive qu'aux autres," casts the polygamous Muslim family and the corporation as protection for people living with HIV. In the segment, Mariam, a young pregnant third wife, agrees to test for HIV during a prenatal visit. After she tests positive, her two co-wives, Djereba and Assiata, avoid any contact with her and then abandon the household. After their husband, Abdul Diallo, also tests positive through his employer and is fired, he tries to commit suicide with Mariam and their child. The destruction of the family is narrowly averted when Djereba and her daughter return to the house and discover Abdul, Mariam, and their child unconscious on the sofa near a discharging cooking gas tank. The segment depicts Djereba's return as literally saving not only Abdul, Mariam, their child, and the family, but also the community. As Djereba explains to Abdul, she has come back because she recognizes that leaving the family can spread the virus, just as returning can contain it: "Abdul, I was wrong to have left. I have come back with your daughter. It was stupid on my part to leave. Maybe I am already contaminated. It's not worth transmitting this virus to others" ("Ça n'arrive qu'aux autres").

In the next scene, a doctor announces to Djereba and Mariam that Djereba and the children have tested HIV-negative. Nevertheless, Djereba has agreed to stay with the household, and as the doctor approvingly declares, she must provide "moral support" to her husband and co-wife (*sa rivale*). The doctor details the precautions necessary: if Adul or Mariam cut themselves, they must clean up the blood themselves and use bleach as disinfectant. As for the "biggest problem, sex," the doctor instructs the two co-wives that Abdul must always use condoms. Dismayed, Djereba asks the doctor: "So, I cannot have any more children [*Je ne peux plus faire d'enfants, alors*]?" ("Ça n'arrive qu'aux autres"). Without referring to Mariam's pregnancy—which is never directly addressed again after Mariam tests HIV-positive—the doctor responds to Djereba that he advises against her reproducing: she can be contaminated by Abdul, and "the child who will be born has a strong chance of being seropositive" ("Ça n'arrive qu'aux autres").

The segment seamlessly redirects Djereba's unpaid reproductive labor into maintenance of the HIV-positive household. As a self-described "good Muslim wife," the HIV-negative Djereba will remain in the household, accept condom usage, and perhaps most importantly, provide her HIV-positive husband and her co-wife with necessary care and support. In other words, the HIV-negative wife who cannot reproduce and who does not participate in the formal economy nevertheless must continue to play a central sustaining role as unpaid laborer in the polygamous household. She not only saves but also preserves the family and protects it by remaining—and enabling her husband and co-wives to remain—firmly enclosed within it.

As in "Au nom d'amour," the private corporation in "Ça n'arrive qu'aux autres" demonstrates its enlightened benevolence by also shouldering responsibility for people living with HIV. The scene with Diallo's two wives at the doctor's office cuts to Diallo entering his boss's office. The editing highlights and simultaneously renders mutually sustaining the divisions between the family and workplace, and between gendered female and male labor. Having undergone HIV education exemplified by the series itself, Diallo's supervisor recognizes that HIV "does not happen only to others. We can all be a victim of it" ("Ça n'arrive qu'aux autres"). The boss informs Diallo that the company will rehire him to perform modified office duties for as long as he remains a "healthy carrier." The boss figures the corporation administration's response as a demonstration of their participation in "the fight against AIDS": "This tact is the workplace's support of people who are seropositive with this new plague [*Ce tact c'est le soutien du monde du travail aux séropositifs de ce nouveau fléau*]" ("Ça n'arrive qu'aux autres"). Reincorporation into the company and sexual self-restraint serve as principal modes of prevention and are constituted as analogous individual and corporate responsibilities. The substitution of the private corporation for the state in public health provision constitutes a neoliberal solution, one that also draws from prior colonial enterprises, which were compelled to provide their workers with the healthcare that the state could not (Bekelynck 132). As the boss reminds Diallo, he should not take advantage of the company's generosity to take a fourth wife or additional mistresses (*d'autres bureaux en ville*). Diallo assures him that he will not, and the segment concludes with Assiata's return and the family's joyful reunification under the restored patriarchal order ("Ça n'arrive qu'aux autres"). The segment reinforces and naturalizes a gendered economic and social order as, paradoxically, under threat, safe, desirable, in need of protection, and ensuring safety.

In the longest, most original, and frankly strangest, segment of the *Les gestes ou la vie* series, "Mon nom est 'la vie,'" an albino girl in a robe and glowing white veil thwarts HIV depicted in a panting voiceover as an invisible ravening beast gleefully searching for victims. The girl, who calls herself "Life," appears magically at a dinner party and then beckons partygoers to the television where she stages interventions in a sequence of scenes: with sex workers on the street, a man and a menstruating woman about to have sex, a man about to have sex with two boys, a man and a woman engaging in anal sex, a dentist cleaning teeth, a male circumciser, women performing a scarification ceremony, and so on ("Mon nom est 'la vie'"). In each scene, HIV howls in frustration as the girl advises different methods of protection: condom usage, sterilized blades, bleach as disinfectant, storing of blood for transfusions, and rubber gloves. The girl repeatedly refers to the advice she dispenses as saving the lives of the people in the scenes, as well as those of the partygoers depicted as in a trance in front of the television.

The director, Touré, described "Mon nom est 'la vie'" as "in the register of religious syncretism" (Déniaud and Touré 123–126, 126), and the segment amalgamates the Gospel and the trance, the angel and the albino, to represent televised HIV education as initiating a successful process of conversion that ensures salvation. After the guests are jolted from their trance, the girl's final words echo those of Christ instructing doubting disciples after his resurrection: "Now that you have been informed, go tell your relatives, your family. Respond boldly without shame [*sans gêne ni fausse pudeur*] to the good news. I will always be among you" ("Mon nom est 'la vie'").[9] The segment's self-referential framing of televised HIV prevention education lends authority to its own messages and further detaches the series from the conditions and contexts of its production. In the series, HIV prevention education, and HIV itself, are not sites of ongoing negotiations and struggle, but supernatural revelations, with the categories of danger and safety—HIV prevention media, such as *Les gestes ou la vie*—constituting divine truths, with prevention a form of redemption.

CONCLUSION

Broadcast on state television, *Les gestes ou la vie* avoids any direct reference to political crises and to conditions of increasing economic precarity. Through its persistent attempts to shape female reproductivity, it nevertheless actively reflects, participates in, and deflects debates around economic retrenchment. According to the series, the central obstacles to perinatal HIV prevention are not structural adjustment policies mandating decreases in public services and intensifying poverty, or the global inequities limiting life chances, in part through the restriction of access to treatment or prophylaxis for HIV, but rather inadequate surveillance of women's bodies and reproductivity. *Les gestes ou la vie* suggests that mother-to-child transmission of HIV instigates a state of emergency to be addressed by the suspension of state laws prohibiting abortion. Confronting a state in crisis, the series proposes abortion and family as forms of prevention, and the patriarchal family in tandem with the corporation as the primary providers of care and support.

NOTES

This chapter was excerpted from Christine Cynn, *Prevention: Gender, Sexuality, HIV, and the Media in Côte d'Ivoire*. Ohio State University Press, 2018, and is reprinted with permission.

1. All translations from the original French to English are by the author.
2. French minister of health at the time, Simone Veil, insisted that "abortion must remain the exception, the last resort for situations with no way out (*l'avortement doit rester l'exception, l'ultime recours pour des situations sans issue*)" (BFM TV).
3. Structural adjustment policies implemented from 1991 to 1993 marked what Anoh, Fassassi, and Vimard describe as a neo-Malthusian shift to population control rather than growth. The focus on a limitation of international migration as a form of population control corresponded with the rise of the exclusionary rhetoric of *Ivoirité*. They attribute the pronatalist perspective of the country to cultural and religious factors as well (Anoh et al. 10, 691).
4. According to Ivorian law, if only one physician resides in the place where the abortion is performed, that physician must certify the procedure. If no other physicians reside in the place where the abortion is performed, the physician "must certify on his or her honor that the life of the mother can only be saved by the surgical or therapeutic operation employed" (Le Code Pénal). See also Ngwena, "Reforming African Abortion Laws," (particularly p. 170); Center for Reproductive Rights.
5. The accompanying article offered different statistics: 18 percent of girls between ages fourteen to sixteen, 72 percent of those between eighteen and twenty-five, and 9 percent of those between twenty-five and thirty-five had had an abortion at least once as an illicit form of birth control (Masoso 5; Ehoura 6–7). An *Ivoir'Soir* article noted: "Despite its prohibition . . . abortion today is extremely commonplace [*banal*]" (Konan 4).
6. As part of a UNAIDS Drug Access Initiative, six "'referral centers'" in Abidjan distributed ARVs to "[s]elected patients." Women who had participated in clinical trials for prevention of mother-to-child HIV transmission received the maximum possible subsidy on ARVs, 95 percent, along with active members of nongovernmental organizations dedicated to people living with AIDS. The plan to distribute ARVs was announced in November 1997 but distribution did not begin until August the following year. In 1996, highly active antiretroviral therapy (HAART) was identified as a significant improvement in treatment of HIV infections, but HAART distribution did not begin in Côte d'Ivoire until October 1999.

7. On the World Trade Organization's (WTO) Trade Related Aspects of International Property Rights (TRIPS), the Doha agreement of 2001, and the "Paragraph 6 solution," which in 2003 (formalized as an amendment in 2005) finally permitted countries that did not have the capacity to manufacture antiretroviral drugs to import generics from developing countries granted compulsory licenses by the WTO, see UNAIDS et al.; On Paragraph 6, see World Trade Organization, General Council; See also Hanefeld and Beall and Kuhn (6); For necessary warnings about the embrace of biomedicine and medical intervention as a quick-fix solution to the HIV epidemic, see Wendland. For a critique of biomedical interventions as likely exacerbating the spread of HIV in Abidjan, see Nguyen.

8. Touré goes on to explain that because of intense fear and stigma around HIV/AIDS, no private (including foreign-owned corporations operating in Côte d'Ivoire) or public company would permit him to film in their workplaces ("SIDA" 81–87).

9. "I am with you always, to the end of the age." [*Et voici que je suis avec vous pour toujours jusqu'à la fin du monde*] (*La Bible de Jérusalem*, Matt. 28:20). The albino girl as Christ might be productively read alongside "black Jesus" of Touré's novel, *Destins Parallèles*.

WORKS CITED

Agamben, Giorgio. *Homo Sacer: Sovereign Power and Bare Life*, translated by Daniel Heller-Roazen. Stanford University Press, 1998.

Anoh, Amoakon, R. Fassassi, and Patrice Vimard. "Politique de Population et Planification Familiale en Cote d'Ivoire." *Les Politiques de Planification Familiale*. Centre Francais sur la Population et le Developpement, 2002.

Ayé, Jean-Pierre. "Avortement: L'Église s'inquiète," *Fraternité Matin*, April 10, 1989, p. 26.

"Au nom d'amour." *Les gestes ou la vie*, directed by Kitia Touré. Kaiola Productions (with RTI TV2), 1993.

Bayer, Ronald. "Perinatal Transmission of HIV Infection: The Ethics of Prevention." *Clinical Obstetrics & Gynecology*, vol. 32, no. 3, Sept. 1989, pp. 497–505.

Beall, Reed, and Randall Kuhn. "Trends in Compulsory Licensing of Pharmaceuticals since the Doha Declaration: A Database Analysis." *Plos Medicine*, vol. 9, no. 1, 2012, pp. 1–9.

Bekelynck, Anne. "Le rôle des entreprises privées dans la lutte contre le VIH/sida en Côte d'Ivoire: des vecteurs d'une utopie sociale aux partenaires d'une action publique." *Lien social et Politiques*, vol. 72, 2014, pp. 129–149. https://doi.org/10.7202/1027210ar.

BFM TV. "Le Discours de Simone Veil en 1974. L'Assemble Nationale." www.bfmtv.com/politique0/texte-le-discours-de-simone-veil-en-1974-a-l-assemblee-nationale-1198272.html.

Boddy, Janice. *Civilizing Women: British Crusades in Colonial Sudan*. Princeton University Press, 2006.

"Ça n'arrive qu'aux autres." *Les gestes ou la vie*, directed by Kitia Touré. Kaiola Productions (with RTI TV2), 1993.

Center for Reproductive Rights. "The World's Abortion Laws Map 2013 Update." reproductiverights.org/sites/crr.civicactions.net/files/documents/AbortionMapFactsheet_2013.pdf.

Centers for Disease Control and Prevention. "Current Trends Recommendations for Assisting in the Prevention of Perinatal Transmission of Human T-Lymphotropic Virus Type III/Lymphadenopathy-Associated Virus and Acquired Immunodeficiency Syndrome." *Morbidity and Mortality Weekly Report 34*, 6 Dec. 1985, pp. 721–726. www.cdc.gov/mmwr/preview/mmwrhtml/00033122.htm.

Connor, Edward M., Rhoda S. Sperling, Richard Gelber, Pavel Kiselev, Gwendolyn Scott, Mary Jo O'Sullivan, Russell VanDyke, Mohammed Bey, William Shearer, Robert L. Jacobson, Eleanor Jimenez, Edward O'Neill, Brigitte Bazin, Jean-Francois Delfraissy, Mary Culnane, Robert Coombs, Mary Elkins, Jack Moye, Pamela Stratton, and James Balsley, for the Pediatric AIDS Clinical Trials Group Protocol 076 Study Group. "Reduction of Maternal-Infant Transmission of Human Immunodeficiency Virus Type 1 with Zidovudine Treatment. Pediatric AIDS Clinical Trials Group Protocol 076 Study Group." *The New England*

Journal of Medicine, vol. 331, no. 18, Nov. 1994, pp. 1173–1180. doi: 10.1056/NEJM199411033311801.
Déniaud, François and Kitia Touré. "Présentation de documents audiovisuels sur la prévention du sida." *Les sciences sociales face au Sida: Cas africains autour de l'exemple ivorien*, edited by Jean Pièrre Dozon and Laurent Vidal, ORSTROM, 1995, pp. 123–26.
Desgrées du Loû, Annabel, Philippe Msellati, Ida Viho, Angèle Yao, Delphine Yapi, Pierrette Kassi, Christiane Welffens-Ekra, Laurent Mandelbrot, François Dabis. "Contraceptive Use, Protected Sexual Intercourse and Incidence of Pregnancies among African HIV-Infected Women. DITRAME ANRS 049 Project, Abidjan 1995–2000." *International Journal of STD and AIDS*, vol. 13, no. 7, July 2002, pp. 462–468.
Deutscher, Penelope. "The Inversion of Exceptionality: Foucault, Agamben, and 'Reproductive Rights.'" *South Atlantic Quarterly*, vol. 107, no. 1, 2008, pp. 55–70. doi: 10.1215/00382876-2007-055.
Ehoura, Awa. "Tous les moyens sont bons." *Ivoire Dimanche*, December 2–8, 1990, p. 6–7.
Ehoura, Awa, and Agnès Kraide Masoso. "Avortement: La calamit." *Ivoire Dimanche*, December 2–8, 1990, p. 4.
Foucault, Michel. *The History of Sexuality, Vol. 1: An Introduction*, translated by Robert Hurley. Vintage-Random House, 1978.
———. *"Society Must Be Defended": Lectures at the Collège de France, 1975–1976*, translated by David Macey. Picador, 2003.
Guillaume, Agnes, and Annabel Desgrées du Loû. "Fertility Regulation among Women in Abidjan, Cote d'Ivoire: Contraception, Abortion, or Both." *International Family Planning Perspectives*, vol. 28, no. 3, Sept. 2002, pp. 159–161. doi:10.2307/3088259.
Hanefeld, Johanna. "Patent Rights vs. Patient Rights: Intellectual Property, Pharmaceutical Companies and Access to Treatment for People Living with HIV/AIDS in Sub-Saharan Africa." *Feminist Review*, vol. 72, no. 1, Sept. 2002, pp. 84–92. doi:10.1057/palgrave.fr.9400057
Hunt, Nancy Rose. *A Colonial Lexicon: Of British Ritual, Medicalization, and Mobility in the Congo*. Duke University Press, 1999.
Knoppers, Bartha Maria, Isabel Brault, and Elizabeth Sloss. "Abortion Law in Francophone Countries." *The American Journal of Comparative Law*, vol. 38, no. 4, Sept. 1990, pp. 889–922.
Knoppers, Bartha Maria, and Isabel Brault. *La Loi et L'Avortement Dans Les Pays Francophones*. Éditions Thémis, 1989.
La Bible de Jérusalem. Éditions du cerf, 1998.
Le Code Pénal. Loi 81-640 du 31 juillet 1981, Titre 2, Chapitre 1, Section 1, Article 343.
McClintock, Anne. *Imperial Leather: Race, Gender, and Sexuality in the Colonial Contest*. Routledge, 1995.
Mikell, Gwendolyn. *African Feminism: The Politics of Survival in Sub-Saharan Africa*. University Pennsylvania Press, 1997.
"Mon nom est 'la vie.'" *Les gestes ou la vie*, directed by Kitia Touré, Kaiola Productions (with RTI TV2), 1993.
Msellati, Philippe, Anne Juillet-Amari, Joanne Prudhomme, Hortense Aka-Dago Akribi, Djeneba Coulibaly-Traore,Marc Souville, Jean-PaulMoatti, and Côte d'Ivoire HIVDrug Access Initiative Socio-Behavioural Evaluation Group. "Socio-Economic and Health Characteristics of HIV-Infected Patients Seeking Care in Relation to Access to the Drug Access Initiative and to Antiretroviral Treatment in Côte d'Ivoire." *AIDS (London, England)*, vol. 17, suppl. 3, July 2003, pp. S63–S68.
Nguyen, Vinh-Kim. "Therapeutic Modernism: Medical Pluralism, Local Biologies, and HIV in Côte d'Ivoire." *Troubling Natural Categories: Engaging the Medical Anthropology of Margaret Lock*, edited Naomi Adelson, Leslie Butt, and Karina Kielmann. McGill-Queen's University Press, 2013, p. 57.
Ngwena, Charles G. "Reforming African Abortion Laws and Practice: The Place of Transparency." *Abortion Law in Transnational Perspective: Cases and Controversies*, edited by Rebecca J. Cook, Joanna N. Erdman, and Bernard M. Dickens. University Pennsylvania Press, 2014, pp. 166–186.

———. "Reforming African Abortion Laws to Achieve Transparency: Arguments from Equality." *African Journal of International and Comparative Law,* vol. 21, no. 3, Oct. 2013, pp. 398–426.
O'Manique, Colleen. "Global Neoliberalism and AIDS Policy: International Responses to Sub-Saharan Africa's Pandemic." *Studies in Political Economy* vol. 73, 2004, pp. 47–68.
———. *Neoliberalism and AIDS Crisis in Sub-Saharan Africa.* Palgrave Macmillan, 2004.
"Raisons de la peur." *Les gestes ou la vie,* directed by Kitia Touré. Kaiola Productions (with RTI TV2), 1993.
Singer, Linda. *Erotic Welfare: Sexual Theory and Politics in the Age of Epidemic.* Routledge, 1993.
Stepan, Jan. "Preface." *La loi et l'avortement dans les pays francophones,* by Bartha Maria Knoppers and Isabel Brault. Éditions Thémis, 1989.
Thomas, Lynn M. "Gendered Reproduction: Placing Schoolgirl Pregnancies in African History." *Africa After Gender?*, edited by Catherine Cole, Takyiwaa Manuh, and Stephen Miescher. Indiana University Press, 2007, pp. 48–62.
———. *Politics of the Womb: Women, Reproduction, and the State in Kenya.* University of California Press, 2003.
Thonneau, P., Y. Djanhan, M. Tran, C. Welfens-Ekra, M. Bohoussou, and E. Papiernik. "The Persistence of a High Maternal Mortality Rate in the Ivory Coast." *American Journal of Public Health,* vol. 86, no. 10, Oct. 1996, pp. 1478–1479.
Toungara, Jeanne M. "Changing the Meaning of Marriage: Women and Family Law in Côte d'Ivoire." *African Feminism the Politics of Survival in Sub-Saharan Africa,* edited by Gwendolyn Mikell. University of Pennsylvania Press, 1997, pp. 53–76.
———. "Inventing the African Family: Gender and Family Law Reform in Côte d'Ivoire." *Journal of Social History,* vol. 28, no. 1, 1994, pp. 37–61.
Touré, Kitia. *Destins parallèles.* Nouvelles Éditions Ivoiriennes, 1995.
———. "SIDA et la liberté." *Cinémas et libertés: contribution au thème de FESPACO 93, Présence Africaine volume special,* 1993, pp. 81–87.
UNAIDS, World Health Organization, UNDP. *Policy Brief: Using TRIPS Flexibilities to Improve Access to HIV Treatment,* Geneva, Switzerland, 2011, www.unaids.org/sites/default/files/media_asset/JC2049_PolicyBrief_TRIPS_en_1.pdf.
UNESCO. *Globalization and Women's Vulnerabilities to HIV and AIDS.* Paris: Division for Gender Equality, 2010. unesdoc.unesco.org/images/0019/001915/191501e.pdf.
UN IGME. "Child Mortality Estimates: Côte d'Ivoire Under-Five Mortality Rate," 2016, www.childmortality.org/index.php?r=site/graph#ID=CIV_CotedIvoire.
Useche, Bernardo, and Amalia Cabezas. "The Vicious Cycle of AIDS, Poverty, and Neoliberalism." *The Wages of Empire: Neoliberal Policies, Repression, and Women's Poverty,* edited by Amalia L. Cabezas, Ellen Reese, and Marguerite Waller. Paradigm, 2007, pp. 16–27.
Wendland, Claire L. "Research, Therapy, and Bioethical Hegemony: The Controversy over Perinatal AZT Trials in Africa." *African Studies Review,* vol. 51, no. 3, 2008, pp. 1–23. www.jstor.org/stable/27667377.
World Health Organization, "HIV/AIDS: Mother-to-Child Transmission of HIV." www.who.int/hiv/topics/mtct/en/
———, UNICEF, UNFPA, World Bank Group, and United Nations Population Division Maternal Mortality Estimation Inter-Agency Group. "Maternal Mortality in 1990–2015: Côte d'Ivoire." www.who.int/gho/maternalhealth/countries/civ.pdf.
World Trade Organization, General Council. *Implementation of Paragraph 6 of the Doha Declaration on the TRIPS Agreement and Public Health, Decision of the General Council of 30 August 2003.* 1 Sept. 2003, WT/L/540 and Corr. 1, www.wto.org/english/tratop_e/trips_e/implem_para6_e.htm.

Chapter Nine

When "Safe" Isn't Safe

Reflecting on the Role of Science in the Production of Harmful Discourse of HIV/AIDS

Alison Patev

SAFE

In HIV/AIDS research and intervention, it is the one word stressed more than almost any other. Individuals are told that they must be "safe," must practice "safe" sex, must get tested to make sure they are "safe," and must ask potential sexual partners about their HIV status to ensure potential partners are "safe." This language emphasizes that in order to keep oneself and one's sexual partners healthy, one must engage in certain practices that help to mitigate the chance of HIV infection. By framing some individuals and behaviors as "safe," it is inherent that individuals who do not engage in "safe" practices have become a danger to themselves and others. In some ways, this dichotomy is helpful; both seronegative and seropositive individuals use condoms and other barriers in an effort to avoid infection of themselves or others. This dichotomy also suggests to individuals that they may put themselves or their partners in harm's way and place them at risk for HIV transmission if they don't engage in "safe" practices.

Thus, this inherent dichotomy of safety/danger that is presented in interventions is not always beneficial and may even perpetuate harmful messages surrounding HIV/AIDS. Cindy Patton, in her seminal text *Inventing AIDS*, examines the multiple meanings of "safe sex" throughout the AIDS epidemic. Patton asserts that the discourse surrounding safety has "become involved in constructing identities around infection or presumption of infection" as HIV antibody testing indicates "safe versus dangerous persons" (48). Presumably, "safe" people have received a negative test result, while "dangerous" individuals are those who have tested positive. Moreover, this message can be extended further to characterize individuals who engage in risky behaviors (i.e., not using a condom, not being tested) as "dangerous."

Ultimately, this dichotomy produces the message that seronegative individuals are good because they cannot infect anyone, and seropositive individuals are bad because they are an imminent threat to nonpositive individuals. This view of people living with HIV (PLWH) or people living with AIDS (PLWA) is detrimental because these views create prejudice toward PLWH/PLWA. Further, as Patton notes, this dichotomy also forces the construction of individual identities as "safe" or "dangerous." Identities can impact individuals' opinions, attitudes, and behaviors. For instance, seronegative individuals may see themselves as being clean, and may be less likely to engage in protected sex acts; Patton writes that "a negative test gives you a 'clean bill of health' and means you do not need to practice safe sex . . . [so after a negative test] others simply do not think about the possibilities of future exposure to HIV" (32). This belief produces the counterbelief that individuals who are seropositive might be stigmatized and viewed (and view themselves) as unclean and a hazard to others.

Perhaps somewhat paradoxically, despite scientists' use of the "safe/unsafe" dichotomy and the messages those terms inherently spread, much work focuses on decreasing the stigma towards people who receive HIV antibody testing, as well as PLWH and PLWA. Decreasing stigma and prejudice toward individuals affected by HIV or AIDS is important, as stigma and perceived discrimination lead to a host of negative outcomes. Perceived HIV/AIDS stigma can affect HIV testing behaviors, such that people who perceive greater stigma toward HIV/AIDS are less likely to get an HIV test (Kalichman and Simbayi). Further, perceived discrimination toward PLWH and PLWA can lead to less treatment adherence among PLWH (Bogart et al.). Despite some of the drawbacks to HIV testing, it can be argued that less testing and less treatment adherence will lead to greater spread of HIV and more deaths from AIDS. Therefore, reducing HIV and AIDS stigma would ultimately improve outcomes for all. Framed in this way, it is easy to believe that science is all benevolent and only perpetuates the best results for society. However, this is not the whole picture. When we consider aspects of intervention and education, such as the "safe/unsafe" dichotomy, the impact of science on HIV/AIDS discourse becomes more complex.

Thus, science, which I have long believed to be capable of doing only good, perpetuates much of the stigma that researchers aim to stamp out. Throughout the course of this chapter, I will employ critical analysis of several texts and discourses in order to demonstrate how science might not be so benevolent. Through critically analyzing the work surrounding science and AIDS discourse, I have come to better understand the effect that intervention work may have on the harmful messages surrounding HIV/AIDS. That is, prevention messages unfortunately, unknowingly, promote ideas that further stigmatize and demonize certain groups, including PLWH and PLWA. In addition, I will critically examine three works of art that disrupt the messages that science is an all-knowing, always-benevolent entity, including two documentaries: *Doctors, Liars, and Women*: *AIDS Activists Say No to Cosmo* (1988), by Jean Carlomusto, and *DiAna's Hair Ego* (1989), by Ellen Spiro. I will also examine Kgafela oa Magogodi's poem "Varara" (2000), which takes on the topic of condom use and HIV/AIDS prevention in South Africa. These works are cultural productions that attempt to drive the production of HIV/AIDS discourse and diminish the harmful effects that science has had on HIV/AIDS messages.

SCIENCE

. . . is broadly defined by the Merriam-Webster dictionary as "the state of knowing, or knowledge as distinguished from ignorance or misunderstanding" ("Science"). As an experimental health psychologist, I put a lot of faith in science and scientific findings. Particularly when it comes to HIV/AIDS, my training has painted science as a benevolent, all-knowing entity aimed at eliminating disease and negative messages surrounding disease. It is common for scientists to view organizations like the Centers for Disease Control and Prevention (CDC) and the National Institutes of Health (NIH) as omniscient authorities. For example, when it comes to implementing education and prevention programs, researchers refer to the CDC's database *Effective Interventions* ("Effective Interventions"). The *Effective Interventions* home page boasts a banner asserting "HIV Prevention That Works" ("Effective Interventions"). This page is infused with a sense of scientific authority. The CDC webpage also touts the role that their "scientific advances" have played in stopping the global AIDS epidemic through providing HIV antibody testing, antiretroviral drugs, and education to millions ("CDC's Role in Global HIV Control"). This idea of science as an authority is taken for granted among the scientific community.

Feminist scholars such as Evelyn Fox Keller and Sandra Harding have critiqued modern Western science as patriarchal and dominating, as well as racist and colonialist. Keller argues that Western science is driven by a goal to be powerful and dominating, which reproduces masculine, androcentric norms about science. Harding agrees about the patriarchal nature of Western science but expands this idea to show how patriarchal science is also colonialist as well. Historically, women make up about half of colonized individuals. Further, colonized men have been seen as less masculine and not as "real men" to Western researchers. Colonized women have been almost erased from scientific discourse about colonized and neocolonized nations (Harding). More generally, Western science's approach to postcolonial regions has been biomedical, technological, and intellectual neocolonization. In this neocolonialism, Western science forces its findings and new technology on postcolonial nations, as these postcolonial nations are thought to be incapable of deriving their own science and technology. These facets of science as patriarchal and colonialist are evident in Western science's impact on the HIV/AIDS epidemic, both in the United States and Africa.

Within the United States, science organizations have attempted to dominate the discourse surrounding HIV and AIDS. By deciding who is "at risk" for HIV and who is "safe," scientists can drive HIV prevention, education, diagnosis, and treatment. In Africa, the domination of Western science is more obvious. Western ideas of African nations as ignorant, unadvanced, and poor have served to reinforce colonialism and render some areas dependent on Western aid. Western science has also painted a picture of "African AIDS," and presumes a monolithic Africa. This homogenizing of "Africa" has allowed Western science to generalize the problems affecting one area as the problems that affect all of Africa; therefore, Westerners can justify interfering in any of the African nations, effectively recolonizing such nations.

For many, particularly scientists like myself, Western science and science organizations like the CDC are the global authority on HIV and AIDS education, prevention, diagnosis, and treatment. Moreover, we assume that scientists operate with the greater good in mind—and often they do! However, the assumption that our empirically based, research-supported interventions and treatments do not reproduce biases and assumptions made by researchers and institutions is a fallacy. What happens when science, a seeming state of knowing, breeds the ignorance and misunderstanding it seeks to combat?

SCIENCE AND HIV IN THE UNITED STATES

As previously described, science and scientific organizations in the United States and Western society have been important drivers of negative messages surrounding HIV and AIDS. Throughout the course of the AIDS epidemic, organizations such as the FDA and CDC have been among the main producers of popular discourse surrounding HIV. Although this has been positive in many ways, it has also been detrimental, as these organizations have produced definitions of "safe" and "risky" behaviors. One of the most pervasive and damaging messages is the idea of safety. Conceptions that some acts or people are "safe" and some are "unsafe" create increased stigma surrounding HIV/AIDS as well as greater prejudice toward PLWH and PLWA. The dichotomy of safe/dangerous promoted by HIV antibody testing is just one example of how science and science organizations produced harmful cultural messages during the HIV/AIDS epidemic. Beyond the "safe/unsafe" dichotomy, science has also produced harmful messages about risk and promoted beliefs about the individuals who contract HIV and AIDS.

First, science has perpetuated negative discourse surrounding HIV/AIDS through the construction of "risk groups" and "risk behaviors." In HIV/AIDS education, intervention, and research, these are commonplace phrases; education and intervention are usually targeted toward certain risk groups. Risk assumes that individuals within a risk group are in control of their behaviors and that their status of "at risk" is somehow their fault. Thus, the term "risk" carries implications for the morality of individuals at risk (Lupton). In the context of HIV, this may imply that "at-risk" individuals are somehow morally deficient, or otherwise complicit in their own risk. Deborah Lupton points out that the word "risk" is not a neutral term. Using this word in relation to a group or behavior carries many negative connotations. "Risk," when used in the context of "risk groups" or "risk behaviors," refers to the consequences of an individual's lifestyle or choices (Lupton 427). This is especially true when it comes to health behaviors. For example, using the term "risk group" to talk about men who have sex with men (MSM) suggests that such people are "at risk" because they engage in sex with other men. Thus, using "risk groups" to refer to certain populations may have dire consequences. For instance, referring to MSM as a risk group may perpetuate homophobic understandings of MSM, as well as stereotypes of MSM as unclean or dangerous. Devine et al. even note that "the public's focus on risk groups may be the single most destructive social component of the AIDS epidemic" (1216). Construction of these risk groups promotes an "us" versus "them" dichotomy through which uninfected individuals are viewed as innocents at the mercy of infected, dangerous others, who are considered menaces to public health.

Using the terms "risk group" and "risk behavior" has two harmful outcomes. The CDC initially developed risk groups to name those who had been identified as the most common victims of AIDS and those who were not. Such grouping encouraged the public to perceive AIDS victims and PLWA as one collective group instead of as individuals (Devine et al. 1215). However, so-called risk groups are often groups that already carry stigmatized identities, such as people of color, MSM, and intravenous drug users. Therefore, the categorization of such groups as at risk further perpetuates their marginalization. When the designation of "at risk" is placed upon these groups, it compounds the stigma that they already face. That is, social narratives and beliefs about underprivileged groups have been altered to include the stereotype that these groups as a whole rampantly contract and spread HIV and are therefore even more dangerous. For example, the association between gay men and AIDS has become so prevalent that individuals' attitudes toward homosexuals are often inseparable from their attitudes toward

PLWH and PLWA (Herek and Capitanio), and each negative view can fuel the other. That is, negative attitudes toward PLWA can exacerbate homophobia, as homophobia can propagate stigmatization of gay men and AIDS (Devine et al. 1220).

In addition to compounding the marginalization experienced by risk groups, defining "risk" drives ideas of whose body is the "social standard" and whose bodies are compromised (Waldby 77–78). Put differently, risk definitions "may therefore be considered hegemonic conceptual tools that can serve to maintain the power structure of society" (Lupton 432). In the context of the AIDS epidemic, Waldby delineates two groups: the general population and the risk groups. The general population, broadly, has been considered to be white, heterosexual, cisgender men. Risk groups, on the other hand, refer to anyone other than white, heterosexual, cisgender men (hereafter called WHCM). Thus, WHCM bodies are considered to be the uniform standard for health in the United States while risk group members are considered to be atypical. Risk group members, by definition, place the WHCM's bodies in harm's way and make them susceptible to contracting HIV/AIDS (Waldby 77–81).

This binary also reinforces ideas about which behaviors are the accepted standard and which behaviors are not. Again, as WHCM are considered the standard, their supposed behaviors are the accepted norm. Any behaviors that are not part of the accepted group of behaviors for WHCM are considered abnormal and risky. For example, anal sex is associated with gay men. Patton notes, "Anality [functions as] . . . a chief Western symbol of homosexuality" (91). Because it is more strongly related to gay men than WHCM, it is considered to be deviant. Because such behaviors are deviant, they are automatically considered a risk to the general population, through the exclusion of gay men. Even when identity terms, such as "gay," are removed from behaviors and risk, seemingly neutral terms like "men who have sex with men (MSM)" promote stigmatizing attitudes toward specific sexual behaviors, like anal sex (Young and Meyer).

Beyond promoting ideas about safety and risk, science and organizations like the CDC have become producers of popular messages surrounding AIDS by defining who is likely to contract HIV. As the medical and scientific community became aware of AIDS in the 1980s, the CDC branded AIDS as a disease only affecting gay men. Cohen writes that the *Morbidity and Mortality Weekly Report* "highlighted the common sexual identity of the patients, suggesting that some aspect of their gay 'lifestyle' might be the underlying cause of the disease" (123). Indeed, AIDS had originally been known by many names, most referencing gay men; for example, AIDS has been called gay pneumonia, gay cancer, and gay-related immune deficiency (Treichler 46). These misnomers produced a series of cultural messages about AIDS and propagated homophobic ideas. Internalized homophobia led doctors and scientists to believe that gay men's deviant existence and rampant promiscuity was the cause of their disease. Early science magazines, such as *Discover*, printed articles referencing the "vulnerable anus," and concluding that AIDS was the price men paid for having anal intercourse (Treichler 17–18). The attitudes of researchers and doctors directly influenced the response to AIDS by spreading the message that gay men were deviants, and that AIDS was the cost of choosing aberrant sexual and romantic preferences (Cohen 133). These messages were passed to the general population and still exist in perceptions of HIV and AIDS today.

Further, the focus on AIDS as a disease that mainly affected gay white men reproduced the message that it was rare (or in some cases impossible) for individuals who were not gay men to contract the disease. As a result, other groups of individuals were erased from the discourse surrounding AIDS. One example is intravenous drug users (IVDUs) who had been dying from AIDS for years. However, they had not been diagnosed with AIDS because IVDUs were already thought to be unhealthy due to their drug usage. Similar to what occurred for gay men, when AIDS was finally acknowledged as an issue for intravenous drug users (IVDUs), the acknowledgment fueled stereotypes that individuals were deviant. Drug users were generally perceived to be unhealthy already, and the discourse surrounding AIDS in IVDUs was affected by "the personal attitudes of researchers, who viewed this population as merely disease vectors and unworthy victims" (Cohen 135). Essentially, scientists and doctors turned a blind eye. Since drug use was a choice, AIDS was just a consequence, a price to pay for choosing to get high. Thus, the scientific community perpetuated the idea of AIDS as a disease of immorality and poor decision making. Scientist and researcher apathy to IVDUs and their risk for AIDS conveyed the message that only some people were worthy of prevention and treatment.

Like IVDUs, individuals of color were initially left out of the conversation surrounding AIDS. In addition to perceptions of AIDS victims as deviant in some way, organizations such as the CDC were reluctant to concede that AIDS was a concern outside the gay, predominantly white, community. Despite the abundance of evidence presented to them that indicated that people of color were also at risk, the stereotype that AIDS was a white gay disease persisted and obscured the fact that individuals of color were contracting the disease as well. Cohen suggests that the misrepresentation about who was contracting AIDS led people of color—black individuals and African Americans in particular—to believe they were not at risk, while also being grossly misinformed about the AIDS epidemic (139). At the start of the AIDS epidemic, the only people of color identified as a risk group were Haitian individuals. This has resulted in a high prevalence of HIV and AIDS diagnoses among individuals of color that persists to this day. In 2015, black and African American individuals accounted for 45 percent of new HIV diagnoses and 48 percent of new AIDS diagnoses (CDC "HIV and African Americans"). These high rates of HIV/AIDS among black individuals can be attributed to a number of influences, including the erasure of people of color from AIDS discourse.

Further, women (especially heterosexual women) were also excluded from the AIDS discourse for much of the epidemic. For a long time, it was actually thought that women could not contract HIV or AIDS; women's "rugged vaginas" protected women from becoming infected (Treichler 17). Women who did contract AIDS were either morally deficient (e.g., they were "prostitutes") or were thought to have contracted it through sex with a man who either had sex with men or was an IVDU. Moreover, women were often seen as "vectors of disease for men and infants more than victims themselves" (Susser 20). Failure to comply with mandatory testing programs for pregnant women and women seeking marriage, established by many states in 1987, was an additional indication of immorality. Indeed, it seemed that scientists were more concerned for men and children than women; this is evidenced by the exclusion of women from drug trials due to the belief that drugs might impact potential, not actual, future pregnancies (Epstein 260). Although women account for roughly 25 percent of all people living with HIV (CDC "Estimated HIV Prevalence"), they have historically been underrepresented in medical trials. Until 1993, any women who were considered to have "child-bearing potential" were excluded from medical trials for fear that exposure to novel medication may be detrimental to women's ability to become pregnant. Recently, a 2016 meta-analysis examined the percentage of women who had been included in AIDS medical research (Curno et al.). Findings showed that women made up only 19.2 percent of participants in ARV studies. It is clear that women are still being erased from AIDS discourse.

The erasure of groups like IVDUs, people of color, and women from AIDS discourse is detrimental for a number of reasons. First, the exclusion of groups breeds harmful social norms and spreads messages about morality, sexuality, and victimhood. For example, the exclusion of women from AIDS discourse has been shown to silence women's sexual agency (Peters et al.). Peters and colleagues explored policies from international organizations, including the World Health Organization, and found that women's sexual agency was mostly deleted from the discourse produced by those organizations. In education and prevention practice, this is evidenced by the female condom; the female condom is the only HIV/AIDS prevention method designed specifically for the female body (Peters et al.). Thus, the erasure of women continues to perpetuate the suppression of women's needs in the context of AIDS.

Moreover, the omission from AIDS discourse of certain, underrepresented groups has had devastating effects for the diagnosis and treatment of HIV/

AIDS among members of those groups. It was believed initially that many groups could not contract AIDS. For instance, "nonpromiscuous" heterosexual women were believed to be incapable of contracting HIV/AIDS (Treichler). In fact, women were excluded as an epidemiological risk category for AIDS, and any woman who contracted AIDS had her gender erased in favor of other risk categories, such as "'transfusion victims,' 'intravenous drug users,' or 'mothers of infants with AIDS'" (Treichler 62). Additionally, so-called promiscuous women were considered immoral due to their promiscuity and, thus, at risk. Therefore, even if a "nonpromiscuous" woman was to present to her doctor with AIDS symptoms, there is a chance she would not be diagnosed. As the symptoms and signs of HIV/AIDS were being determined, many indications that occur solely in female-bodied individuals, such as increased yeast infections or vaginal bacteriosis, were not included in the list of symptoms. Thus, many women living with HIV or AIDS went undetected. As a result of these limited signs, women could spread HIV to future partners and would be likely to die from AIDS. It seems that the exclusion of groups from AIDS discourse could pose a serious threat. If groups are presumed "safe" from HIV/AIDS, then they will be less likely to be diagnosed with AIDS and receive treatment and other benefits (e.g., medical care, housing). They might also be more likely to pass on HIV to sexual partners. This erasure of groups is irresponsible and incredibly dangerous.

Ultimately, Western science and science organizations such as the CDC and NIH have driven a number of negative messages about HIV and AIDS in the United States. The "safe/unsafe" dichotomy perpetuates ideas of PLWH and PLWA as dangerous threats to unsuspecting victims. Using the terms "risk group" and "risk behavior" in reference to groups with high prevalence of HIV further marginalizes those groups and determines which bodies are the social standard and which are not. Lastly, modern science has offered a social construction of specific "at-risk" groups, which is detrimental not only to groups with a high prevalence of HIV, but also to the groups erased from the discourse. However, the United States is not the only location where science has driven negative messages. Science's construction of HIV and AIDS has spread globally; in the next sections, I will examine science's influence on the AIDS epidemic in southern African nations.

WESTERN SCIENCE INTO AFRICA

Western science prompted construction of an "African AIDS" that reinforces colonialist ideals (Patton 77). This construction has created a host of false truths about "African AIDS." Treichler notes that Western discourse about AIDS has twisted the cultures within the landmass of "Africa" into an entity that does not reflect the true nature of the African nations (102). Rather,

Western scientists have interpreted, described, and fought the "African AIDS epidemic" through a Western lens, inscribing Western cultural ideals to Africa. That is, Western scientists assimilate "African culture" into our own, and ascribe Western meanings to African traditions, values, attitudes, and behaviors. This practice completely erases the rich diversity and culture found within the African nations and alters the values or behaviors that differ from our own.

This portrayal of "Africa" through Western perspective has given rise to the three harmful stereotypes about a generalized Africa and Africans, as outlined by Patton. The first stereotype is that people from African nations will not use condoms (Patton 78). This message implies that, unlike Americans or other Westernized individuals, Africans are unable to effectively use one method shown to prevent HIV. The underlying subtext is that Africans do not have access to Western knowledge. The second myth espouses the idea that African nations have underdeveloped science, poor research skills, and subpar medical care (Patton 78). Lastly, Patton describes the myth that "African AIDS" is a disease of poverty. That is, AIDS in Africa stems from a lack of Western-like economic development and opportunity. This text presupposes racist tropes of black Africans as less intelligent and therefore unable to industrialize like Western nations (Patton 81). This also creates the assumption that Western industry is the highest standard that all individuals should aspire to.

The messages perpetuated by Western science about "African AIDS" serve to reinforce colonialist ideals and, in a way, reinstitute colonization in the African nations that have been struck by the AIDS epidemic. By assuming that Africans are less knowledgeable, less advanced medically and technologically, and highly impoverished, Westerners create paternalistic views of African nations. These assumptions also make some believe that when something like an epidemic occurs, Western science has to come in and act as a savior, erroneously assuming that African scientists are incapable of adequately treating disease. Such ideas attempt to make African nations dependent on Western aid, which makes it easier for Western organizations and companies to recolonize some areas. If Keller is correct in suggesting that science's ultimate goal is power and domination, then these messages certainly affirm that. Moreover, by obscuring African nations' cultures, traditions, and actions, Westerners are reinforcing colonialist notions that certain areas are only for Western political and economic gain, and are not unique, independent entities. By driving AIDS discourse in Africa, Western science is essentially recolonizing areas they claim to have released long ago.

Western science, by distorting African cultures and reinscribing them to fit Western ideals about health, science, and sex, has led us to perpetuate a number of myths about "African AIDS." These perspectives and messages about "African AIDS" are detrimental to individuals within the African nations who have been affected by the AIDS epidemic, whether they be the medical professionals, educators, family members, or people living with HIV or AIDS. It is important to recognize these messages and find ways to change them, so that we can stop viewing Africa as one landmass stricken by disease and poverty and start viewing it for what it is—a diverse area with many cultures and practices different from our own.

ART DISRUPTS MESSAGE OF SCIENCE AND AUTHORITY

It is clear that Western science has been a primary driver of the discourse surrounding HIV/AIDS both in the United States and in African nations. Science, while seemingly authoritative, has perpetuated negative messages about safety and risk, and, further, has defined so-called legitimate victims of HIV and AIDS. It has also led to incorrect and detrimental ideas about the AIDS epidemic occurring in African nations; by painting a picture of "African AIDS" as a disease of poverty, ignorance, and underdevelopment, Western science has found a way to reinscribe colonialist ideals into their interference in the "African AIDS" epidemic. As these messages are harmful to people living with HIV (PLWH) or people living with AIDS (PLWA), as well as anyone receiving prevention education or testing, it is important to interrupt these messages. It is vital that individuals produce countermessages that might mitigate some of their effects and change the discourse about HIV/AIDS. Art has played a major role in countering messages about American/Western AIDS or African AIDS. I have witnessed this in two films: *Doctors, Liars, and Women: AIDS Activists Say No to Cosmo*, which disrupts the messages surrounding women and AIDS, and *DiAna's Hair Ego*, which indirectly influences messages surrounding AIDS and black and African American individuals in the South. This is also evident in poetry, specifically the work of Kgafela oa Magogodi, a South African poet.

First, the film *Doctors, Liars, and Women* directly addresses the messages about women and AIDS (Carlomusto). This documentary chronicles a series of attempts by women to counteract science's messages, particularly a misleading article published by a psychiatrist, Dr. Robert Gould, in *Cosmopolitan* magazine, which stated that heterosexual women cannot get AIDS. This message was becoming part of the dominant discourse surrounding HIV and AIDS at the time. Treichler notes that scientists thought that the female anatomy (e.g., "rugged vaginas") helped to protect female-bodied people from contracting this disease. To directly contradict these dominant messages, the filmmakers have included concrete facts, such as "AIDS is the leading cause of death in New York City for women between the ages of 25–34" (Carlomusto). They also include personal accounts of monogamous, heterosexual, non-IVDU women who contracted HIV from vaginal intercourse with a man. At the beginning of the film, a woman named Tema Luff shares that she has contracted HIV from her male partner, and states that what Dr. Gould has written is "nothing short of attempted murder" (Carlomusto). These facts and personal experiences directly demonstrate that the assertion in the *Cosmopolitan* article, that women cannot contract AIDS through heterosexual sex, is false.

The documentary includes a confrontation with Dr. Gould, the writer of the *Cosmopolitan* article. Dr. Gould stands as a representation of science who has produced popular knowledge surrounding AIDS to a wide female audience. In this confrontation, a group of women question Dr. Gould about how he came to understand that women could not contract AIDS and why he published this information in *Cosmopolitan*. This confrontation in the documentary represents a direct challenge to science and the messages produced by science. In the interview with Dr. Gould, the women are calm, well prepared with questions, and well organized, taking turns to ask questions. They quote his "facts" back to him; one woman explicitly says, "That's wrong" (Carlomusto). They also question his data, citing more recent statistics regarding women and heterosexual HIV transmission, and share personal anecdotes of women who only practiced oral sex and still were infected. By being well versed on scientific literature and statistics surrounding HIV/AIDS and women, the women confronting Dr. Gould, although not scientists themselves, demonstrate that community members can be well informed and may even know more than scientists and doctors. This documentary serves to directly counteract the messages perpetuated by scientists and inserts heterosexual women into the discourse surrounding AIDS.

Another documentary, *DiAna's Hair Ego*, does slightly different work but still subverts messages perpetuated by science surrounding AIDS (Spiro). This documentary serves to disrupt messages surrounding AIDS and people of color in the rural United States. The video documents the process of DiAna providing information, education, and even safe-sex materials (e.g., condoms) to her clients who, as a result of the refusal to recognize that people of color were at risk, knew little about HIV, AIDS, and transmission of the virus. First, DiAna's work with her clients, many of whom are black, acknowledges that black individuals are just as much at risk as gay white men. In a time when people of color were being largely ignored by scientists and the CDC, DiAna recognized that people of color were also at risk. Early in the documentary, she speaks about how she knew nothing about AIDS and realized that her clients did not know much either. This is directly in line with Cohen's conclusion that due to scientists' insistence that AIDS was a gay man's disease, people of color were uneducated about AIDS. It also eliminates that supposition that gayness and blackness are not mutually exclusive. Through her hair salon, DiAna is able to reach individuals who may be at risk as they get their hair cut. Through this informal, relaxed setting, she is able to get people to open up about the AIDS epidemic and sex in a way that may have been more difficult in formal, structured interventions.

Indirectly, this work disrupts ideas that scientists, counselors, or medical professionals are the authorities and are therefore best equipped to teach about HIV transmission and prevention. DiAna is a hairstylist, not a scientist, yet she is able to engage her community and provide effective education. Moreover, this documentary demonstrates that community-based, grassroots interventions can be more effective than one-size-fits-all interventions. DiAna is a well-known member of her community able to engage the folks who frequented her salon. She is able to bring up AIDS and educate people because she knows them and is able to connect to those around her. I will note that, to some extent, DiAna does promotes "safe/unsafe" dichotomy to those she educates. In teaching individuals about condom use and other safe-sex practices, and eventually HIV testing, she reproduces some of the discourse that suggests that people can be safe or dangerous. However, DiAna's intervention does not include messages regarding the morality of sex and sexual practices, which thereby avoids perpetuating ideas that specific sexual practices are immoral or wrong. This documentary works to show that all individuals should be educated about AIDS, that scientists or researchers are not always the best qualified to facilitate education, and that community-based, tailored education makes more sense than one-size-fits-all education. The production of this documentary reinforces the work that DiAna is doing; by chronicling her work and showing it to be effective, the documentary demonstrates that community members can do work to combat the spread of HIV/AIDS, educate and raise awareness, and fight the stigma of these diseases.

Beyond documentaries, poetry has also been used to combat dominant ideas about HIV/AIDS outside of the United States. An exemplar of this is the spoken word poetry of Kgafela oa Magogodi, which serves to disrupt messages about AIDS in South Africa. In particular, Magogodi's poem "Varara" touches on the discourse surrounding who gets HIV/AIDS and how HIV is transmitted, as well as on messages about prevention and treatment. In regards to who gets HIV/AIDS, Magogodi uses words that describe dominant Western ideas about people living with HIV/AIDS, such as promiscuous individuals, who he says are "whoring," and gay men, who are "having coffie with a moffie" (Magogodi 56). These references call to mind the groups that scientists had named at risk. By placing these stereotypes at the beginning of the poem, Magogodi reiterates and makes salient dominant knowledge. The acknowledgment of these stereotypes stands in stark contrast to the next section of the poem, which subverts these stereotypes with other examples.

Magogodi quickly switches from naming groups considered most at risk for contracting HIV and AIDS. He notes that "you don't have to be a bitch to get varara," (Magogodi 56) and then proceeds to counter these images of immoral or dirty individuals contracting HIV/AIDS. Magogodi states that a woman contracted HIV from a respected man ("ntate" meaning father), who got the virus from "the nun next door" (Magogodi 56). Varara, he says, can be contracted anywhere, anytime: on the dance floor, standing, or on futon beds. These instances of individuals contracting HIV subvert dominant ideas of who gets HIV and how it is spread. These lines provide counterexamples to the stereotypes at the beginning of the poem that do not fit within the dominant knowledge surrounding HIV. Dominant knowledge maintains that HIV is contracted by immoral individuals like gay men and prostitutes; the examples Magogodi provides here are of moral, religious individuals: a father and a nun. These images directly contradict Western ideals about who is at risk for HIV. It is not something meant for the unclean or sinful, but is something that can affect everyone from prostitutes to religious leaders.

There are also attempts to describe many of the myths of HIV/AIDS transmission, prevention, and treatment throughout the poem. Magogodi acknowledges HIV/AIDS conspiracy theory beliefs with the line "varara is a white man's lie" (Magogodi 57). These conspiracy beliefs, which include notions that HIV/AIDS was created by white individuals to exterminate people of color, were prominent among people of color in the United States and South Africa (Klonoff and Landrine). He also notes the many ways to prevent or treat HIV/AIDS: condoms, doctor's visits, holy site visits, Jesus. By acknowledging the variety of beliefs about HIV/AIDS transmission and treatment, Magogodi demonstrates that he is aware of dominant ideas about HIV/AIDS in South Africa. This is one way through which he is able to connect with his South African audiences. Throughout the poem, it is clear that Magogodi's poems are written and performed for individuals in his community and are intended to impact his family, friends, and peers as opposed to appealing to a wider audience. His use of slang and South African references, like "varara," "moffie," and "Chauke," is meant to reach other South Africans. These references help to build trust between Magogodi and his audiences. They show he is not an outsider, but someone who understands the struggles that South African communities are facing. Compared to interventions and other art, this feels less targeted toward a general audience and more targeted toward South African locals.

Finally, despite acknowledging the assortment of ideas about prevention, Magogodi says that varara is sneaky. He writes that it would elude the police like Collen Chauke, a South African fugitive during the AIDS epidemic. By personifying it and giving it characteristics, the poem makes it seem that HIV/AIDS has its own mind and will not be stopped. He ends the poem by saying that "varara will not stop til thy condom come" (Magogodi 57). This is an educational piece—that is, use a condom and you can prevent HIV/AIDS. However, taken together with the rest of the information given in this work, I'm not sure this line is entirely educational. In a way, it almost seems sarcastic, as if saying, "yeah, they say to use condoms, but that will never happen." It is like Magogodi is saying that, like the Kingdom of God, condoms are something that everyone should work for and pray for but may never be widely used. The end of this poem is rather open, and it lets listeners or readers draw their own conclusions about HIV/AIDS, prevention, treatment, and condom use.

The art engaged with here demonstrates that science organizations and scientists are not always the best drivers of HIV/AIDS knowledge. Even today this is demonstrated by ongoing disputes between communities and scientists on matters of HIV causation, transmission, and treatment access, evidenced in places such as South Africa. These works make clear the gaps that exist between community members' and scientists' understandings of HIV transmission and effects in communities. Rather, members of the community can have a greater influence that mitigates harmful messages and prevents science from dominating. Community members are often separated from science (though sometimes not, as in the case of DiAna) and are better able to understand the harm that science is doing, as in the case of *Doctors, Liars, and Women*. They have a different view on HIV/AIDS science than the doctors and scientists who are entrenched in biomedical and scientific discourses. Community members may have a different connection to HIV/AIDS than most scientists as the community members see the day-to-day effects of HIV/AIDS among people they know. Thus, these artists and their works show me that harmful HIV/AIDS messages can and will be interrupted. A logical follow-up question is: What does the future of HIV/AIDS science look like without these harmful messages?

PRACTICING "SAFE" SCIENCE?

What might it look like to have an intervention or education program that is cognizant of the negative messages current science spreads? Or rather, what might "safe" science look like? Based on many of the points raised in this chapter, there are a number of solutions that can be implemented. For starters, we can remove that "safe/unsafe" dichotomy. Although science has switched to talking about "saf*er* sex," this language still implies that on the flip side of "saf*er*" is "unsafe." Further, using language like "protected sex" also sends messages that using condoms is a way to shield an individual from a potentially untrustworthy partner. Additionally, these messages about safety and protection also do not account for other discourses surrounding condom use; for example, some work has shown that condomless sex is seen as a mechanism for facilitating intimacy, romance, and love (Rosenthal et al.), such that condomless sex is a sign of trust and intimacy between two partners. Scientists and interventionists could use purely descriptive language about sexual practices, like "condom sex" and "condomless sex." While this sounds banal, describing sex as being with or without a condom deletes the use of words like "safe" or "protected" that inherently have connotations of one type of sex being better than others. However, another issue may arise; since condoms are so strongly linked with "safe" or "protection" in modern society, using phrases like "condomless sex" may still carry the implications of "safety," thereby making a switch in language moot. Since nothing exists outside of HIV/AIDS discourse (Edelman), it seems that nothing short of a complete social shift in thinking about HIV/AIDS would serve to change ideas about "safe/unsafe."

In the future, deletion of phrases like "risk groups" and "risk behaviors" when referring to commonly performed sex acts, such as anal sex, may be beneficial. As mentioned earlier, the use of these terms serves to further marginalize and disenfranchise certain communities, such as black communities and gay communities. While categorizing certain groups for being at risk, health researchers can target and provide aid to those communities so that rates of HIV can be reduced. However, such targeted intervention also paints a bullseye on the backs of those communities, making it more likely that they are negatively stereotyped and discriminated against due to their status as a risk group. Switching language to better describe these groups is tough; any connection with HIV/AIDS automatically carries a harsh stigma. Even referring to such groups as "target groups" or "focus groups" means that these groups are being singled out due to high prevalence of disease. Swadener and Lubeck, when referring to so-called "at-risk" children and families, have reframed the ideas about risk into individuals being "at promise." The reframing attempts to change the discourse surrounding disenfranchised individuals and reinforce the idea that all individuals should not be seen as underprivileged and being in need of help, but should be considered as individuals who, with the right opportunities, can flourish. One issue with this phrasing, however, is that it seems to assume that many marginalized individuals have access to the resources that nonmarginalized groups have, which is problematic. It is also problematic that the "at promise" discourse may promote ideal standards that are dictated by the white, heteronormative, patriarchal hegemony. However, this "at promise" discourse views individuals positively, which avoids further negative stereotyping and marginalization.

Lastly, future education and intervention need to become more culturally competent. It is unrealistic, and even detrimental, to think that Western science will stop intervening in African nations. However, it is important that Western scientists do not try to implement interventions there that have only been tested in Western populations. Western science, first and foremost, needs to do better with the research conducted using individuals in African nations. As Patton points out, modern scientists perceive they are taking less risk by using Africans for medical trials, as opposed to using individuals in the Global North. Future research should treat African people with the same risk/benefit lens as is used for people in the Global North and should not devalue the sacrifices made by the African participants (Patton 86–89). Steps should be taken to ensure that education, intervention, and medical testing is specific to individuals in different regions of Africa; for example, Western HIV screening tests are less effective among African individuals as these tests also react to malaria antibodies (Patton 80). It would serve Western scientists well to include scientists, researchers, and doctors from African nations in the development of education and intervention for their own countries or regions; moreover, much like developing interventions here, community members should be involved in the planning and design of such programs to ensure the programs are as effective as possible.

As someone who has dedicated my life to health science, it is strange to see the negative impact that science can have. Science can be colonialist, it can be domineering, and it can often, unwittingly, work against the individuals it is attempting to help. It is even more rare to see scientific entities' messages subverted even, as is the case with the *Doctors, Liars, and Women* video, if the science is absolutely incorrect. In my mind, science has been the authority, the end-all-be-all of health promotion. If you had asked me early in my training as an HIV prevention scientist, I might have told you that everyone should listen to science, as the science is always right. However, it is now clear that while science and science organizations can be beneficial in disease prevention and health promotion, they can also perpetuate damaging messages that can marginalize groups of people and create poor outcomes for many.

The work done in this chapter is not meant to portray science as the enemy, or prove that science and organizations like the CDC promoting "safety" or regular testing is bad. Rather, these readings serve as a wake-up call and a reminder to me that my work and the work of HIV/AIDS scientists and medical professionals are not exempt from producing cultural messages around HIV/AIDS; Edelman makes it clear that nothing is outside the discourse surrounding AIDS. This recognition can help me, in the future, to be cognizant of these messages in my work and the work of my colleagues.

WORKS CITED

Bogart, Laura M., Glenn Wagner, Frank H. Galvan, and Denedria Banks. "Conspiracy Beliefs about HIV are Related to Antiretroviral Treatment Nonadherence among African American Men with HIV." *Journal of Acquired Immune Deficiency Syndromes*, vol. 53, no. 5, Apr. 2010, pp. 648–655. doi:10.1097/QAI.0b013e3181c57dbc.

Carlomusto, Jean, director. *Doctors, Liars, and Women: AIDS Activists Say No to Cosmo*. Directed by Jean Carlomusto, Gay Men's Health Crisis, 1988.

The Centers for Disease Control and Prevention [CDC]. "CDC's Role in Global HIV Control." www.cdc.gov/globalhivtb/who-we-are/about-us/globalhiv/globalhiv.html. Accessed March 23, 2017.

———. "Effective Interventions." effectiveinterventions.cdc.gov/. Accessed March 22, 2017.

———. "Estimated HIV Prevalence and Incidence in the United States, 2010–2016." *HIV Surveillance Supplemental Report*, vol. 24, no. 1, 2018. www.cdc.gov/hiv/pdf/library/reports/surveillance/cdc-hiv-surveillance-supplemental-report-vol-24-1.pdf.

———. "HIV and African Americans." www.cdc.gov/hiv/group/racialethnic/africanamericans/index.html. Accessed April 15, 2017.

Cohen, Cathy J. *The Boundaries of Blackness: AIDS and the Breakdown of Black Politics*. University of Chicago Press, 1999.

Curno, Miriam J., S. Rossi, I. Hodges-Mameletzis, R. Johnston, M. A. Price, and S. Heidari. "A Systematic Review of the Inclusion (or Exclusion) of Women in HIV Research: From Clinical Studies of Antiretrovirals and Vaccines to Cure Strategies." JAIDS: *Journal of Acquired Immune Deficiency Syndromes*, vol. 71, no. 2, Feb. 2016, pp. 181–188. doi:10.1097/QAI.0000000000000842.

Devine, Patricia G., E. Ashby Plant, and Kristen Harrison. "The Problem of 'Us' Versus 'Them' and AIDS Stigma." *American Behavioral Scientist*, vol. 42, no. 7, Apr. 1999, pp. 1212–1228. doi:10.1177/00027649921954732.

Edelman, Lee. "The Plague of Discourse." *Homographesis: Essays in Gay Literary and Cultural Theory*, edited by Lee Edelman. Routledge, 1994, pp. 79–92.

Epstein, Steven. *Impure Science: AIDS, Activism, and the Politics of Knowledge*. University of California Press, 1993.

Harding, Sandra. "Postcolonial and Feminist Philosophies of Science and Technology: Convergences and Dissonances." *Postcolonial Studies*, vol. 12, no. 4, Dec. 2009, pp. 401–421. doi:10.1080/13688790903350658.

Herek, Gregory M., and John P. Capitanio. "AIDS Stigma and Sexual Prejudice." *American Behavioral Scientist*, vol. 42, no. 7, Apr. 1999, pp. 1130–1147. doi:10.1177/0002764299042007006.

Kalichman, Seth C., and L. C. Simbayi. "HIV Testing Attitudes, AIDS Stigma, and Voluntary HIV Counselling and Testing in a Black Township in Cape Town, South Africa." *Sexually Transmitted Infections*, vol. 79, no. 6, Dec. 2003, pp. 442–447.

Keller, Evelyn F. "Feminism and Science." *Signs*, vol. 7, no. 3, 1982, pp. 589–602.

Klonoff, Elizabeth A., and Hope Landrine. "Do Blacks Believe that HIV/AIDS Is a Government Conspiracy against Them?" *Preventive Medicine*, vol. 28, no. 5, May 1999, pp. 451–457.

Lupton, Deborah. "Risk as Moral Danger: The Social and Political Functions of Risk Discourse in Public Health." *International Journal of Health Services*, vol 23, no. 3, 1993, pp. 425–435.

Magogodi, Kgafela oa. "Varara." *Thy Condom Come*. New Leaf Publishing, 2000.

Patton, Cindy. *Inventing AIDS*. Routledge Publishing, 1990.

Peters, Anny J. T. P., Francien T. M. van Driel, and Willy H. M. Jansen. "Silencing Women's Sexuality: Global AIDS Policies and the Case of the Female Condom." *Journal of the International AIDS Society*, vol. 16, no. 1, Jan. 2013, pp. 1–12. doi:10.7448/IAS.16.1.18452.

Rosenthal, Doreen, S. Gifford, and S. Moore . "Safe Sex or Safe Love: Competing Discourses?" *AIDS Care*, vol. 10, no. 1, Feb. 1998, pp. 35–47. doi:10.1080/09540129850124569.

"Science." *Merriam-Webster.com*. Merriam-Webster, 2019. Web. April 9, 2019.

Spiro, Ellen, director. *DiAna's Hair Ego*. Directed by Ellen Spiro, Video Data Bank, 1991.

Susser, Ida. *AIDS, Sex, and Culture: Global Politics and Survival in Southern Africa*. Wiley-Blackwell Publishing, 2009.

Swadener, Beth Blue, and Sally Lubeck. *Children and Families "At Promise": Deconstructing the Discourse of Risk*. SUNY Press, 1995.

Treichler, Paula. *How to Have Theory in an Epidemic*. Duke University Press, 1999.

Waldby, Catherine. *AIDS and the Body Politic*. Routledge Publishing, 2003.

Young, Rebecca M., and Meyer, Ilan H. "The Trouble with 'MSM' and 'WSW': Erasure of the Sexual-Minority Person in Public Health Discourse." *American Journal of Public Health*, vol. 95, no. 7, July 2005, pp. 1144–1149.

Chapter Ten

Exceptional PrEParations

Pharmaceutical Interventions, Neoliberal Queerness, and Truvada

Andy Eicher

INTRODUCTION: EVERYTHING OLD IS NEW AGAIN

In 1981, the *New York Times* published an article now infamous in the cultural history of HIV/AIDS. The headline read: "Rare Cancer Seen in 41 Homosexuals." Less than a month prior, the Centers for Disease Control (CDC) had identified a rare form of pneumonia in five "active homosexuals." While the condition would not come to be called AIDS for another year, 1981 marks what most scholars understand as the beginning of the HIV/AIDS epidemic in the United States. Throughout much of the rest of the decade, the dominant, straight (and white) US society largely ignored the growing epidemic, dismissing it as a "gay cancer" plaguing those deserving of death because of their hedonism, sexual depravity, and unnatural excess.[1] The result was that gay men and lesbians—as well as other populations affected by HIV, including intravenous drug users—organized to demand action from the government, as well as society more broadly (Gould 174–175). The radical acts of these brave people, many of whom were suffering from AIDS-related illnesses, paved the way for overhauls at the Food and Drug Administration (FDA) regarding administration of—and access to—clinical trials, as well as the approval process for new medications (Kaufman 82–86). While many celebrated the regulatory overhauls and increased access to treatment as a victory, the reality is that access was not even. Mostly white gay men benefited from these changes, while women and people of color continued to confront significant barriers to treatment, trials, and healthcare (France). In addition, transformations in the clinical trial and drug approval processes had further unintended consequences that continue to reverberate to the present day.

In this essay, I consider how the initial, radical responses to the crisis gave way to a focus on assimilation of certain queer subjects—namely gay white men—into the mainstream culture of the United States, and oftentimes at the expense of queer and trans people of color and women. This assimilatory process has recently resulted in the coalescing of strange bedfellows, including radical queer activists and community organizers, pharmaceutical conglomerates, and sex-positive factions of the queer community. This coalescing I refer to is due in part to the rise of HIV/AIDS treatment regimen known as "PrEP," the acronym for "pre-exposure prophylaxis." In what follows, I argue that in broad terms, this process of assimilation has meant a shift from the radical demands of early activists advocating for universal access to food, housing, and healthcare, to a shift that prioritizes individual responsibility and an adherence to market-based solutions to maintain personal health. I will first consider PrEP and its current status as a necessary intervention for sexually active gay men in the wider context of "public" health and safety before I then turn to two cultural artifacts: Andy Egelhoff's 2015 video, *A Short History of Truvada*, and John Greyson's 1993 film, *Zero Patience*. In drawing together these two temporally disparate visual productions, I aim to connect the current moment of HIV/AIDS management to a past moment, often understood as markedly more radical. As I close the essay, I contemplate the possibilities for an alternate vision of the future by imagining otherwise and calling for queer world-making practices that reject neoliberal, incremental change. Ultimately, I reject the assertion that revolutionary change will be realized through neoliberal capitalism. Instead, I remain optimistic that the unrealized goals of the early, radical activists are not only possible, but imperative for the future, particularly concerning the role of women, people of color, and queer and trans people in imagining a world outside capitalism.

PREPPING FOR THE FUTURE

In the United States, a marked ambivalence characterizes contemporary approaches to preparation and preparedness. On the one hand, the United States arguably could be viewed as notoriously unprepared. Oftentimes, the federal governmental approach is to take action *after* disaster has occurred, rather than to take preventative measures ahead of the event. This is evident from responses to natural disasters to the method by which healthcare decisions are made. On the other hand, to the extent that preparations are made, they seem to be almost exclusively through privatized, individualized frameworks with little emphasis on the possibilities of communal, concerted action. To the extent that a community is asked to act collectively, such action is still framed as an individual choice, with an emphasis on personal moral responsibility to protect the future self. One example of this kind of thinking can be seen in responses to the HIV/AIDS epidemic.

In the early days of the crisis, to the extent that state policies were enacted, they focused on the individual, and oftentimes on the individual who was seropositive. The burden of disclosing HIV-positive status to potential sexual partners became not just a moral, but also a legal imperative (Bell 212–213). Because the populations most affected by HIV/AIDS in the United States are queer people and people of color, HIV criminalization reproduced and amplified the racism and homophobia inherent in the criminal justice system. Further, rather than engaging communities in terms of their specific needs, prevention policies tended to adopt a one-size-fits-all approach centering on individual behavior change. According to the logic of this model, it is the responsibility of the individual to have less sex, have monogamous sex only with seronegative partners, and guard against exposure, especially through condom usage. Insofar as these "solutions" and suggestions emphasize individual responsibility, they constitute neoliberal solutions. For this essay, I rely on Dean Spade, who describes how "[n]eoliberalism has been used to conceptually draw together several key trends shaping contemporary policies and practices that have redistributed life chances over the last forty years," including "the dismantling of welfare programs" and "the rollback of the gains of the civil rights movement and other social movements of the 1960s and 1970s, combined with the mobilization of racist, sexist, and xenophobic images and ideas to bolster these changes" (22). As Spade argues, the "notions of 'freedom' and 'choice' . . . obscure systemic inequalities and turn social movements toward goals of inclusion and incorporation and away from demands for redistribution and structural transformation" (22). What does any of this have to do with Truvada or, for that matter, HIV/AIDS? In this section, I argue that a queer/feminist lens helps make visible how the subsuming of the queer body into a biopolitical framework fixated on pharmaceutical intervention further coopts radical queer organizing into a neoliberal logic. Thus, I will provide my short history of Truvada before turning to an analysis of *A Short History of Truvada*.

PREP WORK: MY SHORT HISTORY OF TRUVADA

Before—or, perhaps more fittingly put, in preparation for—my discussion of Egelhoff's *A Short History of Truvada*, I begin with my own brief account of Truvada's history. In a 2004 press release, the pharmaceutical conglomerate

Gilead Sciences announced the approval of the antiviral drug Truvada, which it had developed for the treatment of the HIV-1 virus. A combination drug, Truvada enabled people with HIV-1 infections to take a once-daily pill to keep their viral load managed, or "undetectable."[2] In 2012, in another press release, Gilead Sciences reported the FDA's approval of Truvada for use as "pre-exposure prophylaxis," or "PrEP," for "at-risk" populations. When taken as a once-daily prophylaxis, Truvada is up to 99 percent effective at preventing seroconversion between serodiscordant sexual partners ("The Basics"). Officially, the FDA recommends that PrEP regimens be used in conjunction with condoms—the long-standing safer-sex, prophylactic intervention that has been the central pillar of established HIV-prevention efforts.[3] After the completion of a forty-eight-week study in which adolescents between the ages of fifteen and seventeen were given the drug, Gilead Sciences announced in a 2018 press release the FDA's recommendation that Truvada be used as PrEP for "at-risk" adolescents. Unfortunately, FDA and CDC conceptions of risk fail to take into account the risks posed by the structural violence of settler colonialism, white supremacy, and capitalism for "at-risk" youth.

After initial approval of Truvada as PrEP, the uptake to *prevent* seroconversion was sluggish (Highleyman). Initial resistance to PrEP could be attributed to the phrase "at-risk," a not-so-thinly veiled code for gay men who have multiple sexual partners. As noted by scholars such as Cindy Patton,[4] the stigmatizing of gay men as "promiscuous" has made effective preventative measures difficult and fraught for various factions of the politically engaged gay male population responding to the advent of PrEP. On the one hand, conservative factions worried that Truvada as PrEP would produce a new generation of sexually promiscuous "Truvada whores" drawn into a sexuality that promised a "return" to the sexual freedom in the days before the HIV/AIDS epidemic (Duran, "Truvada Whores?"). Critics also argued that Truvada used as PrEP would result in a resurgence of sexually transmitted infections (Duran, "Truvada Whores?"). Further, there was concern that the efforts of conservative gay rights organizing that focused on mainstreaming gay men and lesbians could be threatened. Much of the mainstream gay and lesbian civil rights organizing specifically relied on not making their sexuality and sexual practices part of the conversation, and instead focused on how gay men and lesbians desired monogamy and the protection of "American values," just like their heterosexual counterparts. A return to prioritizing sexual freedom, according to this logic, would reproduce stereotypes of queers as having insatiable libidinal desires, solely focused on their unchecked hedonistic depravity. This stood in sharp contrast to the carefully curated image of gay men and lesbians as respectable individuals interested in having nuclear families and serving their country through military participation.

Still others, such as sex-positive, gay rights advocate Christopher Glazek, suggested that people advancing arguments about the "threat" of Truvada whores were reproducing the all-too-familiar tropes of slut shaming, fear-mongering, and pandering. They argued that the uptake of a PrEP regimen constituted a moral imperative for sexually active gay men who certainly should not be shamed for their significant and varied sexual practices, nor for their desire not to seroconvert. Eventually, the initial controversy dissipated,[5] and after aggressive campaigns targeting gay and bisexual men to initiate a PrEP regimen, the numbers of people on PrEP finally began to rapidly increase (Highleyman). This campaigning has included near unanimous support from an alliance of seemingly disparate allies: government public health agencies, private corporations, geosocial dating applications, community health organizations, activists, and academics—to name a few.

In general, I count myself among those in the sex-positive, pro-public-health faction, who, roughly speaking, adheres to a platform promoting consensual, safer-sex practices. However, I find the response to PrEP—specifically Truvada as PrEP—disappointingly reductive. I certainly understand that the initial possibilities presented by PrEP are very appealing. Indeed, stopping the HIV/AIDS epidemic has long been a goal of community organizers and activists. However, I would suggest that further investigation is required to fully understand the implications of PrEP—as it relates to the queer body specifically, but more broadly speaking, as PrEP has enabled the imbrication of queer politics into neoliberal world-making practices, as well as an uncomfortable alliance with pharmaceutical conglomerates. Again, considering the radical goals of early activists, I am hesitant to cozy up with capitalist power brokers. Moreover, I wonder if PrEP is the solution all communities need; for instance, what resources might better serve trans people of color or people caught up in the prison industrial complex?

On a base level, PrEP functions to remind both queers, as well as broader, straight society, that there is something fundamental about queerness that has been targeted for management through neoliberal medically mediated interventions. I am hardly the first person to make this observation. Cindy Patton, a prolific and longtime scholar of societal responses to HIV/AIDS, co-wrote an essay in 2012 with Hye Jin Kim where they in part comment about long-standing anxieties about gay men's sexuality and resulting desires to pharmaceutically intervene. As they note, "the idea of a pill against HIV and the idea that gay men and women are at such high risk of contracting HIV that condoms and behavior change are insufficiently protective date to the beginnings of the HIV pandemic; indeed, in the context of this epidemic, concepts of risk and ideas of treatment are inextricably linked" (Patton and Kim 297). I would take the assertion by Patton and Kim even further: Truvada reproduces understandings of the male homosexual as some sort of inherently depraved soul who must be recuperated from abject sexuality. Further, Truvada as PrEP dovetails with neoliberal projects of optimization of the body, and, in particular, on the elimination of marginalized and queer sexual practices. In an essay for the *Disability Studies Reader*, Robert McRuer asserts that the fictions of prototypical heterosexuality and able-bodiedness are predicated on the assumption that both queerness and disability are tragic accidents of nature, necessitating both explanation and intervention to "safely contain" them (305). McRuer suggests that the proper execution of compulsory heterosexuality is also free of disability: "[t]he most successful heterosexual subject is the one whose sexuality is not compromised by disability (metaphorized as queerness); the most successful able-bodied subject is the one whose ability is not compromised by queerness (metaphorized as disability)." Through the ongoing practice of medicalizing queer identity, "people with disabilities are often understood as somehow queer . . . while queers are understood as somehow disabled" (304). Moreover, PrEP as a neoliberal intervention not only seeks safely to contain the abject queer body, but also invites rather than rejects participation in neoliberal capitalism and the attendant risks posed to marginalized people. PrEP further shifts expectations about sexuality and sexual practices.

In a special edition of *GLQ*,[6] Jasbir Puar wrote concluding remarks that directly interrogate debility, disability, and sexuality under global capitalism. Her essay, "Coda: The Cost of Getting Better: Suicide, Sensation, Switchpoints," raises important questions about the biopolitical shifts occurring under late capitalism, and details the ways in which queers may be unintentionally implicated or swept up in the tentacles of capitalism. Turning her attention to the media pundit and gay rights activist Dan Savage, Puar specifically critiques his "It Gets Better Campaign," which she characterizes as "a mandate to fold oneself into urban, neoliberal gay enclaves: a call to upward mobility that discordantly echoes the now-discredited 'pull yourself up by the bootstraps' immigrant motto" ("Coda" 151). As Puar argues, this promise does not account for other factors, such as race and class, and furthermore, fails to recognize the ways in which neoliberalism and its accordant logic render all bodies as simultaneously expendable, as well as exploitable sites to be mined for maximum profit ("Coda" 153). In addition, Puar links the catchphrase "it gets better" to a narrative of progress and health whereby white, upwardly mobile gay men enjoy the benefits of patriarchy, settler colonialism, and the exploitation required to sustain this upwardly mobile trajectory ("Coda" 153–154).

Using the example of increased prescriptions of antidepressant drugs in the United States and in the United Kingdom, Puar refers to Nikolas Rose to suggest that the increased use of these drugs has less to do with more people being "hailed" or "interpellated" (in the Althusserian sense) as depressed, and more to do with "the gradation of populations" and "through the evaluation and accommodation of degrees" to which one is depressed ("Coda"

155–156). In other words, the diagnosis is not whether one is depressed, but rather, "to what degree is one depressed?" (Puar, "Coda" 156). These approaches assume people need personalized healthcare solutions, according to broader neoliberal thinking, and imply that all people, even those who are able bodied, stand to be optimized or improved through medical and pharmaceutical intervention.

Puar argues that through this form of medical administration, bodies are "drawn into a modulation of subindividual capacities" so that bodies can be subjected to surveillance not solely rooted in "identity positions" but further sorted through various metrics, including the perceived statistical possibilities of "risk and prognosis" ("Coda" 156). Ultimately, bodies are "further stratified across registers of the medical-industrial complex: medical debt, health insurance, [and] state benefits, among other feedback loops into the profitability of debility" (Puar, "Coda" 156). In other words, bodies are reordered around an identity that is derived on the basis of "risk" or "prognosis" and how one's prognosis or perceived risk further fits into various structures of the neoliberal, late capitalist order. Positive outcomes are measured according to the extent an intervention can maximize performance, or to the extent that an intervention can ameliorate a perceived risk—real or imagined—to increase performance. Ultimately, the aim is to resuscitate a failed body, or to further optimize a nondisabled body, a point that Puar underscores in a different article:

> Neoliberal regimes of biocapital produce the body as *never healthy enough*, and thus *always* in a debilitated state in relation to what one's bodily capacity is imagined to be; aging itself is seen as a debility, as some populations live longer but also live with more chronic illness. ("Prognosis" 167, emphasis mine)

Though Puar's assertion that the body is never healthy enough appears to be at odds with McRuer's claim that the proper heterosexual subject is not compromised by disability, I read this differently. First, the interventions Puar critiques are neoliberal mandates meant to stave off or prevent future disability. Additionally, in the instance that debilitation has happened as the result of capitalist exploitation, the logic becomes, how might a pharmaceutical intervention return the body to a fictive originary state? Pharmaceutical interventions enable bodies to avoid or reverse debility, and thus protect them from the queerness of disability. On the one hand, the queer is constituted as disabled, and on the other, neoliberal regimes seek perpetually to stave off disability. Truvada resolves a certain contradiction—it enables the staving off of disability and, implicitly, of the queerness of the gay man.

As upwardly mobile, middle-class, white gay people (primarily men) have found some measure of acceptance in society, they too must adhere to such neoliberal logic. Even before transmission has occurred, gay men are presumed at grave risk, necessitating an intervention—even if their "menu" of preferred sexual acts does not include behaviors associated with risk of seroconversion. Adherence to a preventative pharmaceutical intervention further confirms in the broader imaginary that there is something inherently "wrong" with gay men: their sexual practices (and the identities conflated with sexual practices) pose broader risks to public health and safety, dangers that must be contained through initiation of PrEP. Ready to work, produce, and consume, the gay man is no longer compromised by his sexuality; pharmaceuticals and capitalism have saved the day once more.

Such approaches to managing community resources are dangerous. The push towards PrEP in the United States makes a lot of assumptions. One of the most visible failures of domestic policy in this country is the continued reliance on a for-profit, private insurance model. In this model, most people gain access to healthcare through employer-subsidized policies in exchange for full-time work. Given the racist and colonial history of the United States, it is perhaps unsurprising that barriers to access remain for both employment and healthcare, especially for people of color. Even when a queer person of color is able to access a doctor, they still face the legacies of historic and continued racism and homophobia in the medical field. In addition to the initial visit to the doctor for a prescription in the first place, PrEP regimen requires HIV/STI screenings every three months to ensure continued seronegativity. Continued adherence to PrEP requires access to insurance-subsidized prescriptions, given the prohibitive cost of the drug if paid for in full— nearly $2,000 per month (Citroner).[7] Undertaking a PrEP regimen further presumes an individual's willingness to be a "good," neoliberal, sexually responsible citizen. This neoliberal "sexual responsibility" is misleading. Rather than prioritizing democratic intimacy and mutual satisfaction[8]— which I argue are the paramount sexual responsibilities—individuals are instead invited to participate in a highly mediated sexuality that is predicated on neoliberal logic of personal responsibility. Responsibilities include having a job that offers insurance and, next, understanding one's body not as a site of possibility and sexual potentiality, but rather as a vessel of perverse depravity, best understood through its proximity to a deadly infectious disease kept at bay only through acceptance of the grim reality that the natural and logical outcome of anal penetration is of course death that is preventable solely through an expensive, pharmaceutical intervention. In the end, PrEP not only functions to prepare the upwardly mobile, white gay male subject for a productive life but it also transforms him into a neoliberal, sexually responsible citizen. The integration into the structures of capitalism facilitated by Truvada forecloses more radical potentials.

ALTERNATIVELY, *A SHORT HISTORY OF TRUVADA*

Brooklyn-based visual artist and DJ Andy Egelhoff—also known as "SPRKLBB"—composed a short, satirical video performance, ostensibly telling the "short history" of Truvada by examining a time "before" and "after" Truvada as PrEP. This video is reminiscent of nature films—for instance, it incorporates close-ups in nature and observation by an omniscient camera lens—and also harkens back to the 1993 film, *Zero Patience*,[9] specifically through the caricature of colonial tropes. Egelhoff's short video is also in part a campy critique of "gay clone"[10] culture within the gay male community. His film pokes fun at the notion that undertaking a PrEP regimen will transform a primordial queer into "the perfect bottom"—hyper-capacitated with pharmaceuticals and ready for a carefree lifestyle of dance parties and anonymous sex. My reading of this video centers on a critique of neoliberal imperatives and rhetoric that insist on long-term interventions to promote "well-being" that bring the body closer to a nonexistent "ideal" originary state, as well as to pacify the potentials for more radical engagement.

As the film opens, a single tablet of Truvada descends from the sky; the smooth, blue pill is cast in relief against the textured backdrop of a statuesque tree with sprawling branches. The pill's origin is unknown, perhaps from a bottle in the sky or the pharmaceutical giant, Gilead Sciences; the camera quickly zooms in before there is time to consider the tablet's genesis. After the title flashes across the screen, the creatures—which I will refer to as "clones"—that are the subject of this short video are introduced. Marching through nature, the clones are identical in appearance: backwards snapback cap, black t-shirt with a graphic across the chest, red underwear, and black sneakers. Though they read as cis, white men, their humanity is unclear because they are not "civilized," a nod to a precolonial (or, pre-PrEP) moment. Their purpose is unclear, but their uniform appearance suggests they are, or will become, "gay clones." Foraging, they find a Truvada tablet nestled amongst plants, awaiting discovery. The manufactured, inorganic tablet—emblazoned with "Gilead"—is in sharp contrast to the organic plant life that surrounds it, reinforcing the dichotomy created between nature and the pharmaceutical industry. In the scenes that follow, the clones take the mysterious tablet back to their cave, where it is presented to a clone still in larva form. After one of the clones takes a bite out of the tablet, a transformation occurs: the clone rubs his stomach before being propelled forward as white smoke is expelled from his ass. Dramatic music gives way to bright colors, dancing clones, and techno music: the perfect bottom is born.

Against a backdrop of flashing neon colors, the word "Truvada" shimmers in the background as clones lightheartedly dance to upbeat techno music. They have been transported from their existence in nature to a synthetic world of electronic music and drugs—a geographic and temporal demarcation that might be read as *after* colonization (or post-PrEP). Pills swirl against the backdrop of bright, flashing colors from one Truvada bottle to the next. In a neon sky, full of feathery white clouds, a clone appears, adorned with angel-like wings. Looking down—from where is unclear: heaven? the sky? space?—and seeing the masses of pre-Truvada clones, the clone reaches into its underwear and pantomimes tossing bottles and bottles of Truvada down to Earth, allowing the other clones to undergo metamorphosis. Now in the mystical domain of a perpetual gay disco dance party, clones dance as empty Truvada bottles float through the neon party. The text, "The Perfect Bottom," appears on top of the screen as a clone exuberantly smiles and gyrates while the next sequence displaying an infomercial-style screen pleads, "Call Now!!!" to secure a perfect bottom for only "¢99 per month [*sic*]" with a small asterisk clarifying this price is "with medicaid [*sic*]." The final scene is a return to the clone flying through the sky, preparing to once again drop Truvada from his crotch. However, before he can accomplish this, he is struck by a fly swatter, splattering blood across the frame with a gravelly voice proclaiming, "I got it!"

Egelhoff's short video deploys campy excess and stereotypically "gay" or "queer" aesthetics and sensibilities to make light of what purports to be the short history of Truvada and its production of the "perfect bottom" within the gay male community. However, a more critical analysis reveals how some of the theoretical concepts raised earlier come together. Before Truvada, the clones are seen as backwards and primitive. This is made evident through their seemingly purposeless wandering, uncoordinated movements, and garbled, throaty communication. Reading this as metaphorically depicting pre-PrEP gay men, I argue that extending my discussion of Puar's and McRuer's analyses of the relationship between neoliberal, late capitalism, disability, and queerness is useful. These pre-PrEPped clones are compromised by queerness as well as proximity to risk, and the implication is that this is in part due to their lack of access to a pharmaceutical intervention. In a sense, the gay bottom is doubly fucked: on the one hand, the penetration of his ass by his partner's penis and, on the other, the possible penetration of the immune system by a deadly virus. These practices are destabilizing to the mainstream order and thus must be *contained*. The discovery of Truvada thus drastically transforms the clones' prospects and capacities. No longer at risk of debilitation by a deadly virus, the clone is free to participate in capitalist commodification. However, this participation comes at a cost: the clone must acquiesce to the conventions of Western life, rooted in white supremacy and colonial violence.

Now, the clones are carelessly dancing to upbeat electronic music in a discotheque where empty bottles of PrEP rain down against a backdrop of flashing neon colors. In undertaking an ongoing and expensive pharmaceutical intervention, the clones are interwoven into the colonial and neoliberal paradigms of progress, strength, and individual responsibility but also the "gradation of populations" Puar describes. Rather than being actually unwell and requiring medical intervention to overcome or manage illness, the clones—a surrogate for gay men in general—are sorted into a particular risk group requiring a particular intervention: PrEP. Instead of understanding HIV as an illness (or disability) to be managed or treated, the logic of PrEP understands queer sexual practices and, by extension, the queer (i.e., gay sex and gay men, respectively) as at grave risk of becoming disabled, thus threatening the neoliberal order. The voluntary adherence to a PrEP regimen recuperates the clones into productive capitalism, safely contains the aberrant sexual practice, sorts populations in terms of risk and prognosis, and maintains the logic of neoliberalism. The dancing, free-spirited clones therefore serve as a visual example of how such pharmaceutical interventions hold transformative promise, while also exemplifying a particular type of queer or gay "lifestyle" that is narrowly permissible. "The perfect bottom" is not only ready for anonymous sex and partying, but also for an expensive, ongoing regimen made possible by a massive pharmaceutical corporation. In other words, the perfect bottom is caught between queer culture and neoliberalism, ready to receive on both accounts: penetration from his partner and penetration into a carefully surveilled, pharmaceutically mediated state.

Beyond the transformation that has occurred with the adherence to a PrEP regimen, the clones have undergone a different kind of (sero)conversion than their earlier clone counterparts. In the 1970s and 1980s, the lifestyle of the gay clone subculture involved frequent, anonymous sexual encounters and the use of illicit drugs to intensify these sexual experiences. A permissive attitude towards both sex and drugs was later blamed, in part, for the early spread of AIDS within the gay community. These behaviors became the basis of homophobic responses to the crisis, which suggested that these people were receiving their rightful punishment for promiscuity. Whereas the earlier clones of the 1970s to 1990s were wiped out by AIDS, Egelhoff's clones are no longer at risk of seroconverting to HIV-positive status and are rendered invincible through adherence to a PrEP regimen. A different kind of conversion has occurred: the clones' blood is protected *against* HIV, and ironically this protection occurs through regular drug use. However unlike in the 1970s and 1980s, these drugs are sanctioned through official medical practitioners: doctor and pharmacist. Whereas illicit drugs were once taken to enhance sexual pleasure and experiences, drugs are now taken out of an anxiety produced by the perceived risk of seroconversion. In other words, the purpose of PrEP appears to be for either serodiscordant couples or sexually active users to help gird against future HIV transmission. Unlike the clones of yesteryear, these clones accept rather than reject the established order, seeking further integration into regimes of neoliberal authority and surveillance. In the end, as the flyswatter splatters the clone across the frame a voice proclaims, "I got it." If the viewer is to assume the "I" is hegemonic society, one is left wondering what exactly *it* is. Does the ominous voice mean to suggest that "it" is the clone? HIV? Truvada? Or perhaps it is more nefarious: with the end of HIV now possible, and the further integration of the (white) gay community into the mainstream, the abject queerness once associated with the gay community is finally contained. The very queerness that once was a site of radical resistance—imagining alternative ways of being and world making as well as a rejection of the status quo—is finally folded into the logics of late capitalism. This symbolic smashing of queerness makes way for the further spread of homonormativity. Ironically, in the era of PrEP, sex and drugs once again enjoy an intermingling, but this time it is with the stamp of approval of the established order and the promise and potential to *end* a global pandemic rather than exacerbate it. In a shift from the current moment of HIV/AIDS management, I return to the 1980s to pay a visit to the now debunked Patient Zero depicted in John Greyson's 1993 film *Zero Patience*.[11]

Greyson's film is best characterized as a satirical musical that in part challenges myths about Patient Zero, while also parodying tropes of colonialism and white supremacy. The film focuses on Victorian sexologist Sir Richard Burton—who, through an unexplained mishap with the Fountain of Youth, is immortal and happens to be chief taxidermist at the Museum of Natural History in 1987 Canada. He begins working on an exhibition about historical "patient zeroes"—including Typhoid Mary—and decides to make a short documentary about Patient Zero for the exhibition. In *Zero Patience*, Patient Zero is French-Canadian flight attendant, "Zero," the person vilified for supposedly introducing and spreading HIV in North America through sexual contact with hundreds of men. Throughout the film, we see Burton interviewing various people who knew Zero and who explain how little was known in the early days of AIDS about who got sick or how, and who further describe how Zero was trying to exist—specifically *not* with malicious intent, as insinuated by Burton. However, Zero not spreading HIV with malicious intent does not fit the narrative sought by Burton; he therefore manipulates their interviews to make it appear as though Zero was a narcissistic, nihilistic serial killer, who fucked with impunity and flaunted his depraved sexual deviance. While filming and postproduction of the documentary are happening, Zero reappears from death, visible only to Burton. As Zero attempts to clear his name, he and Burton eventually pursue a sexual relationship. Ultimately, the film culminates with Zero being able to cross into the afterlife. For the sake of my argument, however, I would like to briefly discuss one key scene from the film.

The scene I would like to discuss is towards the end of the film, when Zero is looking at his own blood under a microscope, which is "full" of HIV antibodies, as well as various other sexually transmitted infections. Notably,

AIDS activist Michael Callen plays the part of "Miss HIV," a campy, saucy, and queer anthropomorphized embodiment of HIV. In this scene, Callen and the other anthropomorphized infections in Zero's blood explain how little was actually understood about AIDS when Zero was alive, including whether or not HIV definitively caused AIDS. Callen and the other infections further explain that in the early days of the epidemic, important epidemiological work[12] was done that established that AIDS—whatever it was[13]—could be transmitted sexually. The realization that the virus was sexually transmitted gave rise to the safer-sex movement. Rather than shaming people for their sexual practices, proclivities, or preferences, safer-sex practices encourage people to participate in low-risk sexual acts, or to use barriers when engaging in "higher-risk" activities. Safer-sex therefore set a tone for radical activism, community building, and lifesaving interventions. These anthropomorphic infections then muse that perhaps Zero should be remembered not as a nihilistic sociopath who spread AIDS, but instead as the person who gave birth to a safer-sex movement. In addition to a shared visual aesthetic and campy, queer sensibility, this scene and Egelhoff's video short are products of their time and, as such, are important artifacts for considering attitudes and approaches to HIV. However, aside from shared aesthetic sensibilities and subject matter (AIDS), the films have different targets. Where Egelhoff's video critiques Truvada as PrEP and pokes fun at the idea of a "perfect" bottom—a position arrived at through adherence to a pharmaceutical intervention with little emphasis on community building—Greyson's film focuses on the possibilities of queer community building, conviviality, and empowered sexuality.

As I have argued, the current approach to fighting HIV/AIDS through campaigns of prevention prioritize individuals adhering to an expensive pharmaceutical regimen widely available only to those with private insurance, a job, and a commitment to capitalism. It articulates the queer body as abject and always already failed, recuperated through a neoliberal healthcare intervention. Egelhoff's video critiques this idea, suggesting that clones are concerned solely with having fun at the expense of community engagement and imagining otherwise. Viewing Egelhoff's video short alongside the earlier AIDS film, *Zero Patience*, makes evident how the current moment is a far cry from the hope of earlier organizers. Greyson's Zero is exonerated from his responsibility in spreading the virus. An entire community is built around him, and he is a part of it. This community is interested not in placing blame, emphasizing personal responsibility, or perpetuating a circumspect morality of monogamy, but instead playfully broaches the painful reality of life during an epidemic. Through the sharing of information and a desire to imagine the world and intimacy otherwise, an earlier community organized around their proximity to a virus and agitated for an end to homophobia, increased access to healthcare, and prioritized collectivity. Rather than seeing the prevention of HIV as an effort best managed privately and for profit, *Zero Patience* understands it as the responsibility of the many, regardless of their means. As I close, I suggest Juana María Rodríguez's call for the necessity of prioritizing "questions of sex and sexual expression" in "our political discussion on public education, militarization, international diplomacy, art and aesthetics, the distribution of resources, sovereignty claims, and urban planning" and to understand these as "pressing social issues that have sexual implications" (16), is fundamental to considering the infrastructure we might need to build and imagine the future.

CONCLUSION: OR, THE GAYS ARE AT IT AGAIN

I think a lot about the future. The current moment is so politically toxic, and I look on in disbelief as mainstream gay rights organizing for the past forty years has accomplished little more than access to same-sex marriage and the "right" of gay men and lesbians to die fighting for a country that doesn't even want to sell them cake for their weddings. It is wild to think about the activists who literally died fighting against the indifference of a country that was happy to watch them die, yet mainstream gay rights organizations were so quick to insist upon an adherence to a politics of respectability. In centering assimilationist politics, organizers asked queer people to abandon their radical dream and vision of the future. The exacerbation of divisions along various demographic lines became the goal. For middle-class white men and women, the promises of social integration led many to become complicit in the very power structures of capitalism so violent for the rest of the world.

But I still have hope. Outside of this capitalist logic, I think the possibilities and potentialities remain to be found. In returning to the moments of radical community collaboration borne from the AIDS crisis, I see the ways in which the goals unrealized then still might be accomplished in the future. Women, queers, and people of color have always known the world as it is currently constituted is not for them. They are asked to participate in the exploitation of their marginalized counterparts globally while simultaneously being exploited by the machinations of global, neoliberal capitalism. What is wonderful about rejecting the status quo is that the possibility to imagine otherwise opens up a possibility to create a world far outside of privatization, neoliberalism, and individual responsibility. Reviewing cultural productions such as *Zero Patience* reminds viewers of the ways that people have tried not to make a broken system work or force themselves into molds that they could never fit. There is a blueprint for a future that makes space for everyone and does not try to blame individuals for their circumstance. So, while there is some work to do, it is my hope that the future we will imagine, build, and yearn for is the queer revolution.

NOTES

1. This has been written about extensively, both at the time, as well as since the start of the crisis. For example, Allen White wrote for the *San Francisco Chronicle* in the wake of Ronald Reagan's death in 2004. Commenting on the rise of the religious right, White notes that "[a] significant source of Reagan's support came from the newly identified religious right and the Moral Majority, a political-action group founded by the Rev. Jerry Falwell. AIDS became the tool, and gay men the target, for the politics of fear, hate and discrimination. Falwell said, 'AIDS is the wrath of God upon homosexuals.' Reagan's communications director Pat Buchanan argued that AIDS is 'nature's revenge on gay men.'"
2. "Undetectable" refers to an HIV serostatus whereby the person has previously tested HIV-positive, but through careful adherence to antiretroviral therapy, their viral load is suppressed such that it is too low to be measured in a blood test and is similarly too low to result in seroconversion of an HIV-negative sexual partner during barrier-free sexual activity (McCray and Mermin).
3. In his 1987 essay, "How to Have Promiscuity in an Epidemic," Douglas Crimp writes about efforts to get gay men to use condoms through the dissemination of sexually explicit safer-sex cartoons by community health organizations like the Gay Men's Health Crisis, as well as public service announcements aimed at demonstrating how to properly put a condom onto a penis through demonstrations on bananas (254–256, 259–263). Both efforts were met by sharp backlash from the religious right as well as "big Banana," respectively (Crimp 256, 259–263).
4. This is a point Patton makes in several publications, including her 1990 book, *Inventing AIDS*, as well as in *Sex and Germs*.
5. The original writer of "Truvada Whores?" wrote a retraction and the various factions largely decided that coalescing around a pharmaceutical intervention that promised to prevent future transmissions of HIV was what was in the best interest of the "community" (Duran, "An Evolved Opinion").
6. The 2011 special issue was entitled "Queer Studies and the Crisis of Capitalism." Contributions were from scholars grappling with what role queer studies should serve critiquing the ongoing exploitation occurring under late capitalism/neoliberalism and the power relations required to sustain these global systems of finance.
7. Recently, Gilead Sciences has announced its intention to donate hundreds of thousands of prescriptions to the CDC for uninsured, "high-risk" individuals to receive at no cost. However, as noted by the *New York Times* editorial board and others, this will still not ensure access for all people at risk of seroconversion ("A Million Americans").
8. My call for "democratic intimacy" and "mutual satisfaction" is a nod to Gayle Rubin's imagining of a "democratic morality" in her infamous essay, "Thinking Sex: Notes for a Radical Theory of the Politics of Sexuality."
9. I would like to thank Dirk Visser, also a contributor to this edited collection, who brought the film *Zero Patience* and its similar aesthetic (at points) to my attention.
10. A "gay clone" refers to a member of a subcultural group within the gay male community, characterized by similar dress and bodily appearance (i.e., hyper masculine, muscular) and exclusiveness within a clique, particularly in the 1970s and 1980s (Levine 1–2, 6).
11. Douglas Crimp, writing in 1987, notes that the concept of Patient Zero—or, the person understood as responsible for bringing AIDS to the United States—was a fabrication of Randy Shilts in his 1987 book, *And the Band Played On*, but a 2016 article in *Nature* by Worobey et al. scientifically "proved" the impossibility of real-life Patient Zero, Gaëtan Dugas, being responsible for introducing the HIV virus to North America.
12. I would also note, to this point about "Zero as '0,'" that "0" literally never existed. In fact, early researchers marked the patient with the letter "O" to indicate he was from outside California. It was only Randy Shilts's depraved desire to place blame on a single person for a crisis that was the result of systemic state failure, as well as his unchecked desperation to sell more copies of his semi-nonfictional book, that produced the fiction of "Patient Zero" (Murphy).

13. As Callen's Miss HIV notes in the scene, the jury was out as to what actually caused AIDS throughout much of the 1980s.

WORKS CITED

Altman, Lawrence K. "Rare Cancer Seen in 41 Homosexuals." *New York Times*, July 3, 1981, www.nytimes.com/1981/07/03/us/rare-cancer-seen-in-41-homosexuals.html.

"The Basics | PrEP." *PrEP Facts*, San Francisco AIDS Foundation, San Francisco Department of Public Health, Project Inform, Be the Generation, Gilead Sciences, 2018, men.prepfacts.org/the-basics/.

Bell, Chris. "I'm Not the Man I Used to Be: Sex, HIV, and Cultural 'Responsibility.'" *Sex and Disability*, edited by Robert McRuer and Anna Mollow. Duke University Press, 2012, pp. 208–228.

Citroner, George. "Truvada Drug Cost and HIV PrEP Treatment." *Healthline*, July 11, 2018, www.healthline.com/health-news/cost-of-hiv-prevention-drug-discouraging-people-from-doing-prep-therapy#1.

Crimp, Douglas. "How to Have Promiscuity in an Epidemic." *October*, vol. 43, 1987, pp. 237–271. doi:10.2307/3397576.

Duran, David. "An Evolved Opinion on Truvada." *The Huffington Post*, March 27, 2014, www.huffingtonpost.com/david-duran/truvadawhore-an-evolved-o_b_5030285.html.

———. "Truvada Whores?" *Huffington Post Voices*, November 2, 2012, www.huffingtonpost.com/david-duran/truvada-whores_b_2113588.html.

Egelhoff, Andy, director. *A Short History of Truvada*, December 18, 2015, www.youtube.com/watch?v=h56bXsLJNkk.

France, David, director. *How to Survive a Plague*. Sundance Selects, 2012.

Glazek, Christopher. "Why I Am a Truvada Whore." *Out Magazine*, May 20, 2014, www.out.com/entertainment/popnography/2014/05/20/why-i-am-truvada-whore.

Gottlieb, M. S., H. M. Schanker, P. T. Fan, A. Saxon, J. D. Weisman, and I. Pozalski. "Pneumocystis Pneumonia—Los Angeles." *MMWR*, vol. 30, no. 21, ser. 1–3, June 5, 1981. *1–3*, www.cdc.gov/mmwr/preview/mmwrhtml/june_5.htm.

Gould, Deborah Bejosa. *Moving Politics: Emotion and ACT UP's Fight against AIDS*. University of Chicago Press, 2009.

Greyson, John, director. *Zero Patience*. Strand Releasing, 1993.

Highleyman, Liz. "PrEP Use Is Rising Fast in US, but Large Racial Disparities Remain." *NAM AIDSMap*, June 24, 2016, www.aidsmap.com/PrEP-use-is-rising-fast-in-US-but-large-racial-disparities-remain/page/3065545/.

Kaufman, Sharon R. *Ordinary Medicine: Extraordinary Treatments, Longer Lives, and Where to Draw the Line*. Duke University Press, 2015.

Levine, Martin P. *Gay Macho: The Life and Death of the Homosexual Clone*, edited by Michael S. Kimmel. New York University Press, 1998.

McCray, Eugene, and Jonathan H. Mermin. "Dear Colleague: September 27, 2017." Received by Colleague, *Dear Colleague: Information from CDC's Division of HIV/AIDS Prevention*, Centers for Disease Control and Prevention, September 27, 2017, www.cdc.gov/hiv/library/dcl/dcl/092717.html.

McRuer, Robert. "Compulsory Able-Bodiedness and Queer/Disabled Existence." *The Disability Studies Reader*, edited by Lennard J. Davis, 2nd ed. Routledge, 2006, pp. 301–308.

"A Million Americans Need This Drug. Trump's Deal Won't Help Enough of Them." *The New York Times*, May 13, 2019, www.nytimes.com/2019/05/13/opinion/truvada-gilead-hiv-trump.html.

Murphy, Tim. "AIDS' Patient Zero Is Finally Innocent, but We're Still Learning Who He Really Was." *The Vindicated*, New York Magazine, October 31, 2016, nymag.com/vindicated/2016/10/aids-patient-zero-is-vindicated-by-science.html.

Patton, Cindy. *Inventing AIDS*. Routledge, 1990.

———. *Sex and Germs: The Politics of AIDS*. South End Press, 1985.

———, and Hye Jin Kim. "The Cost of Science." *Journal of Bioethical Inquiry*, vol. 9, no. 3, 2012, pp. 295–310. doi:10.1007/s11673-012-9383-x.

Puar, Jasbir K. "Coda: The Cost of Getting Better: Suicide, Sensation, Switchpoints." *GLQ: A Journal of Lesbian and Gay Studies*, vol. 18, no. 1, 2011, pp. 149–158. doi:10.1215/10642684-1422179.

———. "Prognosis Time: Towards a Geopolitics of Affect, Debility and Capacity." *Women & Performance: A Journal of Feminist Theory*, vol. 19, no. 2, 2009, pp. 161–172. doi:10.1080/07407700903034147.

Rodríguez, Juana María. *Sexual Futures, Queer Gestures, and Other Latina Longings*. New York University Press, 2014.

Rubin, Gayle S. "Thinking Sex: Notes for a Radical Theory of the Politics of Sexuality." *The Lesbian and Gay Studies Reader*, edited by Henry Abelove, Michèle Aina Barale, and David M. Halperin. Taylor & Francis, 2012, pp. 3–44.

Spade, Dean. *Normal Life: Administrative Violence, Critical Trans Politics, and the Limits of Law*. Duke University Press, 2015.

"U.S. FDA Approves Gilead's Truvada, a One-Tablet, Once-a-Day Fixed-Dose Co-Formulation of Viread and Emtriva as Part of HIV Combination Therapy." *Gilead Sciences, Inc.*, August 2, 2004, www.gilead.com/news/press-releases/2004/8/us-fda-approves-gileads-truvada-a-onetablet-onceaday-fixeddose-coformulation-of-viread-and-emtriva-as-part-of-hiv-combination-therapy.

"U.S. Food and Drug Administration Approves Expanded Indication for Truvada® (Emtricitabine and Tenofovir Disoproxil Fumarate) for Reducing the Risk of Acquiring HIV-1 in Adolescents." *Gilead Sciences, Inc.*, May 15, 2018, www.gilead.com/news/press-releases/2018/5/us-food-and-drug-administration-approves-expanded-indication-for-truvada-emtricitabine-and-tenofovir-disoproxil-fumarate-for-reducing-the-risk-of-acquiring-hiv1-in-adolescents.

"U.S. Food and Drug Administration Approves Gilead's Truvada® for Reducing the Risk of Acquiring HIV." *Gilead Sciences, Inc.*, July 16, 2012, www.gilead.com/news/press-releases/2012/7/us-food-and-drug-administration-approves-gileads-truvada-for-reducing-the-risk-of-acquiring-hiv.

White, Allen. "Reagan's AIDS Legacy / Silence Equals Death." *San Francisco Chronicle*, June 8, 2004, www.sfgate.com/opinion/openforum/article/Reagan-s-AIDS-Legacy-Silence-equals-death-2751030.php.

Worobey, Michael, T. D. Watts, R. A. McKay, M. A. Suchard, T. Granade, D. E. Teuwen, B. A. Koblin, W. Heneine, P. Lemey, and H. W. Jaffe. "1970s and 'Patient 0' HIV-1 Genomes Illuminate Early HIV/AIDS History in North America." *Nature*, vol. 539, no. 7627, 2016, pp. 98–101. doi:10.1038/nature19827.

Chapter Eleven

"We Should Be Embracing the Infected, the HIV-Positive, and Showering Them Not Only with Love, but with Medical Care and Psychosocial Services"

An Interview with Michael Broder

Jennifer J. Lavoie

In March of 2017, at the Northeast Modern Language Association Conference in Baltimore, Maryland, Michael Broder, Jennifer J. Lavoie, Aimee Pozorski, and Travis Alexander participated on a panel discussing representations of the HIV/AIDS crisis, past and present. Broder, Lavoie, and Pozorski had all mentioned the interview between Cathy Caruth, Douglas Crimp, Laura Pinsky, and Greg Bordowitz that Caruth published in her 1995 edited collection, *Trauma: Explorations in Memory*. Entitled "The AIDS Crisis Is Not Over," the earlier interview speaks to us today, over twenty years later (Caruth and Keenan). This interview, conducted during the summer of 2019, is an update and extension of that work.

EMAIL INTERVIEW WITH MICHAEL BRODER, JUNE 2019

Jennifer J. Lavoie: In her book *AIDS-Trauma and Politics: American Literature and the Search for a Witness* (2019), Aimee Pozorski suggests poetry is a practical form in which to address AIDS. As a poet who has written about HIV/AIDS, notably in your two poetry collections, *This Life Now* (2014) and

Drug and Disease Free (2016), what do you think makes poetry, as Pozorski says, so practical for writing about this topic?

Michael Broder: I don't know if I would say that poetry is any more practical a form in which to address HIV and AIDS than any other kind of writing, or, for that matter, than any other form of creative or artistic expression. Poetry is an art form among other art forms: the visual arts and the performing arts, painting, drawing, sculpture, music, dance, theatre, film, and other art forms that play along margins and across boundaries, any of which has an equal claim to addressing HIV and AIDS. I would not want there to be more poetry about AIDS if it meant there had to be less painting by David Wojnarawicz, less theatre by Tony Kushner, less film by Rosa Von Praunheim, less dance by Bill T. Jones, or less music by Queen, Erasure, Pet Shop Boys, Cyndi Lauper, or Madonna (just to mention a few musical artists whose work I feel to be intimately bound up with the AIDS crisis of the 1980s and 1990s, whether directly or obliquely).

That being said, I think that poetry has been a very *powerful* way to address HIV and AIDS, for the same reasons that poetry has great power in taking on any of a number of complex and highly fraught topics. Poetry is allowed to take flight and leave behind certain requisites of other literary forms, such as novels, plays, memoir, biography, and academic, scholarly, or popular nonfiction. Poetry need not worry too much about plot or narrative, characters and characterization, or even accurate facts. Poetry can play freely with (to borrow the four temperaments of poetry identified and elucidated by Gregory Orr) story, structure, music, and imagination. But I would not want to suggest that poetry is a free-for-all. It most certainly is not. Poetry needs coherence of vision—but that vision is free to be ecstatic, vatic, prophetic, allusive, or highly personal and naturalistic, depending on the needs of the poem and the sensibilities of the poet.

As for the very notion of practicality, well, I don't know of many writers or artists in any genre who think of their medium as practical, per se. Rather, I think writers and artists are compelled to make writing and art, and they are going to make it out of whatever content, subject matter, or experience is most meaningful to them. As artists and writers, we work with what we've got, and we make the most of it.

JL: As a scholar, how do you feel writing about HIV/AIDS has changed since the height of the AIDS crisis?

MB: Oh my. A couple of things I have to say about this before I answer the question. I'm okay with being called a scholar, but I think readers of this interview should know that I am not a full-time, practicing scholar; that is, I do not routinely do scholarly research or writing. I have a scholarly academic background. I studied comparative literature as an undergraduate at Columbia University from 1979 to 1983. I earned an MA in classics from the Graduate Center of the City University of New York (CUNY) in 1989. That was en route to a PhD in classics, but I quit that program in 1989, then earned an MFA in creative writing (poetry) at NYU in 2005, and then resumed the long-deferred doctorate in classics, which I completed in 2010. My dissertation was on queer kinship and camp aesthetics in Juvenal's ninth satire. I wrote a chapter called "The Most Obscene Satires: Scholarly Reception and a Queer/Camp Approach to Juvenal 2, 6, and 9" in a volume called *Ancient Obscenities* edited by Dorota Dutsch and Ann Suter. And I wrote an article called "Tradition vs. Reception as Models for Studying the Great Books" in *Classical World*. But that, and some paper presentations at conferences, is about it for my serious academic scholarship. These days, I am a freelance medical writer who also runs a nonprofit poetry press and writes a poem now and then when I'm not feeling overwhelmed, which is rare.

All of that being said, writing about HIV/AIDS has clearly changed since the height of the AIDS crisis, and I hasten to add that we are still at the height of the AIDS crisis, from a global perspective. When we refer to the AIDS crisis as something in the past, we are referring to the AIDS epidemic as it was experienced by primarily gay white men in the developed world in the 1980s and 1990s, particularly in the United States, and particularly in gay white population centers like New York, San Francisco, Los Angeles, Washington, DC, Chicago, Boston, Miami, and a number of other hardest-hit cities. That epidemic began to come under control in 1996 with the advent of effective treatments for HIV infection that could stop or slow disease progression, improve health, and extend life. That's when the nature of the epidemic changed from AIDS as a death sentence to HIV as a more or less chronic manageable condition (although still no walk in the park). But this change in the epidemic has a lot to do with who had access to quality health care, and that tended to be gay white men in wealthy countries, like the United States, the United Kingdom, and the European Union. In the developing world, and in particular in sub-Saharan Africa, the AIDS epidemic continued to rage virtually unabated for many more years. In recent years, great strides have been made in resource-poor countries. But AIDS is still a global health crisis that pushes public and private health systems to the brink. Even in the United States, the epidemic continues to ravage communities of color, particularly the African American community. So it is only with great caution that we should ever refer to the AIDS epidemic in the past tense.

And indeed, writing about HIV/AIDS has changed to reflect this new reality, the reality of a sexually transmitted viral disease that once was a uniform death sentence, but is now something that many people in many places can live with. We have also developed new approaches to HIV/AIDS prevention, including a pill you can take once a day to protect yourself from infection during sexual encounters (PrEP, which stands for "pre-exposure prophylaxis"), as well as a more population-based approach whereby we protect the uninfected by making sure that people with HIV are on medication that completely suppresses their virus, thereby rendering it virtually impossible for them to transmit the virus to a sexual partner (a strategy that has recently come to be called U=U, for "undetectable equals untransmittable"). Thus, much First World writing about HIV/AIDS today includes stories about long-term survival, as well as stories about the lingering shame and stigma that continue to attach to a medical condition that need no longer provoke such responses, but, sadly, does.

JL: While conducting my own research on AIDS narratives, one of the common themes was "bearing witness." In your experience, how has this changed since the 1980s? Does poetry allow the poet and readers alike to bear witness?

MB: Again, any art form can allow the bearing of witness, and this includes poetry, as well as film, dance, music, and the visual arts. But again, how it has changed since the 1980s lies in what we are bearing witness to. In the privileged white West, at least, we are for the most part bearing witness to survival. We are reflecting on the past, and on what it means to have lost so many, so quickly, so young, and to be among the survivors, the ones left behind—an odd formulation, really, as the dead are somewhere real and solid and three-dimensional, while we the living are caught in some kind of time and space apart from reality, a kind of survivor's limbo. I say these things mostly from the perspective of a writer; I'm not sure how poetry, or any other art form, functions in allowing readers or other consumers of art to bear witness. I suspect it does, but they would be the experts on the nature of that witness, not me. Ideally, I would think it has something to do with empathy. I'm not sure that empathy is the same thing as witness, but it does seem to be related. I think it also may matter whether you are a member of the affected community or not. That is, I think a survivor of trauma, reading poetry that addresses that trauma, has a sense of witness being born by the poet on their behalf. Whereas, if the reader is not a survivor of the particular kind of trauma addressed by the poetry, I think the reader can experience empathy, and maybe even be moved to some kind of action, but I feel that puts them more in the position of someone hearing testimony at a trial. The person on the witness stand is bearing testimony. The members of the jury, and the audience in the gallery, are hearing that testimony, and being moved by it, and may take action based on it, but they themselves are not bearing witness. They are, rather, consumers of the witness being born.

JL: You created the HIV Here & Now Project, which started as a yearlong countdown to thirty-five years since the beginning of AIDS. What led you to start this project, and what were your hopes for it?

MB: I was participating in an LGBTQ reading in Minneapolis during a major writers' conference in April 2015, and I noticed that a number of the gay male poets, particularly older gay male poets, including me, were reading poems about being long-term survivors of the AIDS epidemic, about being HIV-positive for a very long time, for decades in fact. And it occurred to me that this had never happened before. This was not Marie Howe writing about her brother who died of AIDS, or Mark Doty writing about his lover who died of AIDS, or any of the amazing poets in David Groff and Philip Clark's incredible anthology, *Persistent Voices*, who wrote about their own experience of AIDS and are now dead. No, this was something different. This was we, the poets who didn't die, the poets who lived. How amazing was that? What did that mean? What was that like? And that's when I decided to put together an anthology of poems by long-term survivors of HIV and AIDS. But by evening, I had decided I wanted much greater breadth—not just old fags like me living with HIV for twenty-five years, but twenty-two-year-old kids newly infected, or on PrEP, or not on PrEP and scared shit they're going to get infected any day now. People of all races, ages, sexes, genders, geographies, HIV statuses. So I got back to Brooklyn after the conference, and started getting out the call for submissions and doing a lot of direct, individual solicitations to as many of my poetry friends and acquaintances as I had or could find emails for or reach on Facebook. And some were down with it right away. But a lot of people didn't understand what I was talking about, and responded in ways that I found surprising. *That's not a topic I write about. That's not something that's part of my experience. I'm flattered, Michael, that you want to include me, but I don't have any relevant work.* So I wasn't really getting the kind of material I wanted. I got discouraged, even angry. Then I got the idea for the HIV Here & Now poem-a-day website. I thought it would give the project greater visibility, and maybe it could also model what the possibilities for a poetics of HIV and AIDS could be, whatever your relationship was to the disease and to the history of the epidemic. As it turns out, the print anthology is still a work in progress. On the website, we now do a poem-a-day series for National Poetry Month every year, and one from November 1 to December 1 as a run-up to World AIDS Day. I still want to produce the print anthology, maybe even in multiple volumes to better reflect the multivalent ways in which poets can relate to and respond to HIV and AIDS. If I wait just a bit longer, we can launch in connection with forty years of AIDS, rather than the original plan of launching in connection with thirty-five years of AIDS.

JL: According to Douglas Crimp in "'The AIDS Crisis Is Not Over': A Conversation with Gregg Bordowitz, Douglas Crimp, and Laura Pinsky," the trauma produced by AIDS, aside from the physical reality, is a "socially produced trauma" (Caruth and Keenan 257). Do you think this view still holds weight in today's society? Or has it changed somehow?

MB: It's a completely socially produced trauma, perhaps now more than ever. When that conversation took place, in 1991, there was still no durable, effective treatment for HIV infection. We had AZT, which is in fact a good drug; but in those days, due in part to its use at unnecessarily high doses, it was associated with devastating side effects that left people feeling the treatment was worse than the disease, and believing that AZT would kill them before AIDS did. Moreover, we had yet to discover that no one drug was going to stop HIV completely. Combination therapy was going to be needed, in particular, combinations of drugs in different classes that inhibited the viral replication process at different points in the viral life cycle. All of that was still five years away. So, with apologies for my wonkiness about HIV treatments, the reason I bring this up is that, back in 1991, we had trauma coming at us from many sides. We were falling sick to a mysterious illness for which there was no effective treatment, stopgap treatments at best, which could fend off a few bouts of one or more opportunistic infections, but let's face it, once you had Kaposi's sarcoma, or pneumocystis pneumonia, you knew the milk train wasn't stopping for you much longer. (Let me interrupt myself to clarify that I tested positive in 1990, so if at times I sound a bit cavalier about some of these realities, it's only gallows humor about my own gallows, albeit gallows that I was fortunate enough to escape. But my own survival was by far never a foregone conclusion. I was lucky AF). So there was the trauma of the mysterious and deadly medical condition itself. Then there was the shame, which I would say had a self-centered, psychological dimension, as well as an other-centered, sociological dimension—the self-centered, psychological shame out of which we asked ourselves: How did I let this happen? Why wasn't I more careful? What did I do to deserve this? And the other-centered sociological shaming, the stigmatization, out of which the noninfected and nonaffected pointed fingers at us and said: *You did something to deserve this, you should have been more careful, you should have known better, and now YOU are putting ME at risk, you the guilty ones are putting us innocent ones at risk.* All of that—the disease itself and the attendant shame and stigma, all were intensely traumatic experiences. And I say this shame and stigma are in some ways more pervasive and more pernicious now than they were then, precisely because there is so little reason for them. We know that HIV/AIDS is not confined to any one stigmatized group, but affects people of every demographic. We know that there are treatments and effective methods of prevention. We should be embracing the infected, the HIV-positive, and showering them not only with love, but with medical care and psychosocial services. This would in fact be the best, surest, most effective way to end the epidemic once and for all, for rich and poor, privileged and marginalized alike. And yet we do not do that. I like to say that HIV is not at all your problem, until that one fateful moment when it suddenly it is so totally your problem that it shapes and colors your entire life, your entire world. If only we could bridge that gap, that denial, that isolationism, we could live in a world not only much more compassionate, but much safer and healthier. But we don't. We are too invested in our own superiority. We need and want scapegoats; we need and want somebody to feel better than, someone to kick to the curb, someone to shove under the bus, in order to maintain our own illusions of safety, security, and strength.

JL: It is beyond unfortunate that, after all this time, we still haven't found a way to, as you say, "bridge that gap." In the same interview, Gregg Bordowitz discusses the representation of HIV-positive people on television, as well as the stigma attached to being openly positive in public (Caruth and Keenan 258–264). Do you think this stigma still exists today?

MB: The stigma of HIV most certainly persists today, and again, I think it may be worse in some respects than ever before. I did not know about this until after I started the HIV Here & Now Project. As I said above, some poets turned down my solicitations. I had never heard of such a thing. I know poets who wrote poems about elements on the periodic table so they could be featured on an episode of the popular public radio program, *Radio Lab*. Poets will write poems about anything if they think it will help them get their work read. I'd never known a poet to turn down a solicitation on the grounds that they did not usually write about that topic. Poets almost by definition can and do write about anything and everything. But when it came to HIV, many were hesitant, and no matter how much shit I take from poets for saying this, I believe that was an example of the stigmatization of HIV. These poets did not want to be guilty by association. They were afraid that if they wrote an "HIV poem" or an "AIDS poem," people would think they had HIV or AIDS, or at the very least, that they were gay. I don't think this happened back in the early 1990s, when poet Michael Klein was editing the groundbreaking anthology, *Poets for Life: Seventy-Six Poets Respond to AIDS* (1992). Seventy-six of the most illustrious names in poetry contributed to that volume, presumably without hesitation, but that was at a time when the creative community felt tremendous compassion for the thousands who were getting sick and dying of an untreatable and uncurable disease whose very cause was unknown just a few years earlier. Much of that compassion, I would argue, has now evaporated, precisely because of the strides we have made in reducing tremendously the number of new HIV infections annually.

It is much easier to blame the victim today than it was twenty-five or thirty years ago, when you could imagine that most people who were sick and dying had become infected before we even knew that an epidemic was in our midst, much less what caused it or how to prevent it. And now there are new levels and layers of stigmatization. We know you can prevent HIV by using condoms, so if you have HIV, you must be a slut who insists on bareback sex. Ironically, perhaps, there is also stigma around using PrEP for HIV prevention, because, by a similar logic, if you need to take a pill to reduce your chances of getting HIV, you must be a slut who cannot be bothered to use a condom. When it comes to HIV today, there is nothing you can do to avoid stigmatization, other than to project the impression that you have no sex at all, or if you do have sex, you have sex only with someone whose sexual purity you have thoroughly investigated and demonstrated, and you are in a strictly monogamous relationship with that person, who is also in a strictly monogamous relationship with you. Anything less, and you are a dirty slut who deserves what he gets. I know that sounds harsh, but I'm only calling what I see and hear.

JL: That actually ties in really well with my next question regarding education about HIV/AIDS. It struck me how Laura Pinsky argues that much of the time, when it comes to AIDS education, it assumes the reader is HIV-negative due to the language used (Caruth and Keenan 260). This interview took place in 1992. Do you think education has improved with regards to HIV/AIDS?

MB: Education around HIV/AIDS has definitely improved in the past twenty-five years. Particularly with regard to the issue you raised, about education being targeted at an assumed HIV-negative person, it's a whole new world, largely because the HIV treatment and prevention paradigm has shifted so dramatically in the past ten years. Of course, we still want to educate people who are HIV-negative, particularly if they are members of high-risk groups, and encourage them to access prevention services. But today, prevention means a lot more than condoms. It even means a lot more than PrEP. In fact, the best HIV prevention method is to move as many HIV-positive people as possible onto effective treatments that will make it impossible for them to infect an HIV-negative sexual partner. So now you get public service announcements that promote the idea not only of PrEP, but of U=U. These ads often show gay male couples, particularly younger ones, and particularly young gay men of color, because young gay men of color remain the group most vulnerable to HIV infection, for a number of socioeconomic and sociocultural reasons. The significance of the couple as the relevant unit is that, as I like to put it, my HIV *treatment* is my boyfriend's HIV *prevention* (except in my case it's actually husband, not boyfriend, but same point). So no longer are we talking to a single young gay male, alone in his room or standing on the periphery of some dance floor at a gay bar, fear and worry and anxiety etched into every line of his desperate face. We are talking to couples who are "safer together." We are talking about the possibility of romance and sexual adventure that no longer has to be equated with reckless abandon and irresponsible self-destruction—we are talking about good sexual choices, and no longer implying that sex in and of itself is a bad, dangerous, potentially life-threatening choice. And let me be completely honest: it doesn't hurt that Gilead Pharmaceuticals, the manufacturer of Truvada (the drug used as PrEP), now has an incentive to spend millions of dollars a year on HIV prevention education. It goes without saying that we live in a capitalist market economy, and the profit motive is never far from front and center. In the early 1990s, when I worked in medical communications, specializing in continuing medical education activities for physicians who treated people with HIV/AIDS or at risk for HIV infection, we were able to do the work we did because GlaxoSmithKline had every reason in the world to spend millions of dollars a year educating physicians on how to use the drugs in their ever-expanding HIV franchise. But once Glaxo began to have some very stiff competition from other drug companies, much of that money quickly shifted from educational spending to promotional spending: advertisements in medical journals, in consumer journals, in subways, on bus shelters, all with a slick visual and verbal iconography suggesting that, if you take our drugs, you will get up off your sickbed and go mountain climbing, with your boyfriend, of course, and you will both be tanned, muscular, and very well dressed. Fortunately, that bullshit no longer flies, for a lot of reasons, ranging from dedicated public servants at the federal Food and Drug Administration, to grassroots activists of whom the drug companies still remain very rightly wary (thank you, ACT UP).

JL: In *Humanwrites* (an interview series in *The Adroit Journal*, for which you were interviewed by Aidan Forster in 2015), you say that "the hardest hit group is young black gay men and transgender women." How can society effect change in this area to decrease the new rates of HIV infection?

MB: What I said about changes in HIV education above is relevant to this question as well. Part of the change we need is to talk directly to the at-risk populations in terms that respect their humanity, including respect for their race, ethnicity, gender identity, and sexual orientation. So in addition to the public service ads I mentioned, with the adorable young gay black and Latino couples, we also need (and may already have) ads that include black transgender women, and frankly, we also need to feature images of black transgender men, and black women assigned female at birth, because all of these groups are at elevated risk for HIV infection in the United States. It's simply another aspect of the racial industrial complex that treats black and brown bodies in this country as dispensable entities. Another tool we have for effecting the necessary change is the HIV care continuum. The HIV care continuum is a model that federal agencies use to track progress towards certain HIV treatment and prevention goals. It's related to the idea of U=U that I mentioned above. The care continuum is based on the idea that people with HIV or at risk for HIV go through a predictable series of steps: accessing prevention services and getting tested regularly if they are HIV-negative, and if they are HIV-positive, being linked to care, getting on treatment, staying on treatment, and achieving an undetectable viral load—a milestone that offers them a better prognosis and quality of life, while also protecting any HIV-negative sexual partners from infection. Now, models are fine, but in order for the model to help us achieve our goals as a society for HIV prevention and treatment, we need to put adequate financial and human resources into the services that provide the infrastructure for the HIV care continuum: health clinics, testing facilities, access to care, access to treatment, and psychosocial support services (housing, education, job training, substance abuse services, and other supportive services) that allow people with HIV or at risk for HIV to proceed successfully through the various stages of the continuum. President Obama in 2015 issued a National HIV/AIDS Strategy document that called for, among other things, increasing the proportion of people with HIV who know their status to at least 90 percent, increasing the proportion of newly diagnosed people linked to medical care within one month of HIV diagnosis to at least 85 percent, increasing the proportion of people with HIV who are virally suppressed to at least 80 percent, and more. Achieving these objectives would go a long way to reducing the rate and the number of new HIV infections among the most vulnerable populations. Unfortunately, I despair of our attaining anything even remotely resembling these goals while our nation continues its current slide into white supremacist ethno-nationalism.

JL: I'm glad you mentioned President Obama and his objectives. Unfortunately, I need now to ask your thoughts about our current state of affairs. With consideration of the current political climate under the Trump administration in the United States, how has HIV/AIDS outreach changed in recent years? Where do we need to go from here?

MB: Trump made a bold proposal in his State of the Union address in 2019 to end new HIV infections in the United States by 2030. Meanwhile, for the past two years, he has zealously gone about rolling back fundamental human rights, civil rights, and healthcare protections for the queer community that includes those most at risk for HIV infection. In November 2018, the Trump administration proposed a rule change that would make it harder for people on Medicare to get coverage for their HIV drugs. Trump has repeatedly asked Congress to repeal Medicaid expansion under the Affordable Care Act, despite the fact that Medicaid is the most important source of access to healthcare for people with HIV. Trump has also tried to foist short-term healthcare plans on the American public—plans that eschew many of the protections of the Affordable Care Act—even though such plans usually don't allow coverage for people with HIV. While federal health officials rightly insist that ending HIV requires reducing the stigmatization of gay people and trans people, so they will be more willing to access testing and treatment services, the Trump administration has spent years now doing its best to roll back protections for gay and transgender people. In 2018, the Trump administration announced plans to roll back a rule issued by the Obama administration that prevents doctors, hospitals, and health insurance companies from discriminating against transgender people. In addition, the Trump Justice Department maintains that an existing civil rights law banning job discrimination based on sex does not protect people who face discrimination based on being lesbian, gay, or transgender. Meanwhile, even as Trump claims he wants to "win" HIV, he is still sowing division. His proposed plan would focus on forty-eight counties in the United States where about 50 percent of new HIV infections occur, saying nothing about how it will address the other 50 percent. I mean, correct me if I'm wrong, but I think, to eliminate HIV, you need to eliminate 100 percent of new infections, not just 50 percent. Meanwhile, eighteen of the forty-eight counties are in states that have yet to expand Medicaid: Florida, Georgia, North Carolina, Tennessee, and Texas. How does he propose to eliminate new HIV infections without the benefit of Medicaid coverage for the people most at risk of HIV infection? Trump's plan envisions a tremendous scaling up of PrEP to achieve his goal of eliminating new HIV transmissions, but who is going to pay for PrEP for people without insurance?

So much for Trump. I wouldn't hold my breath for any breakthroughs in HIV/AIDS policy while he is in the White House. In fact, I would not be surprised if we began to lose ground in areas where we had begun to make progress under previous presidential administrations.

As for where we need to go from here, I would say just look at what Trump is doing, or proposing to do, and we need to be doing the exact opposite. We need to be expanding protections in housing, employment, and healthcare for queer people. We need to be expanding access to Medicaid under the Affordable Care Act in the states that have so far chosen not to do so. We need to maintain and expand protections for people with HIV in healthcare and immigration, not gut them. And so on. Trump says he wants to expand Ryan White funding to the CDC [Centers for Disease Control and Prevention] to pay for his plan to end HIV by 2030. But good luck on that in an environment where there is so much rancor and so little comity in Congress that it looks like we are not even going to be able to fix a pothole while Trump is in the White House, let alone end HIV.

WORKS CITED

Broder, Michael. *Drug and Disease Free.* Indolent Books, 2016.
———. Interview by Aidan Forster. "Humanwrites: Interview with Michael Broder, Founder of HIV Here and Now." *The Adroit Journal,* October 13, 2015, theadroitjournal.org/2015/10/13/humanwrites-interview-with-michael-broder-founder-of-hiv-here-and-now. Accessed June 29, 2019.
———. *Mensura Incognita: Queer Kinship, Camp Aesthetics, and Juvenal's Ninth Satire.* 2010. The Graduate Center of the City University of New York, PhD dissertation.
———. "The Most Obscene Satires: A Queer/Camp Approach to Juvenal 2, 6, and 9." *Ancient Obscenities: Their Nature and Use in the Ancient Greek and Roman Worlds,* edited by Dorota Dutsch and Ann Suter. University of Michigan Press, 2015, pp. 283–309.
———. *This Life Now.* A Midsummer Night's Press, 2014.
———. "Tradition vs. Reception as Models for Studying the Great Books." *Classical World,* vol. 106, no. 3, 2013, pp. 505–515.
Caruth, Cathy, and Thomas Keenan. "'The AIDS Crisis Is Not Over': A Conversation with Gregg Bordowitz, Douglas Crimp, and Laura Pinsky." *Trauma: Explorations in Memory,* edited by Cathy Caruth. Johns Hopkins University Press, 1995, pp. 256–271.
Clark, Philip, and David Groff. *Persistent Voices.* Alyson Books, 2010.
Klein, Michael. *Poets for Life: Seventy-Six Poets Respond to AIDS.* George Braziller, 1992.
Orr, Gregory. "Four Temperaments and the Forms of Poetry." *The American Poetry Review* vol. 17, no. 5, 1988, pp. 33–36.
Pear, Robert. "Talk of Ending H.I.V., but Actions Aren't Helping." *The New York Times,* New York ed., February 13, 2019. www.nytimes.com/2019/02/12/us/politics/trump-hiv-plan.html. Accessed June 29, 2019.
Pozorski, Aimee. *AIDS-Trauma and Politics: American Literature and the Search for a Witness.* Lexington Books, 2019.
The White House. *National HIV/AIDS Strategy for the United States: Updated to 2020.* Federal Action Plan. December 2015. www.hiv.gov/sites/default/files/nhas-2020-action-plan.pdf. Accessed on June 29, 2019.
———. *Remarks by President Trump in State of the Union Address.* Delivered 5 Feb. 2019. Issued 6 Feb. 2019. www.whitehouse.gov/briefings-statements/remarks-president-trump-state-union-address-2. Accessed June 29, 2019.

Index

ACT UP, 1, 3, 10n1, 10n2, 11, 68, 69, 160, 170
"ACT UP, Haitian Migrants, and Alternative Memories of HIV/AIDS," 10n2
ACT UP New York: Activism, Art, and the AIDS Crisis, 1987-1993, 10n1
Adelson, Naomi, 123
The Adroit Journal, 171, 174
"The Aesthetics of Rage and Civility in Poetry about AIDS," 36, 41
After Silence, 10n2
"Against Transcendence: AIDS and the Elegy," 36
Agamben, Giorgio, 109, 110, 111, 122, 123
AIDS and Its Metaphors, 28, 32, 41, 46, 59, 103
"AIDS as Metaphor," 32, 41
AIDS: Cultural Analysis, Cultural Activism, 3, 33
The AIDS Epidemic: Private Rights and the Public Interest, 3
"AIDS, Memory, and Desire," 63, 75
AIDS: The Literary Response, 4, 36, 41
"AIDS to Remembrance: The Uses of Elegy," 36
"AIDS Writing and the Creation of a Gay Culture," 46, 59
Alexander, Travis, vii, 163
Almond, Marc, 37

Altman, Lawrence K., 14, 27, 160
American Comparative Literature Association, vii, 2
Angels in America, 10n1
Anoh, Amoakon, 110, 121n3, 122
Apostrophes, 77, 85n5, 87
Armstrong, Walter, 62
Art AIDS America, 10n1, 11
As Is, 4
Assmann, Aleida, 5, 11, 13, 14, 26, 27
Atlantis, 50, 59
"Au nom d'amour," 106, 115, 116, 117, 119, 122
Ayé, Jean-Pierre, 111, 122

Bayer, Ronald, 108, 122
Bay Windows, 41
Beall, Reed, 122
Before Pictures, 10n2
Bekelynck, Anne, 119, 122
Bell, Chris, 147, 160
Bergman, David, 43, 50, 59
Berlant, Lauren, 37, 41
Bersani, Leo, 4, 11, 47, 59
"Between Two Deaths: AIDS, Trauma, and Temporality in the Work of Paul Monette," 4
BFM TV, 121n2, 122
Bishop, Elizabeth, 37
Bishop, Michael, 58
The Blue Star, 50, 59

Boddy, Janice, 111, 122
Body Counts, 6, 61, 62, 67, 69, 70, 71, 74, 75, 76
Bogart, Laura M., 126, 141
Borgman, C. F., 58
Borderlands: Texas Poetry Review, 36, 41
Bordowitz, Greg, 9, 163, 168, 169, 174
Borger, Irene, 40
Borrowed Time, 6, 46, 61, 63, 64, 65, 67, 69, 70, 71, 74, 76
"Borrowing Time: Writing and Resisting Viral Narratives in Novels about AIDS," 63, 76
Boucheron, Robert, 39
Boulé, Jean-Pierre, 81, 82, 83, 85n7, 86, 86n22
Bram, Christopher, 58
Branigan, Tania, 101, 103
Brault, Isabel, 109, 110, 123, 124
Broder, Michael, vii, 9, 163, 164, 174
Bronski, Michael, 48, 59
Brooks, Franklin, 58, 59
Bryan, Jed A., 58
Buchanan, Pat, 159n1
Bull, Chris, 27
Butters, Ronald R., 3, 11

Cabezas, Amalia, 114, 124
Cady, Joseph, 34, 35, 41
Callen, Michael, 68, 74, 156, 160n13
Campbell, Alyson, 20, 27
Campo, Rafael, 40
Camus, 97
"Ça n'arrive qu'aux autres," 106
Candide, 51
Capitanio, John P., 129, 142
Carlomusto, Jean, 8, 126, 135, 136, 141
Carlson, Marvin, 26, 27
Caron, David, 6, 61, 63, 70, 71, 72, 73, 74, 75
Cartwright, Lisa, 10n2
Caruth, Cathy, 9, 163, 164, 165, 174
Castiglia, Christopher, 10n2
Centers for Disease Control (CDC), 8, 9, 11, 11n3, 108, 122, 127, 128, 129, 130, 131, 133, 136, 141, 142, 145, 147, 159n7, 160
Center for Reproductive Rights, 121n4, 122

Champagne, John, 58
Chauke, Collen, 138
Chávez, Karma, 10n2
Chesley, Robert, 5, 14, 20, 21, 22, 23, 24, 25, 26, 27, 27n1, 28
The Children's Hour, 23, 28
Christopher Street, 41
Chronicle of a Blood Merchant, 91
Chronicle of Higher Education, 32, 41
Ciscel, Dennis, 10, 11, 39
Citroner, George, 152, 160
Claire, Thomas, 39
Clark, Philip, 167, 174
Clum, John M., 3, 15, 16, 17, 20, 23, 28, 63, 75
Le Code Pénal, 110, 121n4, 123
Cohen, Cathy J., 130, 131, 136, 142
Cohler, Bertram, 61, 75
Cole, Catherine M., 124
The Compassion Protocol, 78, 83, 85n6, 85n7, 86
Conrad, Ryan, 10n2, 11
Connor, E. M., 106, 122
Cook, Rebecca J., 123
Cosmopolitan, 135, 136
Crimp, Douglas, 3, 4, 10n2, 11, 32, 33, 41, 159n3, 159n11, 160, 163, 168, 174
Cruel Optimism, 37, 41
Cruising Utopia: The Then and There of Queer Futurity, 37, 41
Cruising, 22, 28
"Current Status 1/22/87," 35
Cultural Memory and Western Civilization: Arts of Memory, 11
"Cultural Studies and its Theoretical Legacies," 4, 11
Cultural Studies Review, 70
Curno, Miriam J., 132, 142
Cytomegalovirus, 78, 86

Dallas Buyers Club, 10n1
The Darker Proof: Stories from a Crisis, 58n1
Darrieussecq, Marie, 79, 86
Davis, Christopher, 43, 50, 58, 59
A Deeper Dive, 10n1
Déniaud, François, 120, 123
Deng Hanmei, 103, 103n5
Deng Xiaoping, 95

de Jongh, Nicholas, 15, 16, 28
Denneny, Michael, 46, 59
Dent, Tony, 39
Desgrées du Loû, Annabel, 112, 123
Deutscher, Penelope, 109, 110, 111, 123
Devine, Patricia G., 129, 142
Diaman, N. A., 58
DiAna, 136, 137, 139
DiAna's Hair Ego, 8, 126, 135, 136, 142
Diedrich, Lisa, 4, 62, 64, 75
Displacing Homophobia: Gay Male Perspectives in Literature and Culture, 3, 11
Doctors, Liars, and Women, 8, 126, 135, 139, 141
Dollimore, Jonathan, 22, 28
Donoso, José, 49
Don't Call Us Dead, 38, 41
Doty, Mark, 39, 167
Dream of Ding Village, 7, 89, 90, 91, 92, 94, 95, 96, 97, 101, 103
Dugas, Gaëtan, 159n11
Dunne, Dominick, 58
Duran, David, 148, 159n5, 160
Dutsch, Dorota, 164, 174

Edelman, Lee, 3, 4, 11, 47, 139, 141, 142
editorial board, 159n7, 160
Egelhoff, Andy, 8, 9, 146, 147, 153, 154, 155, 156, 157, 160
Ehoura, Awa, 123
Eisner, Douglas, 61, 76
Epstein, Steven, 132, 142
Erasure, 164
Ermo, 91
Esposito, Roberto, 95
"Estimated HIV Prevalence," 132, 142
The Evergreen Chronicles, 41
"Fact Sheet—Latest Statistics on the Status of the AIDS Epidemic," 11n3

Faggots, 21, 22, 28
Falwell, Jerry, 159n1
The Family of Max Desir, 50, 59
Fang Fang, 93, 103
Fan Jiayang, 90, 98, 103
Fast, Howard, 58
Feinberg, David B., 35

Ferro, Robert, 6, 43, 44, 45, 48, 49, 50, 51, 52, 53, 54, 55, 56, 57, 58, 58n3, 58n4, 58n5, 59
Finkelstein, Avram, 10n2, 11
Fish, Stanley, 45, 59
Food and Drug Administration (FDA), 8, 30, 31, 66, 114, 128, 145, 147, 161, 170
Forster, Aidan, 171, 174
Forty Years Later, 30
Foucault, Michel, 78, 90, 91, 94, 95, 103, 109, 123
France, David, 145, 160
Fraternité Matin, 111
French Studies, 70
Fries, Kenny, 39

Gao Yaojie, 7, 91, 96, 103
Garmire, Lisa, 63, 64, 76
Gay Sex in the 70s, 22, 28
Genon, Arnaud, 85n1, 86
The Gentrification of the Mind, 10n2, 12
Les gestes ou la vie, 7, 105, 106, 108, 115, 118, 120, 121, 122, 123, 124
Ghost Letters, 29, 40
Gilead Sciences, 8, 147, 153, 159n7, 160, 161, 170
Gindt, Dirk, 20, 27
GlaxoSmithKline, 170
Glazek, Christopher, 149, 160
GLQ, 11, 150, 161
Gottlieb, M. S., 63, 160
Gould, Deborah, 10n2, 11, 145, 160
Gould, Robert, 135, 136
Gran Fury: Read My Lips, 10n1
Granta, 58n1
Greyson, John, 146, 155, 156, 157, 160
Groff, David, 167, 174
Grumley, Michael, 50, 58n3, 59
Guibert, Hervé, 6, 77, 78, 79, 80, 81, 82, 83, 84, 85n1–85n7, 85n10–86n26, 86–87, 185
Guillaume, Agnes, 112, 123
Gunn, Thom, 36, 39, 41

Haas, Astrid, 20, 28
Hadas, Rachel, 40
Hall, Stuart, 4, 11
Hall, Tom, 15, 28
Hamilton, Patrick, 23

Hanefeld, Johanna, 122n7, 123
Hard as Water, 97
Harding, Sandra, 127, 142
Harold, John, 40
The Haunted Stage, 26, 27
Hellman, Lillian, 23, 28
Helms, Jesse, 24
Hemphill, Essex, 40
The Henry J. Kaiser Family Foundation, 11, 11n3
Herek, Gregory M., 125, 129
Herkt, David, 70
Hervé Guibert: Voices of the Self, 81, 85n7, 86
Hilderbrand, Lucas, 10n2, 11
Highleyman, Liz, 148, 149, 160
Hitchcock, Alfred, 23
"HIV among African Americans," 11n3
"HIV and African Americans," 131, 142
"HIV at 30: A Public Opinion Perspective," 11n3
HIV Here & Now Project, 167
Hoctel, Patrick, 43, 48, 59
Holland, Walter, 39
Holleran, Andrew, 35, 46, 59
Horowitz, Roger, 34, 35, 37, 41, 61, 63, 64, 65, 66, 67, 68, 69, 71, 72, 73, 74
Houphouët-Boigny, Félix, 106
Howe, Marie, 167
How to Have Theory in an Epidemic: Cultural Chronicles of AIDS, 33
How to Survive a Plague, 10n1
Humanwrites, 171, 174
Hunter, B. Michael, 40
Hunt, Nancy Rose, 111, 123
Hushka, Rock, 11

If Memory Serves, 10n2
Illness as Metaphor, 32
Illness as Narrative, 62, 76
Incognito, 6, 77, 78, 79, 81, 82, 83, 84, 85n7, 85n8, 86
Indiana Review, 36, 41
The Inheritance, 16, 28
"Introduction," 10
Inventing AIDS, 33
"Is the Rectum a Grave?," 4, 11, 59
Ivoire Dimanche, 112, 123

The James White Review, 41
Jarraway, David, 61, 76
Jerker, 5, 22, 25, 27
John, 37
Johnson, Greg, 39
Jones, Bill T., 164
Jones, James W., 47
Jurecic, Ann, 62, 76
Juvenal, 164, 174

Kagan, Dion, 18
Kalichman, Seth C., 126, 142
Katz, Jonathan David, 11
Kaufmann, Vincent, 85n7, 87
Kaufman, Sharon R., 145, 160
Keenan, Thomas, 9, 174
Keller, Evelyn Fox, 127, 134, 142
Kikel, Rudy, 39
Kim, Hye Jin, 149, 161
Klein, Michael, 40, 169, 174
Klonoff, Elizabeth A., 138, 142
Knoppers, Bartha Maria, 109, 110, 123, 124
Kramer, Larry, 4, 5, 10n1, 13, 14, 17, 18, 20, 21, 22, 24, 25, 27, 28, 59
Kuhn, Randall, 122, 122n7
Kushner, Tony, 164

La Bible de Jérusalem, 123
"Lament," 36

Landrine, Hope L., 138, 142
"Landscape," 93, 103
Lassell, Michael, 39
Lauper, Cyndi, 164
Lauretis, Teresa de, 49, 59
Lavoie, Jennifer J., 30
Larry Kramer in Love and Anger, 10n1
"Learning from Philadelphia," 10n2
Lenin's Kisses, 102n1, 103
Levine, Martin P., 159n10, 160
Library Journal, 70
Lopez, Matthew, 16, 28
Love Alone: Eighteen Elegies for Rog, 34, 37
Lubeck, Sally, 140, 142
Luff, Tema, 135
Lupton, Deborah, 129, 130, 142
Lynch, Michael, 39

MacDonald, Jr., John W., 37
Madden, Ed, 36, 37, 41
Madonna, 164
Mae West is Dead, 58n1
Magogodi, Kgafela oa, 8, 126, 135, 137, 138, 142
The Man in the Red Hat, 6, 77, 78, 83, 84, 85n7, 86
Masoso, Agnès Kraide, 112, 121n5, 123
Mars-Jones, Adam, 44, 45, 58n1, 59
Mayes, Susan, 58
McBain, Ed, 58
McCann, Richard, 29, 40, 41
McClintock, Anne, 115, 123
McCray, Eugene, 159n2, 160
McMillen, Liz, 32, 41
McRuer, Robert, 149, 151, 154, 160
Mermin, Jonathan H., 159n2, 160
Meyer, Ilan H., 130, 143
Micklowitz, Gloria D., 58
Mikell, Gwendolyn, 111, 123, 124
Miller, Andrew, 40
Miller, Tim, 15
"The Mirror and the Tank: 'AIDS,' Subjectivity, and the Rhetoric of Activism," 4, 11
Misove, Michael, 69
Mitchell, Larry, 58
Monette, Paul, 4, 6, 34, 35, 36, 37, 39, 40, 41, 46, 59, 61, 62, 63, 64, 65, 66, 67, 68, 69, 71, 72, 73, 74, 75, 76
"Mon nom est 'la vie,'" 106
Moon, Michael, 3
Morbidity and Mortality Weekly Report, 122, 130
Moving Politics, 10n2
Msellati, Philippe, 114, 123
Muñoz, José Esteban, 37, 41
Murphy, Tim, 159n12, 160
Murphy, Timothy, 4, 11, 41, 58, 59, 103

NAMES Project AIDS Quilt, 4
National Institutes of Health (NIH), 127, 133
The Nearness of Others, 6, 61, 70, 71, 74, 75
Nelson, Emmanuel S., 4, 11, 41
New England Journal of Public Policy, 3
Newman, Lesléa, 40

New York Times, 14, 18, 104, 145, 159n7, 160, 174
Nguyen, Vinh-Kim, 122n7, 123
Ngwena, Charles G., 121n4, 123
"Nights of 1990," 29
Night Sweat, 5, 22, 23, 24, 25, 27n1, 28
The Normal Heart, 4, 5, 10n1, 13, 14, 16, 17, 18, 19, 20, 21, 22, 23, 24, 25, 26, 27, 28
Northeast Modern Language Association, vii, 2, 163

Obama, Barack, 61, 171, 172
October, 3, 11, 33, 160
O'Malley, Padraig, 3, 11
O'Manique, Colleen, 124
"One Art," 37
Orr, Gregory, 31, 41, 164, 174
The Others, 50, 59

Pastore, Judith Laurence, 59
Patton, Cindy, 32, 33, 41, 125, 126, 130, 133, 134, 140, 142, 148, 149, 159n4, 160, 161
Pear, Robert, 174
Persistent Voices, 167, 174
Persons of Interest, 10n1
Peters, Anny J. T. P., 132, 142
Peter Wall Institute of Advanced Studies, 4
Pet Shop Boys, 164
Picano, Felice, 61
Pinckney, Tim, 16, 28
Pinsky, Laura, 9, 163, 168, 170, 174
Pivot, Bernard, 87
The Plague, 97
"The Plague of Discourse: Politics, Literary Theory, and AIDS," 3
Pleasure, 89, 101
Poets for Life: Seventy-Six Poets Respond to AIDS, 169, 174
Poirier, Suzanne, 4, 11, 41, 58, 59, 96, 103
Policing Desire, 14, 28
Pozorski, Aimee, 163, 174
Prevention: Gender, Sexuality, HIV, and the Media in Côte d'Ivoire, 121
Puar, Jasbir K., 150, 151, 154, 161
Puccia, Joseph, 58

Queen, 164

Radio Lab, 169
Raoul, Valerie, 4, 11
"Raisons de la peur," 7, 105, 106, 107, 108, 113, 114, 115, 124
Reagan, Ronald, 30, 61, 65, 159n1, 161
Rebels Rebel , 10n2
Redick, Alison, 19, 28
Redon, Joel, 58
Reed, Christopher, 10n2
Reed, Jeremy, 39
Reed, Paul, 58
"Refusing the Name: The Absence of AIDS in Recent American Gay Male Fiction," 47, 59
"Retroactivism," 10n2
"Revisiting AIDS and Its Metaphors," 10n2
Rodríguez, Juana María, 157, 161
Rojas, Carlos, 91, 94, 102n1, 103, 103n4, 104
Román, David, 20, 28
Rope, 23
Rose, Nikolas, 150
Rosenthal, Doreen, 139, 142
Rubin, Gayle S., 159n8, 161
Rubin, Martin, 58

Savage, Dan, 150
Schildcrout, Jordan, 23, 24, 28
Schulman, Sarah, 10n2, 12
Schreiber, Ron, 37, 39, 41
Second Son, 6, 43, 45, 48, 50, 51, 52, 53, 55, 56, 57, 58, 58n4
Shilts, Randy, 159n11, 159n12
A Short History of Truvada, 8, 146, 147, 160
Simbayi, L. C., 126, 142
Sinfield, Alan, 15, 20, 28
Singer, Linda, 113, 115, 124
Sepretta, Tommaso, 10n2, 12
"Slim," 44, 58n1
Smith, Danez, 38, 41
Sontag, Susan, 14, 28, 32, 41, 46, 47, 58n2, 59, 63, 96, 103
Spade, Dean, 147, 161
Spiro, Ellen, 8, 126, 142
SPRKLBB, 8, 153
Stambolian, George, 59
Stepan, Jan, 111, 124

Stevenson, Robert Louis, 22, 23, 28
Still at Risk, 16, 28
Stonewall, 16
Stray Dog Story, 5, 21, 22
Streams of Light, 89, 101, 104
A Streetcar Named Desire, 23
Strong, Beret E., 36, 41
Strub, Sean, 6, 61, 63, 67, 68, 69, 70, 71, 72, 73, 74, 75, 76
Sturken, Marita, 19, 20, 27, 28
The Suicide Club, 22, 28
Susser, Ida, 132, 142
Suter, Ann, 164, 174
Swadener, Beth Blue, 140, 142

Taking Liberties: AIDS and Cultural Politics, 33
Test, 10n1
Thomas, Lynn M., 111, 124
Thonneau, P., 114, 124
Thy Condom Come, 8
Tiny Stories, 10, 11, 39
To the Friend Who Did Not Save My Life , 77, 78, 81, 82, 83, 85n3, 85n5, 85n6, 85n7, 87
Toungara, Jeanne M., 115, 124
Touré, Kitia, 7, 105, 108, 118, 120, 122, 122n8, 122n9, 123, 124
Treichler, Paula A., 32, 33, 41, 130, 132, 133, 135, 142
Trump, Donald, 9, 160, 172, 173, 174
Truvada, 8, 9, 147, 148, 149, 151, 152, 153, 154, 155, 156, 160, 161, 170
Tsai, Chien-hsin, 98, 101, 103
Turnbull, Peter, 58

UNAIDS, 11n3, 12, 121n6, 122n7, 124
Uncle Howard, 10n1
UNESCO, 124
Unfitting Stories: Narrative Approaches to Disease, Disability, and Trauma, 4
UN IGME, 113, 124
United in Anger, 10n1
Useche, Bernardo, 114, 124

Valley of the Shadow, 43, 50, 58, 59
"Varara," 126, 137, 142
Veil, Simone, 121n2, 122
The Violet Quill, 46, 49, 58n4, 59

Voltaire, 51
Visser, Dirk, 159n9
Vito, 10n1
Von Praunheim, Rosa, 164

Waldby, Catherine, 130, 142
Wang Jinping, 103, 103n3
Watney, Simon, 14, 28, 32, 33, 34, 35, 41
Watts, Jonathan, 101, 103
Wendland, Claire L., 122n7, 124
We Were Here, 10n1
When We Rise, 10n1
White, Allen, 159n1, 161
White, Edmund, 35, 59
The White House, 173, 174
White, Ryan, 55, 59n7, 173
Whitehead, Bill, 50
Why We Fight: Remembering AIDS Activism, 10n1
Williams, Tennessee, 23
"'Without us all told': Paul Monette's Vigilant Witnessing to the AIDS Crisis," 62, 75
Wojnarawicz, David, 164
Wolfe, Tom, 58
Woods, Gregory, 36, 37, 41
Woolverton, Terry, 39
World Health Organization, 105, 107, 114, 124, 132
Worobey, Michael, 159n11, 161
Writing AIDS: Gay Literature, Language, and Analysis, 4, 11, 34, 58, 59, 103

Yang Jisheng, 103n2, 104
Yan Lianke, 7, 89, 90, 91, 93, 96, 97, 98, 100, 101, 102n1, 103, 103–104, 104
Young, Rebecca M., 130, 143
Yuan Weijing, 89, 104
Yu Hua, 91, 104

Zedong, Mao, 94
Zero Patience, 8, 9, 146, 153, 155, 156, 157, 158, 159n9, 160
Zhou Xiaowen, 91, 103

About the Contributors

Michael Broder holds a doctorate in classics from the Graduate Center of the City University of New York, an MFA in creative writing from New York University, and a BA in comparative literature from Columbia University. Michael has taught classics and comparative literature at the University of South Carolina, Montclair State University, and within the City University of New York at Brooklyn College, Hunter College, York College, Queens College, and the Graduate Center. He is the author of the poetry collections *Drug and Disease Free* and *This Life Now*, which was a finalist for the 2015 Lambda Literary Award for Gay Poetry. His poems have appeared in numerous journals and anthologies. Michael is the founding publisher of Indolent Books and the creator of the HIV Here & Now Project.

Ryan Calabretta-Sajder is currently a visiting assistant professor of Italian at the University of Arkansas, Fayetteville, where he teaches courses in Italian, film, and gender studies. He is the author of *Divergenze in celluloide: colore, migrazione e identità sessuale nei film gay di Ferzan Ozpetek* (*Celluloid Divergences: Color, Migration, and Sexual Identity in the Gay Series of Ferzan Ozpetek*) with Mimesis editore and editor of the collection of essays, *Pasolini's Lasting Impressions: Death, Eros, and Literary Enterprise in the Opus of Pier Paolo Pasolini* with Fairleigh Dickinson University Press (2018). His research interests include the integration of gender, class, and migration in both Italian and Italian American literature and cinema. He has recently been awarded one of four Fulbright Awards for the Foundation of the South to conduct research and teach at the University of Calabria, Arcavacata, for the spring of 2017. His next research project examines the visual, semiotic, and affect foodways provoked in Italian and Italian American cinema.

About the Contributors

Shelley W. Chan is professor of Chinese language and cultural studies at Wittenberg University. She earned her PhD from University of Colorado-Boulder, her MA from University of Wisconsin-Madison, and her BA from Hong Kong Baptist University. She is the author of *A Subversive Voice in China: The Fictional World of Mo Yan* (New York: Cambria Press, 2011), and the editor of *Mo Yan—Year 2000 Series: Close Readings on China* (Hong Kong: Ming Pao, 1999). Her articles, translations, and book/film reviews on Chinese literature and culture have appeared in the United States, France, Germany, Australia, Sweden, China, Hong Kong, and Taiwan.

Christine J. Cynn is an associate professor at Virginia Commonwealth University where she is completing a book manuscript on HIV prevention media in Côte d'Ivoire. She has published a number of articles on Francophone HIV prevention media and on US representations of Chinese immigrants as sexually deviant sources of contamination. She has been a Fulbright scholar/researcher in Abidjan, Côte d'Ivoire, and an Andrew W. Mellon postdoctoral fellow at Barnard College in New York. Her interest in video extends to production—she has co-produced, produced, directed, and edited documentary and prevention videos.

Andy Eicher is a PhD student in women's, gender, and sexuality studies at Stony Brook University. Broadly speaking, his research is interested in a critical examination of HIV/AIDS through the lenses of queer and feminist theory, critical disability studies, and crip theory. His project aims to contextualize this examination in the broader context of the "neoliberalization" of healthcare.

Nels P. Highberg is an associate professor of English and modern languages at the University of Hartford. He was the university's Distinguished Teaching Humanist for 2016–2018 and a former director of the Program in Gender Studies. His academic work has appeared in *Feminist Formations*, *Feminist Teacher*, *Performing Ethos*, *Medical Humanities Review*, and other places. His creative essays have appeared in *Concho River Review* and *Riding Light Review*. His essay, "Waiting," about the experience of waiting two weeks to learn the results of an HIV test, which was standard in the early 1990s, was nominated for a 2016 Pushcart Prize.

Jennifer J. Lavoie is an English teacher and young adult author living in Connecticut. She currently teaches ESL to students in China through an online platform while attending Central Connecticut State University for an MA in literature. Her previously published young adult titles include *Andy Squared* and *The First Twenty*, which feature LGBT themes and characters.

Mariarosa Loddo studied comparative literature at the University of Eastern Piedmont (Vercelli, Italy), where she is currently working on illness narratives for her PhD thesis. Her research interests include Hervé Guibert's work, narrative medicine, ethical aspects in illness memoirs, representations of the suffering body, and conceptualization of death. She has published and attended several seminars; she is also member of the editorial board of *Enthymema*, international journal of literary criticism, literary theory, and philosophy of literature.

Alison Patev is a doctoral student in the health psychology program at Virginia Commonwealth University. She received her BA in psychology from Stonehill College in 2013, and her MS in experimental psychology from Mississippi State University in 2015. Currently, Ms. Patev's research interests focus on gender inequity. She has completed projects that explore gender-inclusive language, attitudes toward transgender or gender nonconforming individuals, women's reproductive healthcare, and abortion knowledge. She is currently creating a program designed to promote gender equity among young adults. Ms. Patev has also completed work on sexual health and STI and HIV prevention. She has worked with her mentor, Kristina Hood, to conduct intervention sessions that promote condom use, condom use discussions, and regular STI and HIV testing among young African American women. This work aims to improve the sexual health of women in their community, and reduce high rates of new HIV infection among young African American women.

Aimee Pozorski is professor of English and director of English graduate studies at Central Connecticut State University. She is author of *Roth and Trauma: The Problem of History in the Later Works* (2011) and *Falling after 9/11: Crisis in American Art and Literature* (2014). She has edited *Roth and Celebrity* (2012), the Critical Insights edition of *Philip Roth* (2013), and co-edited, with David Gooblar, *Roth after 80: Philip Roth and the American Literary Imagination* (2016). She co-edited, with Maren Scheurer, the spring 2017 special issue of *Philip Roth Studies* entitled "Philip Roth's Transdisciplinary Translation," which focused on Roth's international appeal as an ethical writer. She was president of the Philip Roth Society from 2009–2015. Her current research focuses on AIDS, trauma, and politics in contemporary American literature.

Dirk Visser studied English language and literature at the University of Groningen, the Netherlands. Following an extensive teaching career, he is currently a PhD candidate at Vrije Universiteit Amsterdam, where he is completing his thesis on the theatrical response to the AIDS crisis.

www.ingramcontent.com/pod-product-compliance
Lightning Source LLC
Chambersburg PA
CBHW020121010526
44115CB00008B/926